DSM-III-R
TRAINING GUIDE

FOR USE WITH THE
AMERICAN PSYCHIATRIC ASSOCIATION'S
DIAGNOSTIC AND STATISTICAL
MANUAL OF MENTAL DISORDERS
(THIRD EDITION - REVISED)

DSM-III-R
TRAINING GUIDE

**For Use with the
American Psychiatric Association's
Diagnostic and Statistical
Manual of Mental Disorders
(Third Edition - Revised)**

by

William H. Reid, M.D., M.P.H.
*Clinical Professor of Psychiatry
University of Texas Health Science Center
San Antonio, Texas*

and

Michael G. Wise, M.D.
*Associate Professor of Psychiatry
University of Texas Health Science Center
San Antonio, Texas*

Brunner/Mazel, *Publishers* • New York

2 Note: *"DSM-III," "DSM-III-R,"* and the contents of the American Psychiatric Association's *Diagnostic and Statistical Manuals of Mental Disorders* are copyrighted by the American Psychiatric Association.

Library of Congress Cataloging-in-Publication Data
Reid, William H.
   DSM-III-R training guide.

   Bibliography: p.
   Includes index.
      1. Mental illness—Classification.   2. Mental
illness—Diagnosis.   I. Wise, Michael G.
II. Title.
RC455.2.C4D54   1987   616.89'0012   88-35186
ISBN 0-87630-505-2
ISBN 0-87630-507-9 (pbk.)

Copyright © 1989 by Brunner/Mazel, Inc.

Published by
BRUNNER/MAZEL, INC.
19 Union Square
New York, New York 10003

MANUFACTURED IN THE UNITED STATES OF AMERICA

10   9   8   7   6   5   4

To students and trainees
in the mental health professions,
and to their careers

Foreword

In my visits to psychiatric institutions, academic facilities, and medical and psychiatric societies throughout the world, the topic that is foremost on the minds of mental health clinicians is DSM-III-R. "How can it be used in our particular setting, situation, or clinical practice?"

When I returned home from a recent trip, I was pleased to find a copy of the *DSM-III-R Training Guide* on my desk. This is exactly the kind of volume that is needed to assist those who lecture and educate—professors and clinicians alike—who need to teach others how to use the DSM-III-R, as well as to learn how to use it ourselves. This volume is also for those who learn best from self-instruction.

This volume builds upon the very successful *DSM-III Training Guide* published in 1981. However, there are many improvements in the current edition. For example, all of the individual diagnostic criteria are included, and extra ICD-9-CM V Codes and E Codes not listed in DSM-III-R have been added as well. These codes are very useful clinically. Also, a glossary of terms used in DSM-III-R and in the volume has been developed.

As a past chair of the American Psychiatric Association Ad Hoc Committee on DSM-III-R as well as the APA past president during the term DSM-III-R was approved by the APA Board of Trustees, I want to thank Drs. William H. Reid and Michael G. Wise for their significant service to the mental health professions.

Robert O. Pasnau, M.D.
Los Angeles, CA

Contents

SECTION I. THE BASICS

SECTION II. THE DISORDERS

Preface

Psychiatric diagnosis is a complex proposition. The third editions of the American Psychiatric Association's Diagnostic and Statistical Manual of Mental Disorders are, arguably, the most significant steps ever taken toward reliable diagnosis of mental disorders. Whether or not one agrees with it, the system defined by DSM-III and DSM-III-R is necessary to clinical practice and mental health administration, and it is here to stay.

Unlike the diagnostic schema used in some other medical fields, the psychiatric nomenclature is widely used by nonphysicians. This update of the original *DSM-III Training Guide* is written for everyone who must become familiar with DSM-III-R. We have not "watered down" the diagnostic concepts. We have, however, tried to clarify DSM-III-R principles and content for medical students, psychiatric residents, and practicing physicians, as well as for counseling students, practicum trainees, psychology interns, and non-medical psychotherapists.

Like the original *DSM-III Training Guide*, this book can (and often should) be used with specially produced 35 mm slides and videotapes. The numbers in the margin of the text refer to these slides, which are available from the publisher. Although this *GUIDE* can be used alone, the complete *DSM-III-R Training Program*,* including the audiovisual materials, is recommended for educational settings.

ACKNOWLEDGMENTS

Finally, the authors would like to express their appreciation and high regard for the work done by the original *DSM-III Training Guide* editors. Linda J. Webb, Dr. P.H., Carlo C. DiClemente, Ph.D., Edwin E. Johnstone, M.D.,

---

*For more information about the *DSM-III-R Training Program* write to Brunner/Mazel Publishers, 19 Union Square West, New York, NY 10003.

Joyce L. Sanders, R.N., M.S.H.P., and Robin A. Perley, M.P.H., did a fine job, which made creation of this update much easier. Unfortunately, the institution which supported much of their work, the Texas Research Institute of Mental Sciences (TRIMS), ceased to exist a few years ago. The subsequent scattering of those original authors made it impossible to enlist their expertise in this revision. The current authors hope this volume lives up to the standard set in the first *Guide*.

William H. Reid, M.D., M.P.H.
Michael G. Wise, M.D.
San Antonio, TX

DSM-III-R

TRAINING GUIDE

FOR USE WITH THE
AMERICAN PSYCHIATRIC ASSOCIATION'S
DIAGNOSTIC AND STATISTICAL
MANUAL OF MENTAL DISORDERS
(THIRD EDITION - REVISED)

Section I

The Basics

Chapter 1

History and Evolution of DSM-III-R

INTRODUCTION

Practitioners' desire to classify symptoms and signs of disease into discrete disorders dates back thousands of years. The need to classify disorders, which is fundamental to their study, has led to the creation, revision, and demise of numerous classification systems. Fortunately, the health professional needs to be familiar with only two current classification systems to properly categorize patients with mental disorders or mental conditions. The first, published by the American Psychiatric Association, consists of a series of Diagnostic and Statistical Manuals of Mental Disorders (DSMs). The latest manual in this series is DSM-III-R, published in 1987. The second system is the International Classification of Diseases (ICD), which is published by the World Health Organization. The ICD is a worldwide statistical disease classification system for all medical conditions, including mental disorders.

HISTORY

It was only recently that an official U.S. classification for mental disorders was attempted. The 1840 census classified all mental illness in a single category, "Idiocy." This early attempt was expanded in the 1880 census, in which eight mental disorder categories were listed (1). By the late 1920s, almost every medical teaching center used a different classification system for mental disorders. The result was a diverse nomenclature that often led to meaningless communications and arguments between professionals.

3

The 1933 Standard Classified Nomenclature of Disease (SCND) attempted to bring order to the terminology. This nomenclature functioned reasonably well until World War II created a crisis in psychiatric terminology: Only 10% of the total cases seen by military psychiatrists could be classified using the SCND (2). In addition, during the postwar period, three separate U.S. nomenclatures existed (the SCND, the Armed Forces nomenclature, and the Veterans Administration system). None of these nomenclatures was consistent with the International Diagnostic Classification (IDC) system.

DSM-I

As a result of the aforementioned confusion over terminology, the Committee on Nomenclature and Statistics of the American Psychiatric Association proposed a revised classification system. After much deliberation, the Diagnostic and Statistical Manual of Mental Disorders (DSM) was published in 1952. The manual later became known as DSM-I when it became apparent that revisions would be needed. DSM-I was reprinted 20 times, was distributed widely, and did much to stabilize mental health nomenclature.

DSM-II

DSM-II was the result of an international collaborative effort that also culminated in the mental disorders section in the Eighth Revision of the International Classification of Diseases (ICD-8). Both DSM-II and ICD-8 went into effect in 1968.

DSM-III

Work on DSM-III began in 1974, in anticipation of ICD-9's 1979 scheduled publication date. Unfortunately, the mental disorders section proposed for ICD-9 was not sufficiently detailed for research and clinical work, so the American Psychiatric Association Task Force on Nomenclature and Statistics developed a new classification system. The development process was complicated and included 14 advisory committees, consultants from allied fields, liaison committees with professional organizations, conferences, and field trials. The field trials included tests of diagnostic reliability, the results of which were published in Appendix F of DSM-III. DSM-III was a dramatic depature from previous DSMs. Innovations included:

- Definition of the term *mental disorder*
- Presentation of diagnostic criteria for each disorder

- Diagnosis according to a multiaxial evaluation system
- Redefinition of major disorders
- Addition of new diagnostic categories
- Hierarchical organization of diagnostic categories
- Systematic description of each disorder
- Decision trees for differential diagnosis
- Glossary of technical terms
- Annotated comparative listing of DSM-II and DSM-III
- Discussion of ICD-9 and ICD-9-CM
- Publication of reliability data from field trials
- Indices of diagnostic terms and symptoms

DSM-III-R
DSM-III-R's development and stated goals were similar to those of DSM-III. Twenty-six advisory committees were formed, each with membership based on expertise in a particular area. In addition, the experience gained in using the DSM-III diagnostic criteria, particularly in well-conducted research studies, played a significant role in proposed modifications. Two draft proposals of DSM-III-R were made available for critical review, and field trials were conducted. The following new appendices were added to DSM-III-R: proposed diagnostic categories needing further study (e.g., late luteal phase dysphoric disorder, sadistic personality disorder, and self-defeating personality disorder), an alphabetic listing of DSM-III-R diagnoses and codes, a numerical listing of DSM-III-R diagnoses and codes, and an index of selected symptoms.

DSM-IV and Beyond
The American Psychiatric Association seems committed to rely on data generated through research for modification of the diagnostic system. As more and more specific information becomes available on mental disorders, a transition from a descriptive classification system to an etiological classification system may be possible. It is anticipated that ICD-10, expected to be published in 1992, will be completely compatible with DSM-IV.

International Classification of Diseases (ICD)
The First Revision Conference of the International List of Causes of Death was held in Paris in 1900. Since the first ICD, which was used strictly for the coding of causes of death, revisions have been made about every 10

years. The ICD did not provide a separate section for mental disorders until the fifth revision (1938), and later revisions expanded the classification system to include causes for morbidity. The 1978 revision, ICD-9, was further modified for use in the United States for collection of morbidity data, collecting research data, indexing medical records, reviewing cases, and for administrative purposes. The result was ICD-9-CM (Clinical Modification) published in 1979 by the U.S. Department of Health and Human Services. Because of close collaboration, DSM-III-R numerical classification codes (Chapter 5) are compatible with ICD-9-CM numeric classification codes. This simplifies the task for the clinician, who can refer to DSM-III-R for the coding of all mental disorders, and to ICD-9-CM, if necessary, for the coding of other medical disorders.

REFERENCES

1. Williams, J. B. W. (1988). Psychiatric classification. In: J. A. Talbott, R. E. Hales, and S. C. Yudofsky (Eds.), *The American Psychiatric Press textbook of psychiatry.* Washington, DC: American Psychiatric Press.

2. American Psychiatric Association (1952). *Diagnostic and statistical manual of mental disorders*, (1st ed., revised). Washington, DC: American Psychiatric Association.

3. American Psychiatric Association (1968). *Diagnostic and statistical manual of mental disorders* (2nd ed.). Washington, DC: American Psychiatric Association.

4. American Psychiatric Association (1980). *Diagnostic and statistical manual of mental disorders* (3rd ed.). Washington, DC: American Psychiatric Association.

5. American Psychiatric Association (1987). *Diagnostic and statistical manual of mental disorders* (3rd ed., revised). Washington, DC: American Psychiatric Association.

Chapter 2

Multiaxial Classification

INTRODUCTION

The multiaxial diagnostic system began in 1980 with DSM-III and, with minor modifications, continues as an integral part of DSM-III-R. The use of the five axes ensures that information needed for treatment planning, prediction of outcome, and research is recorded. Table 1 (p. 8) presents an overview of the multiaxial system.   **6**

AXES I AND II

Axis I and Axis II are used to describe the patient's current condition. When necessary, multiple diagnoses, or diagnoses on both axes, are made. Axis I lists clinical syndromes present, or, if no mental disorder is present, reflects that fact (Chapter 6). Axis II lists personality disorders or developmental disorders. Axis II can also be used to record personality traits, repetitive defense mechanisms that impair the patient's ability to cope, or premorbid personality disorders.   **7**

AXIS III

The clinician lists all physical disorders or conditions on this axis. The physical condition may be causative (e.g., hypomanic or manic symptoms due to a patient's hyperthyroidism), or the physical disorder may provide information important for treatment of the patient. Other notations, such as "frontal release reflexes present," are acceptable.   **8**

TABLE 1
Multiaxial System

Axis I	Clinical Syndromes; Additional Codes/V Codes
Axis II	Personality Disorders; Developmental Disorders
Axis III	Physical Disorders/Conditions
Axis IV	Severity of Psychosocial Stressors
Axis V	Assessment of Global Functioning

AXIS IV

Page 11 of DSM-III-R contains two Severity of Psychosocial Stressors
9 Scales, one for adults and the other for children and adolescents. The Axis
IV rating is based on the clinician's judgment as to the degree of stress
present. Numerous factors are taken into account, including the number
of stressors, the change accompanying the stressor(s), and the desirability
of the change. For example, an impending divorce may be a severe
psychosocial stressor when accompanied by unwanted changes and financial hardship, or it may be a mild stressor if it represents termination of a
tumultuous, destructive relationship.

AXIS V

On this axis, the clinician estimates the patient's level of function at the
10 time of evaluation and the patient's highest level of function during the
past year. Page 12 of DSM-III-R contains the Global Assessment of Functioning Scale (GAF Scale) for this purpose. The assigned codes are self-
explanatory and consider the psychological, social, and occupational
functioning of the patient.

DIFFERENCES BETWEEN DSM-III AND DSM-III-R MULTIAXIAL CLASSIFICATION

- Mental retardation, specific developmental disorders, and pervasive developmental disorders are now listed on Axis II.
- On Axis IV, the severity of psychosocial stress is still rated as it was
  in DSM-III; however, psychosocial stressors are now also classi-

fied as either acute (duration less than six months) or enduring (duration greater than six months).

- The "minimal" rating level of the Axis IV Psychosocial Stressor Scale was eliminated in DSM-III-R.
- Axis V in the DSM-III-R multiaxial system now uses a Global Assessment of Functioning Scale (GAF Scale, DSM-III-R, page 12). The GAF Scale is a composite of psychological/social/occupational function on a continuum from 1 (seriously ill) to 90 (excellent mental health).
- Two GAF ratings are now listed on Axis V: (1) the current GAF rating; and (2) the highest GAF rating during the past year (based on level of functioning for at least a few months).

Chapter 3

Summary of the Features of DSM-III-R

GENERAL INFORMATION

DSM-III-R itself provides a great deal of information useful to the understanding of its diagnostic system. Some highlights are summarized below.

The **Introduction** briefly discusses the history and development of the diagnostic and statistical manuals, up to DSM-III-R. It defines "mental disorder" as

> a clinically significant behavioral or psychological syndrome or pattern that occurs in a person and that is associated with present distress (a painful symptom) or disability (impairment in one or more areas of functioning) or with a significantly increased risk of suffering death, pain, disability, or an important loss of freedom. (p.22)

In addition, the syndrome or pattern "must not be merely an expectable response to a particular event," nor solely a deviant behavior or conflict with society, unless the latter are symptoms of the personal dysfunction described above. Persons with a given diagnosis need not be similar in other ways and, in fact, may be dissimilar in ways that affect one's choice of treatment.

The Introduction discusses other basic features of DSM-III-R and mentions several topics that are expanded upon in this Guide (regarding treatment planning, use by nonclinicians, use in nonclinical settings, and use in different cultures). It particularly directs the reader to the "Cautionary Statement" on potential for improper use.

Chapter 1 of DSM-III-R is a nonannotated outline of the Axis I and II categories and codes, with scales of psychosocial stressors and global functioning for coding on Axes IV and V. **Chapter 2** provides a discussion of the "multiaxial" system which, in DSM-III-R, defines the diagnosis(es) (Axes I, II, and III) and modifiers (Axes IV and V) relevant to greater understanding of the patient, treatment planning, statistical tasks, and/or research. It explains some of the conventions used in the text and a few commonly used terms. These are generally addressed, and often expanded upon, in this GUIDE. **Chapter 3** contains all of the current diagnostic criteria and explanatory text.

Appendix A describes three proposed diagnostic categories that are not included in the official nomenclature. **Appendix B** contains "decision trees," which are designed to help the clinician eliminate superfluous disorders and narrow the diagnostic focus (although one should not feel pressed to arrive at only one diagnosis, or even only one per axis). This GUIDE avoids the rote "decision tree" approach in favor of encouraging the clinician to be more comprehensive in his or her consideration of history, signs, and symptoms.

Appendix C is a short glossary of terms used commonly in DSM-III-R. It does not contain many terms found elsewhere in clinical practice, and its definitions may conflict in part with definitions found elsewhere (cf. explanations of "defense mechanisms"). There is some overlap with the somewhat more comprehensive glossary found at the end of this GUIDE. **Appendix D** is an annotated comparison of DSM-III and DSM-III-R.

Appendix E contains a discussion of the International Classification of Diseases (ICD), as well as a copy of the Mental Disorders chapter of the 1978 ICD-9 and a list of the 1979 ICD "clinical modification" psychiatric codes. **Appendix F** lists DSM-III-R field trial participants. **Appendices G** and **H** are alphabetic and numerical listings of the DSM-III-R disorders.

There are two indices in **DSM-III-R**. One, the Symptom Index, lists symptoms and helps the reader to locate disorders for which they are listed. The other lists the diagnoses (and some other diagnostic terms) alphabetically with page numbers.

Chapter 4

The Diagnostic Process

GENERAL INFORMATION

Unsophisticated readers of DSM-III-R commonly misunderstand it to be
13 a "cookbook" of psychiatric diagnosis. While its format promotes this
misconception, and even some pseudoclinical "computer diagnosis" programs use it to sales advantage, it is not intended for such use (see the
"Cautionary Statement" on p. xxix of the full text). Similarly, DSM-III-R
has been called a "phenomenological" manual, but careful reading of the
criteria and accompanying chapters discloses encouragement of a comprehensive clinical approach to evaluation and diagnosis.

Anyone using DSM-III-R to carry out clinical, statistical, research,
14 legal, or reimbursement purposes related to accurate diagnosis should
first be fully trained in the clinical fields relevant to each of the five axes.
This implies a biopsychosocial foundation for assessing the medical,
emotional, and social characteristics of the patient; interviewing skills;
and expertise at obtaining and interpreting information about the patient
from other sources (e.g., family interviews, medical history, physical
examination, specialty consultation, psychological testing, laboratory
procedures). It further suggests, with no prejudice intended, that individuals with incomplete biopsychosocial background or training may be
inherently limited in their use of this diagnostic system.

Assurance of valid, effective use of DSM-III-R almost always requires
a clinical setting. Although it finds use in other settings—the social
sciences, reimbursement procedures, legal environments, etc.—its clinical
purpose must always be understood as overriding. A clinician may prop-

erly use DSM-III-R terminology to help interpret findings to, for example, an insurance company or court; however, he or she should guard against inappropriate translation of medically relevant information to other settings, whose needs, rules, and vocabularies are often quite different from those of psychiatry.

OTHER KEY DIAGNOSTIC ISSUES
The text of DSM-III-R draws attention to several other important concepts which should be discussed before proceeding:

1. **Coexistence of more than one disorder in the same patient.** Although the principle of parsimony—trying to fit all the patient's symptoms and signs into one disorder—is a good clinical tool, the complexities of patients' physical, emotional, and interpersonal lives often lead to more than one diagnosis. DSM-III-R "decision trees" and similarly designed computer programs should not cause one to forego considering multiple diagnoses. **15**

2. **Frequent lack of discrete division between disorders (or between a disorder and lack of disorder).** The current state of diagnostic art, and the nature of patients themselves, precludes clear-cut borders between closely related syndromes and disorders, and sometimes between normalcy and psychopathology. **16**

3. **"Hierarchical" precedence of some diagnoses over others, including preempting of some diagnoses by organic or pervasive mental disorders with competing symptoms.** Hierarchies, as described in DSM-III-R, increase the clinical accuracy and practicality of the named disorders by **17**

- raising doubt about a second diagnosis when the patient's symptoms are all likely to be related to the first (e.g., depression in a schizophrenic patient often remits as the thought disorder is adequately treated), and
- encouraging the clinician or treatment team to attend to the most acutely important disorder(s) before devoting time and resources to relatively trivial or stable problems (e.g., dealing with a drug withdrawal syndrome in a patient with a somatoform disorder).

4. **Limitations in transcultural application of DSM-III-R disorders and techniques.** Many persons live in, or come from, cultures different

18 from that of the evaluating clinician or that on which most of the DSM-III-R criteria are based. A clinician involved in transcultural assessments should understand both normal and psychopathological aspects of individuals in the "foreign" group and be sensitive to the possibility of misunderstanding, even when he or she has considerable experience with it. This caveat applies even to traditionally distressing symptoms (e.g., certain hallucinations experienced during bereavement in some Native American cultures).

Chapter 5

Axes I and II

INTRODUCTION

The clinician records all mental disorders on either Axis I or Axis II. In **19** some cases the patient will not have a mental disorder, or a mental disorder is not considered to be the reason for evaluation or treatment. In patients without a mental disorder, special codes or V codes are recorded (see Table 2). The basic task of the clinician is to describe the patient's current mental condition using diagnostic Axes I and II of DSM-III-R.

MULTIPLE DIAGNOSES

Multiple diagnoses are made on Axis I and II whenever necessary. Axis I lists clinical mental disorders and syndromes, and Axis II lists personality disorders and developmental disorders. The clinician can also record personality traits or maladaptive defense mechanisms on Axis II. Personality traits/maladaptive defenses are not coded but are useful in treatment planning and may aid other mental health workers during future contacts with the patient.

DIAGNOSTIC HIERARCHY

Four general rules limit the use of diagnoses. These are:

- When an organic disorder is present, it precludes the diagnosis of **20** any other mental disorder that could produce similar symptoms.

For example, if a patient with no previous history of depression becomes depressed secondary to medication (e.g., reserpine) prescribed for hypertension, the correct diagnosis is organic mood syndrome. Even though the patient meets the diagnostic criteria for major depression, that diagnosis would not be made.

21   • When a patient has a "major" disorder such as schizophrenia, associated symptoms (e.g., dysphoria, anxiety, hypochondriacal concerns, etc.) are often present. These symptoms are not diagnosed as separate disorders (e.g., dysthmia, anxiety disorder, hypochondriasis).

22   • When a patient receives more than one diagnosis, the condition that is chiefly responsible for clinical attention or treatment may be labeled the *principal diagnosis*. The principal diagnosis can be either an Axis I or Axis II disorder.

23   • When multiple diagnoses are made on either Axis I or II, they are listed in the descending order of immediate clinical attention.

TABLE 2

	Code	Terminology Used on Axis	Amount of Information Available
24	799.90	Deferred (Axis I or II)	Insufficient Information is available.
	*	Axis I or II diagnosis followed by "(provisional)"	Information strongly suggests a diagnosis, but some doubt exists.
	300.90	Unspecified Mental Disorder (nonpsychotic)	Enough information is available to rule out a psychotic mental disorder.
	298.90	Psychotic Disorder Not Otherwise Specified	A psychotic disorder is present, but further specification is not possible.
	*	(Class of Disorder) Not Otherwise Specified	Enough information is present to indicate a class of disorder (e.g., anxiety). Either information is insufficient or disorder does not meet more specific diagnostic criteria.
	*	V Codes	Specifies the focus of attention of treatment. There may be insufficient information present to specify a disorder.
	V71.09	No diagnosis (Axis I or II)	Sufficient information is available to state that no mental disorder exists.

*A specific code for a disorder is entered here.

DIAGNOSTIC CERTAINTY

A clinician's certainty about a diagnosis is directly proportional to the amount of information available. Unfortunately, information is sometimes lacking, particularly early in the evaluative process. DSM-III-R allows flexibility in such cases. The clinician has several options, which are contained in Table 2.

Apply the information in this chapter to the following case examples.

CASE VIGNETTE

A 20-year-old man presents to the emergency room accompanied by his family. He is combative, smells of alcohol, is obviously quite intoxicated, and was arrested three weeks ago for driving while intoxicated. His wife reports that he has been drinking increasing amounts of alcohol since marital problems developed two months ago. For three days he has been tearful and reported to another family member that he "felt hopeless about the marriage." His appetite, concentration, interest and energy levels, and sleep pattern are normal. He denies suicidal ideation. Past history is significant for poor academic performance during high school (i.e., he was enrolled in special-education classes). His parents state that no learning disabilities were ever identified, but "his I.Q. is low."

Before reading the case discussion, test yourself by filling in the diagnoses below.

List the Axis I disorders present (all mental disorders or conditions):

Axis I _____

_____

_____

_____

List Axis II disorders (personality and/or developmental disorders):

Axis II _____

_____

Discussion

A number of clinical problems are present or are potentially present. **Axis I:** 303.00, Alcohol Intoxication; 305.00, Alcohol Abuse; V61.10, Marital Problem (primary diagnosis); and probably 309.00, Adjustment Disorder with Depressed Mood. **Axis II:** 317.00, Mild Mental Retardation (provisional).

The patient presented to the emergency room in an intoxicated state. He had consumed excessive amounts of alcohol for longer than one month, and he meets the diagnostic criteria for psychoactive substance abuse (DSM-III-R, p. 169), in this case, alcohol abuse. Marital problem is listed as the "primary diagnosis" because it seems to have led to both the alcohol abuse and the adjustment disorder. The use of a primary diagnosis also helps identify a major focus for treatment. On Axis II, a developmental disorder is *possibly* present. However, complete information is not available, so "(provisional)" is added to "mild mental retardation" to indicate that doubt exists. Further clinical information will be needed prior to final Axis II diagnosis.

CASE VIGNETTE

The patient is a 30-year-old male with a history of multiple prior psychiatric hospitalizations. His family brings him to you for evaluation. According to the family, he is not sleeping at night and is very suspicious. The patient reports auditory hallucinations. The voices constantly warn him about the "intentions of people." During the interview he stares intently at you, occasionally becomes angry at your questions, and appears suspicious. His affect varies from appropriate to angry, and his mood is euthymic. He denies depressive symptoms. His associations are not loose; however, he is preoccupied with the idea that the Mafia is going to kill him. At times during the interview he appears quite anxious.

Past history is significant for numerous similar episodes beginning when the patient was 18. He has been psychiatrically hospitalized many times and frequently stops medications following discharge. He has never had a major depressive or manic episode. The family described the patient during childhood as a quiet "loner" who never had any friends. He never dated. The family expresses surprise about his angry outbursts because "he never showed any emotions as a child."

List the Axis I disorders present (all mental disorders or conditions):

Axis I _____

_____

List Axis II disorders (personality and/or developmental disorders):

Axis II _____

_____

Discussion

This patient presents a classic history. The **Axis I** diagnosis is Schizophrenia, Paranoid Type. The course of the disorder is chronic (i.e., duration greater than two years), and the patient is experiencing an acute exacerbation. The DSM-III-R code is 295.34. Although the patient is anxious and paranoid, separate diagnoses, such as anxiety disorder or paranoid disorder, would not be made. As mentioned earlier, symptoms commonly associated with major psychiatric disorders are not listed as separate disorders. Premorbid personality characteristics can be listed on Axis II. Simply write: "(premorbid)" following the personality disorder diagnosis.

The **Axis II** diagnosis is Schizoid Personality Disorder, 301.20 (Premorbid). In other words, prior to developing schizophrenia, the patient's preexisting personality was schizoid.

Chapter 6

Axis III

INTRODUCTION

AXIS III is where the clinician lists all the patient's medical/physical disorders or conditions. ICD-9-CM (Chapter 1) contains an exhaustive list of medical conditions, along with appropriate classification codes. Axis III ensures that medical or physical conditions that can directly or indirectly affect management and treatment are not forgotten.

At times, the Axis III disorder will cause an Axis I or II abnormality. For example, if a patient with alcohol dependence develops signs and symptoms of a delirium (acute confusional state), it is likely that the patient's delirium is caused by the alcohol (e.g., alcohol withdrawal or Wernicke's encephalopathy). Sometimes the Axis III condition will not directly cause the psychiatric disorder, but knowledge of the medical problem is essential to proper management of the case (e.g., in the case of a pregnant woman who is severely depressed, suicidal, and an insulin-dependent diabetic). Failure to properly manage the medical condition during treatment of the mental disorder could have disastrous consequences. The clinician is also encouraged to list other observations on Axis III, such as "frontal release signs present." If no significant medical or physical disorders are present, state "None Known" on Axis III. ICD-9-CM also lists E codes for accidental injuries, poisonings, and suicide attempts.

The combination of Axes I, II, and III presents an immediate overview of the patient's mental and physical condition. For example,

Axis I	295.35	Schizophrenia, Paranoid Type
	305.00	Alcohol Abuse

Axis II   301.20   Schizoid Personality Disorder (premorbid)
Axis III   Liver cirrhosis

In this example, we know the patient is a chronic paranoid schizophrenic, who has a significant problem with alcohol. The patient has liver cirrhosis, in all likelihood caused by the alcohol, and had a premorbid schizoid personality.

Chapter 7

Axis IV

INTRODUCTION

The clinician lists on Axis IV the psychosocial stressors encountered by the patient during the 12 months prior to evaluation. In addition, the level of psychosocial stressors experienced during the last year is rated on Axis IV,* using one of two Severity of Psychosocial Stressors Scales. One scale is used to rate adults and the other scale is used to rate children or adolescents. Both scales are found on page 11 of DSM-III-R. In addition to occurring during the previous year, the stressor(s) must also have contributed to either the

- development of a new mental disorder,
26   - recurrence of a previous mental disorder, or
- exacerbation of an ongoing mental disorder

The evaluator must remember certain guidelines prior to rating the severity of psychosocial stressors. First, rate according to how an "average" individual with similar sociocultural values would react to a particular stress. For example, a 25-year-old distraught man presents for evaluation. The primary stressor is a reduction in this individual's spending allowance from $1,000 per week to $500 per week. For the "average" individual, having $500 per week for miscellaneous expenses would not be stressful;

---

*In the case of Post-traumatic Stress Disorder, the stressor should be listed and rated on Axis IV regardless of when the traumatic event occurred.

therefore, in spite of the strong reaction of the individual, the degree of stress rating on Axis IV would be none. Second, the evaluator should not consider the individual's vulnerability to stress, as in the case just described, but rather the severity of the stressor itself. Third, judgment of stress severity also includes:

- the amount of change in the individual's life as a result of the stressor   27
- the degree to which the event (stressor) is desired
- the degree to which the event (stressor) is under the individual's control
- the number of stressors

RATING THE STRESSOR'S SEVERITY (TABLE 3)

The clinician rates the severity of a psychosocial stressor on a scale from 0 (inadequate information) to 6 (catastrophic). In case of multiple stressors, the most severe stressor is usually rated. If there are multiple severe stressors, a higher rating should be considered. As stated previously, there are separate Severity of Psychosocial Stressors Scales (SPSS) for adults and for children/adolescents. Table 3 is the SPSS for adults. DSM-III-R makes a distinction between acute stress, defined as stress that lasts less that six months, and enduring circumstances, defined as stress that lasts six months or more. The duration of the stress is listed on Axis IV as either

TABLE 3
Rating the Severity of the Stressor

Degree of Stress	Code	Examples of Stressors	
		Acute Events	Enduring Circumstances
	0	Inadequate information	Inadequate information 28
None	1	No acute events	No enduring stressors
Mild	2	Broke up with boyfriend	Job dissatisfaction
Moderate	3	Marriage; retirement	Single parent
Severe	4	Divorce	Unemployment
Extreme	5	Death of spouse	Sexual/physical abuse
Catastrophic	6	Suicide of spouse	Hostage

acute or enduring. When several stressors of varied duration are involved, the clinician lists the stress as either predominantly acute or predominantly enduring.

TYPES OF PSYCHOSOCIAL STRESSORS TO BE CONSIDERED
The following kinds of stressors may be considered:

- conjugal (e.g., marriage, engagement, separation)
- developmental (phases of life such as menopause, puberty)
- family (inconsistent parenting, foster family)
- financial (bankrupcy)
- legal (malpractice suit, arrest)
- living circumstance (move to different neighborhood)
- occupational (unemployment, retirement)
- other interpersonal (death of good friend)
- other psychological (natural disaster, rape)
- parenting (birth of child, parent-child discord)
- physical illness or injury (illness, surgery)

CASE VIGNETTE
B. G. is a 39-year-old, never-married man who works as an accountant in a retail business. He has a long history of poor self-esteem and his mood is usually mildly dysphoric. His co-workers describe him as a dependable, quiet man. For the last nine months the business has slowly declined and bankruptcy is a remote possibility. Since the downturn in business, B. G.'s mood is more dysphoric and he blames himself for the financial condition of the company. He presents for evaluation after his boss insists that he seek assistance.

List the patient's known stressors and rate his degree of stress using the scales on page 11 of DSM-III-R.

Discussion
The only environmental stressor evident from this history is a change in B. G.'s work situation. The degree of stress is rated as mild (code=2), and the circumstances are enduring (duration greater than six months). It is likely that B. G.'s individual vulnerability (his poor self-esteem) magnifies

the impact of this stressor so that his response is more than that expected of the "average" individual; however, individual vulnerability is not a factor in rating Axis IV.

> Axis IV: Psychosocial stressors—Business where he is employed is in financial difficulty
> Severity: 2—mild (enduring circumstances)

CASE VIGNETTE

E. W. is a 14-year-old girl who is the only child currently living with her parents. She is a good student and is known as an outgoing child. Five months ago her maternal grandfather, who had been living with the family for 10 years, died. E. W.'s mother has had difficulty with the loss of her father and is quite depressed, but will not seek professional assistance.

Three months ago E. W.'s school performance began to drop and she began coming home early from school because of stomach pain. E. W., the identified patient, presents for evaluation.

List the patient's known stressors and rate her degree of stress using the scales on page 11 of DSM-III-R.

Discussion

E. W.'s stressors include a mother with a possible mental disorder, and the death of her grandfather. The degree of stress would likely be rated as severe (code=4). It is possible, depending on specific facts in this case, that the stress might be rated as extreme. For example, if E. W. had a very close relationship with the deceased grandfather, and her depressed mother was suicidal and constantly neglecting her, the combined stressors would warrant a rating of extreme (code=5).

> Axis IV: Psychosocial stressors—Mother quite depressed, death of maternal grandfather
> Severity: 4—severe (acute events)

Chapter 8

Axis V

INTRODUCTION

The clinician rates the individual's overall or global level of functioning on Axis V of DSM-III-R. The specific scale used is the Global Assessment of Functioning (GAF) Scale, which is found on page 12 of DSM-III-R. The GAF Scale is a composite index that considers psychological, social, and occupational functioning. GAF Scale ratings are continuous and range from 1 (pervasive severe difficulties) to 90 (symptoms absent).

At the time of evaluation the clinician lists two ratings on Axis V. The first rating is the patient's current level of function. The current GAF establishes a baseline so that results of therapeutic interventions can be measured. The second rating represents the highest level of function (for at least a few-month period) during the year prior to evaluation. The highest GAF during the past year may have prognostic significance because the person will often return to that level of functioning after the episode of illness.

RATING THE LEVEL OF ADAPTIVE FUNCTION

Rating the patient's level of functioning according to the GAF Scale is relatively easy. Simply refer to page 12 of DSM-III-R and locate a verbal description that accurately portrays the individual. Each verbal description has an associated range of numbers or codes (e.g., the person with serious impairment is rated from 41 to 50). The clinician selects a number in that range which best represents the patient's level of function. For example, a 29-year-old male presents for evaluation in a catatonic state. He is mute and will not follow any commands. According to the GAF Scale, a person who has gross impairment in communication falls into a rating range between 11 and 20. The clinician would rate the patient's current level of function within that range. (See Table 4.)

CASE VIGNETTE
M. J. is a 39-year-old, married, female clerical worker with three children. Her problems began about six months ago, after her husband had an affair with a neighborhood woman. Since that time M. J. has experienced increasing paranoid ideation and during the last two months, her job performance deteriorated. She recently started withdrawing from friends, but continues her role as a mother without obvious difficulty. She is not suicidal. Prior to her husband's affair she reportedly had "lifelong" mild anxiety, longstanding insomnia, and a good work record. She is brought for evaluation by her husband because of worsening problems.

TABLE 4
Abbreviated Version of the GAF Scale

Range of Rating	Level of Functioning in Social, Occupational, or School Situations
81–90	Absent or minimal symptoms, only everyday problems and concerns
71–80	Only slight impairment, symptoms are transient
61–70	Mild symptoms, but functioning generally well
51–60	Moderate symptoms (e.g., occasional panic attacks)
41–50	Serious symptoms (e.g., thought of suicide, unable to keep job)
31–40	Some impairment in reality testing of communications, or major impairment in several areas, such as work or school, family relations, judgment, thinking, or mood
21–30	Behavior is considerably influenced by delusions and hallucinations, or serious impairment in communications or judgment, or inability to function in almost all areas
11–20	Some danger of harming self or others, or occasionally fails to maintain minimal personal hygiene, or gross impairment in communication
1–10	Persistent danger of harming self or others, or persistent inability to maintain minimal personal hygiene, or serious suicidal act with clear expectation of death

Discussion

M. J. has significant impairment in many areas. Her paranoid ideation impairs her psychologically, she is isolating herself from friends (social dysfunction), and her job performance is declining (occupational difficulty). According to the GAF Scale, her adaptive function is in the range of 31–40. If on examination she is quite paranoid and she is about to lose her job, one might rate current level of function on Axis V as 31 or 32. Her level of functioning during the last 12 months was clearly higher than her current level, probably in the 61–70 range. If her anxiety level before the current episode was very mild, or intermittent, and she had only minimal insomnia, a rating of 70 on Axis V would be appropriate.

Axis V Current GAF—32
        Highest GAF last year—70

CASE VIGNETTE

A. K. is a 10-year-old boy who is brought by his mother for evaluation. According to the mother, A. K. was an excellent student (mostly A's with a few B's) until about two months ago, when she and A. K.'s father separated. Since the father's departure, the boy has complained of stomach pains associated with going to school. According to A. K.'s teacher, his conduct in school has changed from "excellent" to "needs improvement." During the last two months the father visited the boy once and telephoned him two times. The mother describes the previous relationship between the father and son as "very close." The mother reports that prior to his father's departure A. K. occasionally fell behind in his schoolwork but responded quickly to encouragement. The mother believes that these lapses in schoolwork occurred during times of increased marital discord.

Discussion

A. K.'s history indicates that his highest level of functioning during the last year was relatively good. He had symptoms prior to his father's departure, but the symptoms were transient and were understandable in the setting of marital discord. Therefore, his highest GAF Scale rating would be in the 71–80 range. Whether the evaluator places an individual at the top or the bottom of a particular range depends on the specifics of the case. With A. K.'s history, a rating of 80 seems appropriate. His current level of function is obviously lower, although his symptoms are moderate and understandable given the close relationship he has had with his father. The appropriate GAF Scale range is 51–60. The specific code given by this examiner was 54.

Axis V Current GAF—54
Highest GAF last year—80

Chapter 9

Diagnostic Codes

INTRODUCTION

30   DSM-III-R diagnostic codes provide an easy method for recording diagnoses for administrative and statistical purposes. Each diagnosis has a code number. DSM-III-R lists these code numbers in several locations: Axis I and II categories and codes, pages 3–9; Appendix G (alphabetic listing of DSM-III-R diagnoses and codes), pages 499–506; and Appendix H (numeric listing of DSM-III-R diagnoses and codes), pages 509–515.

Besides the diagnostic codes, additional codes and V codes are available for other clinical situations. In addition, fifth-digit codes are added to certain diagnostic categories. Three diagnostic categories require a fifth digit: organic mental disorders, schizophrenias, and mood disorders.

DSM-III-R's Axes III, IV, and V are also coded. Axis III, which lists physical conditions or other pertinent medical information, is coded according to ICD-9-CM. Axis III codes are not listed in DSM-III-R. The mental health clinician usually writes medical diagnoses or information on Axis III, and medical records personnel will code the information. Axis IV lists the severity of psychosocial stressor(s) in accordance with scales found on page 11 of DSM-III-R, and Axis V lists the individual's level of functioning in accordance with the Global Assessment Functioning (GAF) Scale on page 12 of DSM-III-R. Chapters 5 through 8 in this book contain a complete discussion of DSM-III-R's five axes.

Additional codes (DSM-III-R, p. 363) are used when insufficient diagnostic information is available. For example, code 799.90 on Axis I and/or Axis II signifies that the diagnosis is deferred.

V CODES

V codes (DSM-III-R, pp. 359–361) specify a condition not attributable to a mental disorder that is the focus of attention or treatment. For example, a male adolescent is brought by his parents for evaluation after several heated arguments over his choice of friends. The clinician evaluates the adolescent and finds no mental disorder. The issue, and the focus for treatment, is a Parent-Child Problem (code V61.20). The V codes in DSM-III-R are taken from a large list found in ICD-9-CM. With the exception of V71.09 (no diagnosis), which can be listed on both Axis I and II, V codes are only used on Axis I. Chapter 27 in this book lists V codes.

FIFTH-DIGIT CODES

Whenever an "x" appears in the fifth digit of the diagnostic code, the "x" indicates that additional information is required. The following is a list of diagnoses requiring a fifth-digit designation, as well as the meaning of the fifth-digit code.

Organic Mental Disorders

Code "x" in fifth digit: 1 = with delirium; 2 = with delusions; 3 = with depression; 0 = uncomplicated.

> 290.1x   Primary Degenerative Dementia of the Alzheimer's Type, Presenile Onset
>
> 290.4x   Multi-infarct Dementia

Schizophrenia

Code "x" in fifth digit: 1 = subchronic; 2 = chronic; 3 = subchronic with acute exacerbation; 4 = chronic with acute exacerbation.

> 295.1x   Schizophrenia, Disorganized
>
> 295.2x   Schizophrenia, Catatonic
>
> 295.3x   Schizophrenia, Paranoid (specify if stable)
>
> 295.6x   Schizophrenia, Residual
>
> 295.9x   Schizophrenia, Undifferentiated

Mood Disorders

Code "x" in fifth digit: 1 = mild; 2 = moderate; 3 = severe, without psychotic features; 4 = with psychotic features (specify mood-congruent or mood-incongruent); 5 = in partial remission; 6 = in full remission; 0 = unspecified.

296.2x Major Depression, Single Episode
296.3x Major Depression, Recurrent
296.4x Bipolar Disorder, Manic
296.5x Bipolar Disorder, Depressed
296.6x Bipolar Disorder, Mixed

DIFFERENCES BETWEEN DSM-III AND DSM-III-R DIAGNOSTIC CODES

33

- A small number of DSM-III's diagnostic codes were not ICD-9-CM codes, which caused some problems in record keeping. In contrast, all DSM-III-R codes are legitimate ICD-9-CM codes.
- Some DSM-III-R codes (DSM-III-R, pp. 3-9) are followed by an "*." The codes with an "*" are used more than once in DSM-III-R to maintain compatibility with ICD-9-CM.
- DSM-III's fifth-digit subclassification of mental retardation, pervasive mental disorders, substance abuse disorders, and psychosexual disorders no longer exist in DSM-III-R.
- DSM-III Code V62.89 (Borderline Intellectual Functioning) on Axis I is now coded V40.00 and is listed on Axis II with other pervasive development disorders.

OVERVIEW OF THE DSM-III-R CATEGORIES

It will be helpful to examine briefly each of the major diagnostic categories before beginning a detailed discussion of the over 240 DSM-III-R disorders and V codes. They are addressed in the order in which they are found in the text.

Note that all disorders are coded on Axis I *except* the "Developmental Disorders" portion of the first section, the Personality Disorders, and the V code for "Borderline Intellectual Functioning."

Disorders Usually First Evident in Infancy, Childhood, or Adolescence

There is often no arbitrary age for separating infants, children, adolescents, and adults. "Adolescence" may extend into the late twenties for many college students, for example. Some of the disorders in this category appear late in adolescence or may present during adulthood. *Many are properly diagnosed in adults* (e.g., mental retardation, eating disorders, gender identity disorders).

Conversely, although one should first consider diagnoses in this section when assessing children and adolescents, it is also appropriate to consider most of the other disorders in DSM-III-R. Of course, disorders which specify that the patient be an adult (e.g., antisocial personality) should not be used for children or adolescents.

This very large category is divided into three Developmental Disorders, coded on Axis II:

- Mental Retardation
- Pervasive Developmental Disorders
- Specific Developmental Disorders

and seven Axis I disorders:

- Disruptive Behavior Disorders
- Anxiety Disorders of Childhood or Adolescence
- Eating Disorders
- Gender Identity Disorders
- Tic Disorders
- Elimination Disorders
- Speech Disorders Not Elsewhere Classified

Organic Mental Syndromes and Disorders
The essential feature of all disorders in this large, heterogenous group is "psychological or behavioral abnormality associated with transient or permanent dysfunction of the brain" (DSM-III-R, p. 98). One should note that the term *organic* in DSM-III-R does not imply that many (or most) of the other disorders do not have a biological component. One should not arbitrarily separate "psychiatric" diagnoses from "medical" ones.

There are two common means of arriving at an "organic" diagnostic impression: (1) recognizing one of the disorders or syndromes by its diagnostic criteria, and (2) demonstrating a physical illness or other organic factor(s) which can reasonably be established as the source of the patient's symptoms and signs. It is important to assess and understand the pathophysiologic mechanism insofar as possible, since most psychological and behavioral symptoms are "final common pathways" for many different illnesses. Similarly, many organic disorders and syndromes mimic nonorganic ones; differentiating them is often crucial to treatment.

DSM-III-R differentiates organic mental "syndromes" from organic mental "disorders." In "disorders," the etiology is known or presumed
38 (e.g., the withdrawal deliria). In "syndromes" no reference is made to etiology, although the source is understood to be organic (as opposed to "functional" or primarily psychosocial). "Disorder" implies the presence of an Axis III disorder or condition, which should be specified and coded as such when possible.

For example:

> Axis I 290.00 Primary Degenerative Dementia (Alzheimer's), Senile Onset
> Axis II V71.09 No diagnosis or condition
> Axis III 331.00* Alzheimer's Disease

This category is divided into three subcategories:

39
- Dementias Arising in the Senium and Presenium
- Psychoactive Substance-Induced Organic Mental Disorders
- Organic Mental Disorders Associated with Axis III Physical Disorders or Conditions, or Whose Etiology Is Unknown

Psychoactive Substance Use Disorders
This category includes symptoms and maladaptive behavioral changes
40 associated with use (often regular use) of a substance (including alcohol) that affects the central nervous system. A diagnosis in this category implies an undesirable behavioral change and should not be primarily based on whether the substance use is illegal or socially undesirable. These conditions are separate from symptoms associated with appropriate medical use of the substances described. The term *dependence*, when used here, does not necessarily imply physiological dependence.

Psychoactive Substance Use Disorders are separate from the above organic mental disorders related to substance use and should be coded separately from any Axis III physical damage that has occurred.

---

*"331.00" is the ICD-9 code for Alzheimer's disease.

Schizophrenia

Schizophrenia is coded as one of five subtypes, each of which meets the criteria described later in the text. Characteristic psychotic symptoms during the active phase of illness, lowered functioning, and a specified duration of illness are all essential features.

If the symptoms of Schizophrenia are an outgrowth of either an organic mental disorder or a mood (affective) disorder, the organic or affective diagnosis should prevail unless or until it can be clearly shown that two separate disorders exist.   **41**

Delusional (Paranoid) Disorder

This is a category limited to patients who show persistent, "nonbizarre" delusions, not apparently due to any other mental disorder or organic factor.

Psychotic Disorders Not Elsewhere Classified

This category is designed to account for psychotic disorders that appear separate from organic, schizophrenic, delusional, or mood disorders. Some of the diagnoses (Brief Reactive Psychosis and Schizophreniform Disorder) have criteria related to symptom duration which, in part, separates them from Schizophrenia. A third, Schizoaffective Disorder, incorporates some characteristics of Mood Disorders.

Mood Disorders

Mood Disorders ("Affective Disorders" in DSM-III) share a disturbance of mood that is accompanied by symptoms of a manic or depressive syndrome not due to any other physical or mental disorder. The prolonged   **42** emotion that forms the mood generally affects one's entire life and is usually either depression or elation. There are two subcategories of mood disorders: bipolar and depressive.

Anxiety Disorders (Anxiety and Phobic Neuroses)

Anxiety Disorders are not to be confused with *symptoms* of anxiety in other disorders. In order to qualify for a diagnosis of anxiety disorder,   **43** the anxiety and avoidance behavior that characterize this category must be primary.

Somatoform Disorders

These seven disorders have in common physical symptoms for which there is a lack of organic or physiologic findings and there is significant evidence that psychological factors are involved. It is important to note that these disorders are not voluntary (unlike Factitious Disorder or Malingering). Although the patient may experience "primary gain" or "secondary gain" for unconscious reasons, the symptoms are not directly related to material reward. Some of the disorders are referred to in earlier diagnostic schemata as "hysterical."

Dissociative Disorders

The Dissociative Disorders, sometimes called "hysterical neuroses, dis-
44   sociative type," are manifested by some disturbance or alteration in the integrative functions of identity, memory, or consciousness, not related to organic illness or other psychoses. The symptoms may appear suddenly or gradually and may be transient or chronic. The patient may forget his own identity (as in the Multiple Personality Disorder), lose the feeling of reality (as in Depersonalization Disorder), or experience disturbance of memory (as in Psychogenic Amnesia or Psychogenic Fugue). Sleepwalking, in some ways a Dissociative Disorder, is coded with the Sleep Disorders (see below).

Sexual Disorders

The Sexual Disorders are divided into two groups, the Paraphilias and the Sexual Dysfunctions. The Paraphilias are disorders characterized by recurrent, intense sexual urges for which the object or process involved is socially and/or emotionally deviant. The fantasies and activities range from relatively harmless ones to those which are intrusive and/or harmful to others.

The Sexual Dysfunctions are disorders of normal, consenting sexual function described in DSM-III-R as "inhibition in the appetitive or psychophysiologic changes that characterize the complete sexual response cycle" (p. 290). There are four phases of that cycle: appetitive, excitement, orgasm, and resolution.

Sleep Disorders

The Sleep Disorders are divided into the Dyssomnias and the Parasomnias. The Dyssomnias are disorders of amount, quality, or timing of sleep (e.g.,
45   insomnia, hypersomnia). The Parasomnias are characterized by abnormal events during sleep (e.g., sleepwalking, sleep terrors). Some other disorders related to the neurophysiology of sleep are either not coded in this category (e.g., Functional Enuresis) or not found in DSM-III-R.

Factitious Disorders
Factitious Disorders are characterized by physical or psychological symptoms that are produced voluntarily, primarily for a psychologically grati- **46** fying purpose rather than for obvious personal gain. They are thus distinguished from Malingering. The process by which factitious symptoms are produced may be quite complex and sophisticated.

Impulse Control Disorders Not Elsewhere Classified
The essential features of these disorders are failure to resist an impulse, drive, or temptation to do something harmful to oneself or others; an increasing sense of tension or arousal before the driven behavior; and a sense of pleasure, gratification, or "release" while committing the act. The patient may or may not try to resist committing the act, plan it, or regret it afterward.

Adjustment Disorders
Adjustment Disorders are maladaptive emotional reactions to identifiable psychosocial stressors, manifested by disturbances of mood, conduct, social and interpersonal relationships, or physical health. Adjustment Disorders remit with decrease or disappearance of the stressor, or with improvement in adaptation. They are thus separated from Post-Traumatic Stress Disorders, and should not be mistaken for exacerbations of other mental disorders or simple overreactions to stress.

Psychological Factors Affecting Physical Condition
This category codes psychological factors that contribute to the initiation or exacerbation of a physical condition. The physical problem should be coded on Axis III. The category is separate from Somatoform Disorders, in which no pathophysiology is demonstrable. Some psychological factors affecting physical condition may, however, describe "psychosomatic" or "psychophysiological" symptoms (e.g., psychological factors exacerbating dermatitides, asthma, ulcerative colitis).

Personality Disorders (Coded on Axis II)
DSM-III-R Personality Disorders are characterized by chronic, maladaptive personality traits which pervade both the patient's recent past and his functioning since early adulthood. Diagnostic criteria vary from somewhat vague to highly specific. Most personality disorders are best diag-

nosed only in adults. Some have corresponding diagnostic categories which may be chosen from the Disorders Usually First Evident in Infancy, Childhood, or Adolescence. The Personality Disorders are divided into three "clusters." Patients with cluster A disorders often appear odd or
47   eccentric; those with cluster B disorders may appear dramatic, emotional, or erratic; and those with cluster C disorders may appear anxious or fearful much of the time.

V Codes for Conditions Not Attributable to a Mental Disorder That Are a Focus of Attention or Treatment

The V codes classify problems or symptoms which are apparently not due to any mental disorder—and thus do not merit any "diagnosis"—but which nevertheless cause personal or social distress that has brought them to clinical attention. Although treatment may be indicated, overdiagnosis (e.g., coding as a mental disorder) should be avoided.

Additional Codes
48   The "Additional Codes" in the DSM-III-R should not be ignored. They should be used when diagnostic information is lacking, when diagnosis should be deferred, or when no diagnostic category on a particular axis is appropriate. One should use these codes in lieu of incomplete preliminary diagnoses, in spite of common administrative pressures to the contrary.

Proposed Diagnostic Codes
These codes should not be used in any official clinical context, whether or not one agrees with their criteria. One may use them for personal reference or research.

Section II

The Disorders

Chapter 10

Disorders Usually First Evident in Infancy, Childhood, or Adolescence

This large classification describes disorders that usually begin or become evident in infancy, childhood, or adolescence. Any clinician using this **49** category should have a basic knowledge of normal development in order to be able to distinguish between normal variations due to age or developmental stage and true clinical syndromes.

If appropriate diagnoses cannot be found in this section, disorders described elsewhere in DSM-III-R should be considered, provided there is no proscription against their use in children or adolescents.

Many of these disorders can present after adolescence (e.g., gender identity disorders, eating disorders). The proper coding is nevertheless within this category.

A. DEVELOPMENTAL DISORDERS (AXIS II)

The essential feature of this group of disorders is a disturbance—general **50** or specific—in the acquisition or retention of cognitive, language, motor, or social skills. These disorders are coded on Axis II because they tend to be chronic and may persist into adult life without remission.

Mental Retardation (Axis II) (317.00, 318.00, 318.10, 318.20, 319.00)

Essential features. Significantly subaverage general intellectual functioning and significant deficits or impairments in adaptive functioning, both of which present before the age of 18. Although a valid and reliable

51 intelligence quotient (IQ) measurement is a major indicator of retardation, the IQ should be treated with some flexibility in order to allow for unusual additional deficits or to acknowledge unusually good adaptation.

When a known biological factor is present, it should be noted on Axis III. For persons who become functioning retarded after a period of normal intelligence, both Dementia and Mental Retardation should be diagnosed.

Complications of Mental Retardation may include Depression, Personality Disorders, and—less commonly—Psychotic Disorders. One should separate symptoms related to the Mental Retardation from those associated with "functional" disorders.

Differential diagnosis. Mental Retardation should be diagnosed when
52 the criteria are met, regardless of the presence of other diagnoses. Specific Developmental Disorders reflect a delay or failure of development in a specific area, in contrast to Mental Retardation's general developmental delays. Pervasive Developmental Disorders reflect *abnormal* development, as opposed to Mental Retardation's *delay* in development. Borderline Intellectual Functioning does not imply Mental Retardation.

Diagnostic criteria for Mental Retardation (317.00–319.00):

A. Significantly subaverage general intellectual functioning, usually based on valid and reliable IQ tests.
B. Accompanying deficits in functioning with respect to social skills, communication, skills of daily living, and/or self-sufficiency.
C. Onset before age 18.

Mild Mental Retardation (317.00)—IQ 50–55 to about 70.
Moderate Mental Retardation (318.00)—IQ 35–40 to 50–55.
53 **Severe Mental Retardation (318.10)**—IQ 20–25 to 35–40.
Profound Mental Retardation (318.20)—IQ below 20–25.
Unspecified Mental Retardation (319.00)—Strong presumption of Mental Retardation in a patient who is untestable by standard methods (e.g., because of severe impairment, lack of cooperation, or very young age).

These categories do not apply to people suspected of meeting V code criteria for Borderline Intellectual Functioning.

Pervasive Developmental Disorders (Axis II)

Essential features. These disorders are characterized by qualitative   54
impairment in the development of reciprocal social interaction, verbal
and nonverbal communication skills, and imaginative activity. There is
often a severely restricted repertoire of activities and interests, which
may be stereotyped and repetitive.

Associated features. Often increasing with severity of handicap and
younger age of the child, these may include uneven abnormalities in
development of cognitive skills, stereotypies and other abnormalities of
posture and motor behavior, odd or absent responses to sensory input,
abnormalities in preferred diet or sleep pattern, anxiety, abnormalities of
mood, and self-injurious behavior. Other mental disorders frequently
occur, but are often difficult to diagnose because of the patient's communication deficits.

Predisposing factors. A great many pre-, peri-, and postnatal organic
conditions predispose infants to development of Pervasive Developmental Disorders.

Differential diagnosis. Mental Retardation (which may coexist with
it), Schizophrenia (although extremely rare in childhood), hearing or
visual impairment, and Specific Developmental Language and Speech
Disorders. Tic Disorders and Stereotypy/Habit Disorder are characterized
by stereotyped body movements, without qualitative impairments in
reciprocal social interaction.

Autistic Disorder (299.00)
Diagnostic criteria for Autistic Disorder:

Severe Pervasive Developmental Disorder with onset in infancy or
childhood, plus at least *eight* of the following (including *two* from
group *A*, *one* from group *B*, and *one* from group *C*). A criterion is
considered met *only* if the behavior is abnormal for the child's
developmental level.

A. Reciprocal social interaction.
    1. Marked lack of awareness of the existence of feelings of
       others

    2. No or abnormal seeking of comfort at times of distress

    3. No or impaired imitation behavior

    4. No or abnormal social play

    5. Gross impairment in ability to make peer friendships

B. Verbal and nonverbal communication, imaginative activity.

    1. No mode of communication

    2. Markedly abnormal nonverbal communication

    3. Absence of imaginative activity (e.g., fantasies, acting out adult roles, interest in stories about imaginary events)

    4. Marked abnormalities in speech production

    5. Marked abnormalities in form of content of speech (including stereotyped or repetitive speech)

    6. Marked impairment in the ability to initiate or sustain a conversation, despite adequate speech

C. Repertoire of activities and interests.

    1. Stereotyped body movements

    2. Persistent preoccupation with parts of objects

    3. Marked distress over changes in trivial aspects of the environment

    4. Unreasonable insistence on following routines in precise detail

    5. Markedly restricted range of interests, with preoccupation with a narrow interest

D. Onset during infancy or childhood.

Specify whether childhood onset (after 36 months of age)

Pervasive Developmental Disorder Not Otherwise Specified (299.80)
This is a residual disorder for patients with qualitative impairment and development of reciprocal social interaction and verbal and nonverbal communication skills, but for whom criteria are not met for Autistic Disorder, Schizophrenia, or Schizotypal or Schizoid Personality Disorder.

Specific Developmental Disorders (Axis II)

    Essential features. These disorders are characterized by inadequate development of specific academic, language, speech, and/or motor skills not due to demonstrable physical or neurological disorders, Pervasive

Developmental Disorder, Mental Retardation, or lack of education opportunity.

Predisposing factors are similar to those for Pervasive Developmental Disorders.

Complications include Academic Skills Disorders and Conduct Disorders.

Developmental Arithmetic Disorder (315.10)

Essential feature. Marked impairment of development of the arithmetic skills.

Associated features. Other Specific Developmental Disorders, especially academic skills disorders.

Differential diagnosis. Mental Retardation, inadequate schooling.

Diagnostic criteria for Developmental Arithmetic Disorder:

A. Arithmetic skills markedly below expected level, as measured by standardized, valid, and reliable tests, given adequate schooling and intellectual capacity.
B. Significantly interferes with academic achievement or activities of daily living requiring arithmetic skills.
C. Not due to a defect in visual or hearing acuity, or a neurologic disorder.

Developmental Expressive Writing Disorder (315.80)

Essential features. Marked impairment in the development of expressive writing skills.

Associated features. Other Specific Developmental Disorders, especially academic skills disorders.

Differential diagnosis. Mental Retardation, impaired vision or hearing, impaired motor coordination, inadequate schooling.

Diagnostic criteria for Developmental Expressive Writing Disorder:

A. Writing skills, as measured by standardized, valid, and reliable tests, given adequate schooling and intellectual capacity.
B. Significantly interferes with academic achievement or activities of daily living requiring writing.
C. Not due to a defect in hearing or visual acuity or a neurologic disorder.

Developmental Reading Disorder (315.00)

Essential feature. Marked impairment in the development of word recognition skills and reading comprehension.

Associated features. Other developmental deficits, commonly Expressive or Receptive Language Disorder or Disruptive Behavior Disorders.

Differential diagnosis. Mental Retardation, which is more a general than a specific impairment in intellectual functioning; inadequate schooling; impaired vision or hearing.

Diagnostic criteria for Developmental Reading Disorder:

A. Reading achievement, appropriately measured, markedly below the expected level given adequate schooling and intellectual capacity.
B. Significantly interferes with academic achievement or activities of daily living requiring reading skills.
C. Not due to a defect in visual or hearing acuity, or a neurologic disorder.

Developmental Articulation Disorder (a language and speech disorder) (315.39)

Essential feature. Consistent failure to make correct articulations of speech sounds, given development appropriate for age. A number of speech sounds involving consonants, often those which are acquired later in development, may be affected, but not vowel sounds.

Associated features. Other Specific Developmental Disorders, including Coordination Disorder, Functional Enuresis, delayed speech milestones.

Differential diagnosis. Physical abnormalities causing misarticulation, hearing impairment, dysarthria or apraxia, Mental Retardation, Pervasive Developmental Disorder.

Diagnostic criteria for Developmental Articulation Disorder:

A. Consistent failure to make or use developmentally expected speech sounds, especially consonant sounds.
B. Not due to Pervasive Developmental Disorder, Mental Retardation, defective hearing acuity, disorders of oral speech mechanism, or neurologic disorders.

Developmental Expressive Language Disorder (a language and speech disorder) (315.31)

Essential feature. Marked impairment in the development of expressive language.

Associated features. Frequent Developmental Articulation Disorder, school and learning problems, delay in motor development milestones, occasional Developmental Coordination Disorder or Functional Enuresis. Emotional problems, social withdrawal, and behavioral difficulties may be present.

Differential diagnosis. Mental Retardation, impaired hearing, Pervasive Developmental Disorders, Elective Mutism (for which comprehension is usually found to be within normal limits upon formal testing), and acquired aphasia (differentiated by its history of onset associated with head trauma, intracranial abnormality, or significant neurologic signs).

Diagnostic criteria for Developmental Expressive Language Disorder:

A. Substantially lowered scores on standardized measures of expressive language, when compared to the patient's scores on individual, nonverbal tests of intellectual capacity.
B. Significantly interferes with academic achievement or activities of daily living requiring the expression of verbal (including sign) language.

C. Not due to Mental Retardation, Pervasive Developmental Disorder, inadequate schooling, defect in hearing acuity, or neurologic disorder (e.g., aphasia).

Developmental Receptive Language Disorder (a language and speech disorder) (315.31)

Essential feature. Marked impairment in the development of language comprehension.

Associated features. Developmental Articulation Disorder and Developmental Expressive Language Disorder; Academic Skills Disorders. Functional Enuresis, Developmental Coordination Disorder, Attention-Deficit Hyperactivity Disorder, EEG abnormalities, and other social/behavioral problems are less common.

Differential diagnosis. Mental Retardation, hearing impairment, Pervasive Developmental Disorders, Elective Mutism (in which comprehension is found to be within normal limits upon careful testing), acquired aphasia (distinguished by its history of significant head trauma, intracranial abnormalities, or significant neurological signs).

Diagnostic criteria for Developmental Receptive Language Disorder:

A. Standardized measures of receptive language show scores substantially below those of standardized measures of nonverbal intellectual capacity on individually administered intelligence tests.
B. Significantly interferes with academic achievement or activities of daily living requiring comprehension of verbal (or sign) language.
C. Not due to Mental Retardation, Pervasive Developmental Disorder, inadequate schooling, defect in hearing acuity, or neurologic disorder (e.g., aphasia).

Developmental Coordination Disorder (a motor skills disorder) (315.40)

Essential feature. Marked impairment in the development of motor coordination not explainable by Mental Retardation or known physical disorder.

Associated feature. Delays in nonmotor developmental milestones, Developmental Articulation Disorder, and Developmental Receptive and Expressive Language Disorders are common.

Differential diagnosis. Specific neurologic disorders, Attention-Deficit Hyperactivity Disorder, Mental Retardation, Pervasive Developmental Disorders.

Diagnostic criteria for Developmental Coordination Disorder:

A. Performance in daily activities requiring motor coordination is markedly below the expected level, given the patient's chronological age and intellectual capacity.
B. Significantly interferes with academic achievement or activities of daily living.
C. Not due to Mental Retardation or known physical disorder (including neurologic disorders).

Specific Developmental Disorder Not Otherwise Specified (315.90)
These are disorders in the developmental language, speech, academic, and motor skills that do not meet any of the above criteria, but are clinically significant and cannot be coded adequately elsewhere. Examples in DSM-III-R include aphasia with epilepsy acquired in childhood ("Landau syndrome") and specific developmental difficulties (e.g., spelling).

Other Developmental Disorders (Axis II)

Developmental Disorder Not Otherwise Specified (315.90)
This is a residual category for clinically significant disorders of development that do not meet criteria for either Mental Retardation or other pervasive Specific Developmental Disorders and are not adequately coded elsewhere.

B. DISRUPTIVE BEHAVIOR DISORDERS
These disorders are characterized by socially disruptive behavior, often more distressing to others than to the patient.   56

Attention-Deficit Hyperactivity Disorder (ADHD) (314.01)

Essential features. Developmentally inappropriate inattention, impulsiveness, and hyperactivity. Manifestations generally appear in more than one setting (e.g., home, school, work, social situations), often in varying degrees. Rarely, the signs are seen in only one setting (e.g., home or school). The disorder tends to worsen when sustained attention is required, such as during school or chores at home. When one-to-one attention is given or external controls are strict, the signs may decrease significantly.

In preschool children, gross motor overactivity is usually the most prominent feature. In older children and adolescents, restlessness, inattention, and impulsiveness prevail, and lack of task completion or careless performance of assigned work is often the rule. In older adolescents, impulsive diverting of one's energies away from required activities (e.g., socializing instead of doing schoolwork) is common.

Associated features vary with age and may include poor self-esteem, lability of mood, poor frustration tolerance, and temper outbursts. Academic underachievement is characteristic. Symptoms of Oppositional Defiant Disorder, Conduct Disorder, and Specific Developmental Disorders are often seen. Functional Encopresis or Enuresis is occasionally seen. In clinical samples, Tourette's disorder is often accompanied by ADHD. "Soft" neurological signs and motor-perceptual deficits may be present.

Predisposing factors include central nervous system abnormalities, especially intracranial ones. Child abuse or neglect and chaotic developmental environments are overrepresented in these patients.

Differential diagnosis. Age-appropriate overactivity (which is generally better organized and less random than is seen in ADHD); social reaction or adjustment reaction to inadequate, disorganized, or chaotic environments; Mental Retardation; Pervasive Developmental Disorders; Mood Disorders. The latter should always be considered before making the diagnosis of ADHD. In Undifferentiated Attention-Deficit Disorder, impulsiveness and hyperactivity are not present.

Diagnostic criteria for Attention-Deficit Hyperactivity Disorder:

The following criteria must be considerably more frequent than for most children of the same mental age:

A. At least *eight* of the following present for at least six months:
1. fidgeting, squirming, or restlessness
2. difficulty remaining seated when required to do so
3. easily distracted by extraneous stimuli
4. difficulty awaiting one's turn in games or groups
5. often blurts out answers before questions are completed
6. difficulty following through with instructions from others
7. difficulty sustaining attention in tasks or play
8. often shifts from one uncompleted activity to another
9. has difficulty playing quietly
10. often talks excessively
11. often interrupts or intrudes on others
12. often does not seem to listen to what is being said to him or her
13. often loses things necessary for tasks or activities at school or at home
14. often engages in physically dangerous activities without considering possible consequences (but not for the purpose of "thrill seeking")

B. Onset before age seven.
C. Does not meet criteria for Pervasive Developmental Disorder.

DSM-III-R's optional "severity criteria" are as follows:

Mild—barely meets the diagnostic requirements; minimal impairment in school or social functioning.

Moderate—symptoms or functional impairment intermediate between "mild" and "severe."

Severe—many symptoms in excess of those required to make the diagnosis, *and* significant and pervasive impairment in home and school functioning and with peers.

57

Conduct Disorder (312.xx)

Essential features. The essential feature for each of the three types below (Group, Solitary Aggressive, and Undifferentiated) is a persistent pattern of conduct in which the basic rights of others and major age-appropriate societal norms or rules are violated. The behaviors are typically present in many environments—home, school, with peers, in the community—and are more serious than those seen in Oppositional Defiant Disorder (below). Physical aggression is common, which may include cruelty and deliberate destruction. Violent and/or antisocial behavior may become more serious as the child ages.

Associated features. Substance use or abuse or sexual behavior beginning unusually early for the child's peer group; lack of concern for the feelings and well-being of others; lack of guilt or remorse, low self-esteem (although the patient may appear "tough"), poor frustration tolerance, temper outbursts, provocative recklessness; anxiety, depression, and/or low academic achievement which may justify additional diagnoses.

Predisposing factors. Attention-Deficit Hyperactivity Disorder and Oppositional Defiant Disorder have been associated with Conduct Disorders, as have parental rejection, inconsistent parenting, early institutional placement, paternal absence or social deviance, large family size, and association with delinquent subgroups.

Differential diagnosis. Isolated antisocial behavior (which may be coded as a V code); Oppositional Defiant Disorder; Attention-Deficit Hyperactivity Disorder and Specific Developmental Disorders (the last two of which should be diagnosed separately).

Diagnostic criteria for Conduct Disorder (312.xx) (code type as defined below):

A. A history of at least six months of persistent conduct disturbance which includes at least *three* of the following:
   1. two or more incidents of stealing without confronting the victim (including forgery)
   2. running away from home overnight at least twice (or once without returning)
   3. frequent lying (other than to avoid physical or sexual abuse)
   4. deliberate firesetting
   5. frequent truancy or absence from work
   6. breaking into others' property
   7. deliberate destruction of others' property (other than by firesetting)

8. physically cruel to animals
9. forced sexual activity
10. more than one fight in which a weapon has been used
11. frequent initiation of physical fights
12. stealing with confrontation of the victim (e.g., mugging)
13. physically cruel to people

B. If 18 or older, does not meet the criteria for Antisocial Personality Disorder.

Optional Severity Criteria:

Mild—barely meets the diagnostic criteria and has caused only minor harm to others.
Moderate—intermediate between "mild" and "severe."
Severe—problems considerably in excess of the above criteria, *or* considerable harm caused to others.

Specify:

Group Type (312.20) (conduct problems occurring mainly as a group 58 activity with peers, with or without physical aggression)
Solitary Aggressive Type (312.00) (predominance of aggressive physical behavior, usually toward both adults and peers, initiated individually [not as a group activity])
Undifferentiated Type (312.90) (children or adolescents with mixed clinical features, unable to be classified as either solitary aggressive or group type)

Oppositional Defiant Disorder (313.81)

Essential feature. A pattern of negativistic, hostile, and defiant behavior, but without the serious violations of rights of others seen in Conduct Disorder. May not be manifest in school or outside the family, but almost always seen at home.

Associated features. Low self-esteem, mood lability, low frustration tolerance, temper outbursts, and substance abuse, varying with age. Attention-Deficit Hyperactivity Disorder is often present.

Differential diagnosis. Conduct Disorder and oppositional behavior as a result of Psychotic Disorder or Affective Disorder.

Diagnostic criteria for Oppositional Defiant Disorder:

A. At least *five* of the following for at least six months, each considerably more frequent than in most people of the same mental age:
   1. often loses temper
   2. often argues with adults
   3. often actively defies adult requests or rules
   4. often deliberately annoys other people
   5. often blames others for own mistakes
   6. often touchy or easily annoyed
   7. often angry and resentful
   8. often spiteful or vindictive
   9. frequent use of swearing or obscene language
B. Does not meet criteria for Conduct Disorder or occur exclusively during the course of Psychotic Disorder or Affective Disorders.

Optional severity criteria:

Mild—barely meets the above criteria, and only minimal impairment in school and social functioning.

Moderate—between "mild" and "severe."

Severe—many symptoms in excess of those required, and significant and pervasive impairment in functioning at home and at school, with adults and peers.

C. ANXIETY DISORDERS OF CHILDHOOD OR ADOLESCENCE

Anxiety is the predominant clinical feature, whether it is focused on specific situations or generalized.

Separation Anxiety Disorder (309.21)

Essential feature. Excessive anxiety concerning separation from those to whom the child is attached. The anxiety is beyond that expected for the child's developmental level. Children often show fears of real or imaginary objects or extreme homesickness. Older children and adolescents, especially boys, may deny their overconcern, yet exhibit symptoms of anxiety. Although a form of phobia, it is not included among the Phobic Disorders. When no demands for separation are made, the symptoms are typically absent.

Associated features. Fear of the dark, fixed fears that may appear bizarre, depressed mood (which may justify an additional diagnosis of a Mood Disorder).

Predisposing factors. The disorder frequently is associated with a life stress, typically a loss (which may be a death, divorce, family move, or any other change in the environment). Close-knit families are overrepresented in this diagnostic category, while neglected children are underrepresented.

Differential diagnosis. Normal separation anxiety of early childhood, Overanxious Disorder (in which anxiety is not focused on separation), Pervasive Developmental Disorders or Schizophrenia (either of which preempts the Separation Anxiety diagnosis), Mood Disorders (which are diagnosed concomitantly if both criteria are met), Panic Disorders. In Conduct Disorder, the child stays away from home as well as school and usually does not show signs of anxiety about separation.

Diagnostic criteria for Separation Anxiety Disorder:

A. Excessive anxiety concerning separation from those to whom the child is attached, as evidenced by at least *three* of the following:
   1. unrealistic and persistent worry about possible harm befalling the major attachment figure or fear that he or she will leave forever
   2. unrealistic and persistent worry that a calamitous event will separate the child from the major attachment figure
   3. persistent reluctance or refusal to go to school in order to stay with the major attachment figure(s)
   4. persistent reluctance or refusal to go to sleep without being near the major attachment figure
   5. persistent avoidance of being alone, including clinging to major attachment figures

6. repeated nightmares involving separation themes
7. frequent complaints of physical symptoms on schooldays or at other times of anticipated separation from major attachment figures
8. recurrent signs or complaints of excessive distress in anticipation of separation from home or major attachment figures (e.g., temper tantrums, crying, pleading with parents not to leave)
9. recurrent signs or complaints of excessive distress when separated from home or major attachment figures

B. Duration of disturbance at least two weeks.

C. Onset before the age of 18.

D. Occurrence not exclusively associated with Pervasive Developmental Disorder, Schizophrenia, or other Psychotic Disorder.

Avoidant Disorder of Childhood or Adolescence (313.21)

Essential feature. Excessive shrinking from contact with unfamiliar people. The child frequently appears socially withdrawn, embarrassed, and timid. If the anxiety is severe, the child may become regressed or even mute, even if communication skills are unimpaired.

Associated features include a general lack of assertiveness and self-confidence. In adolescence, inhibition of normal psychosexual activity is common. The disorder usually coexists with other anxiety disorders.

Predisposing factors. Specific Developmental Disorders involving language or speech.

Differential diagnosis. Simple social reticence, Separation Anxiety Disorder, Overanxious Disorder, Major Depression or Dysthymia, Adjustment Disorder with Withdrawal. The diagnosis should not be made if the disturbance meets criteria for Avoidant Personality Disorder.

Diagnostic criteria for Avoidant Disorder of Childhood or Adolescence:

A. Excessive shrinking from contact with unfamiliar people, for six months or longer, sufficiently severe to interfere with social functioning in peer relationships.

   B. Desire for social involvement with familiar people and generally warm and satisfying relations with family members and other familiar figures.

   C. Age at least two and one-half years.

   D. Does not meet criteria for Avoidant Personality Disorder.

Overanxious Disorder (313.00)

Essential feature. Excessive or unrealistic anxiety or worry. Extreme self-conciousness and worry about future events, injury, peer approval, and so forth and concern about past behavior are characteristic. Physical complaints, sometimes almost to the point of obsession, are common.

Associated features. Social or Simple Phobia, perfectionistic tendencies, excessively conforming and approval seeking, anxiety about activities that demand certain levels of performance.

Predisposing factors. Eldest children in small families, upper socio-economic groups, family concerns about achievement even if the child is functioning quite adequately.

Differential diagnosis. Separation Anxiety Disorder, Attention-Deficit Hyperactivity Disorder (in which the child is not particularly concerned about the future). Each may be diagnosed concomitantly with Overanxious Disorder. Adjustment Disorder with Anxious Mood (associated with a recent stressor and lasting less than six months); Psychotic Disorders or Mood Disorders.

Diagnostic criteria for Overanxious Disorder:

   A. Excessive or unrealistic anxiety or worry, for six months or longer, indicated by frequent occurrence of at least *four* of the following:

      1. excessive or unrealistic worry about future events

      2. excessive or unrealistic concerns about the appropriateness of past behavior

      3. excessive or unrealistic concern about competence in one or more areas

      4. somatic complaints for which no physical basis can be established

     5. marked self-consciousness

     6. excessive need for reassurance

     7. marked feelings of tension or inability to relax

  B. If another Axis I disorder is present, the focus of symptoms in "A" above is not limited to it.

  C. If the patient is 18 or older, he or she does not meet criteria for Generalized Anxiety Disorder.

  D. Occurrence does not occur exclusively during the course of a Pervasive Developmental Disorder, Schizophrenia, or any other psychotic disorder.

D. EATING DISORDERS

60   These are gross disturbances in eating behavior, typically beginning in adolescence or early adult life (except Pica and Rumination Disorder of Infancy). Simple obesity is coded as a physical disorder and is not included in this section unless emotional symptoms merit inclusion under Psychological Factors Affecting Physical Condition (316.00).

Anorexia Nervosa (307.10)

61   **Essential features.** Refusal to maintain body weight over a minimal normal weight for age and height; intense fear of gaining weight or becoming fat, even though underweight; distorted body image; and amenorrhea in females. The disturbance of body image is manifested in the way in which the patient's weight, size, and shape are experienced (often as "I feel fat").

    Associated features include self-induced vomiting or use of purgatives (but the primary mode of weight loss is reduction in food intake). Weighing less than 85% of one's expected weight is a rough landmark, frequently followed by metabolic signs such as hypothermia, bradycardia, hypotension, edema, lanugo (neonatal-like body hair), and amenorrhea. Bulimic episodes, often followed by vomiting, frequent focus on food as a topic of thought or fantasy, and unusual hoarding or concealing of food are also seen. Patients almost always deny or minimize the severity of their illness and are resistant to therapy. Delayed psychosexual development is common in adolescence, as is decreased libido in adults. Compulsive behaviors may be present and may justify an additional diagnosis of Obsessive Compulsive Disorder.

Predisposing factors. Occasionally, stressful life situations are associated with onset. Perfectionistic behavior and mild obesity are common before onset. About 95% of patients are female.

Differential diagnosis. Weight loss from depressive disorders or physical disorders, Schizophrenia with bizarre eating patterns (if the full Anorexia Nervosa syndrome is present, both diagnoses should be given), Bulimia Nervosa without associated Anorexia Nervosa (both diagnoses may be appropriate).

Diagnostic criteria for Anorexia Nervosa:

A. Refusal to maintain body weight above minimum normal weight for age and height (sometimes arbitrarily established at 85% of expected weight) or failure to gain weight routinely during periods of body growth, leading to body weight at least 15% below that which is expected.
B. Intense fear of gaining weight or becoming fat, even though underweight.
C. Disturbance in the way in which one's body weight, size, or shape is experienced (e.g., feeling "fat" even when emaciated, unrealistically feeling that one part of the body is "too fat").
D. In females, absence of at least three consecutive menstrual cycles which would otherwise be expected to occur. Amenorrhea is said to exist if periods occur only following hormone administration.

Bulimia Nervosa (307.51)

Essential feature. Recurrent episodes of binge eating (rapid eating of 62 large amounts of food over a short period of time), with a feeling of lack of control over eating behavior during these binges. The food consumed is often sweet and of high caloric content. It is usually eaten inconspicuously or secretly, followed by abdominal discomfort, sleep, social interruption, or (frequently) induced vomiting to decrease the physical pain and distention. Vomiting allows either continued eating or termination of the binge and often reduces unpleasant feelings.

Associated features. Obesity (although not required), depressed mood, substance abuse or dependence.

Predisposing factors. Obesity in adolescence. About 90% of patients are female.

Differential diagnosis. Anorexia Nervosa (which may coexist with it), Schizophrenia with unusual eating behaviors (but usually without the full bulimic syndrome), certain rare forms of "epileptic equivalent seizures," intracranial tumors, Kleine-Levin syndrome, and other neurological diseases. Binge eating is often a feature of Borderline Personality Disorder in women, and both diagnoses may be given if full criteria are met.

Diagnostic criteria for Bulimia Nervosa:

A. Recurrent binge eating episodes (defined above).
B. A feeling of lack of control over eating behavior during the binges.
C. Regular engagement in self-induced vomiting, use of laxatives or diuretics, strict dieting or fasting, or vigorous exercise in order to prevent weight gain.
D. Minimum of two binge-eating episodes per week, planned or impulsive, for at least three months.
E. Persistent overconcern with body shape and weight.

Pica (307.52)

Essential feature. Persistent eating of a nonnutritive substance. Infants typically eat paint, plaster, string, hair, and so forth. Older children may eat animal droppings, sand, insects, leaves, and so forth. There is no aversion to food.

Complications. Lead poisoning, infections, bezoars.

Predisposing factors. Mental Retardation, child neglect, poor supervision. Pica is rare in adults but is occasionally seen in the mentally retarded and in pregnant females.

Differential diagnosis. Autistic Disorder, Schizophrenia, certain physical disorders (e.g., Kleine-Levin syndrome). Pica should not be additionally coded in these disorders.

Diagnostic criteria for Pica:

A. Repeated eating of a nonnutritive substance for at least one month.
B. Does not meet criteria for Autistic Disorder, Schizophrenia, or Kleine-Levin syndrome.

Rumination Disorder of Infancy (307.53)

Essential feature. Repeated regurgitation of food, with weight loss or failure to gain expected weight, which develops after a period of normal functioning. Nausea, retching, disgust, or associated gastrointestinal disorders are not present. The food may be ejected or chewed and reswallowed. There is a characteristic straining and arching position, with the head held back. The infant appears to experience satisfaction from this activity.

Associated features. Irritability or hunger between episodes of regurgitation. The disorder usually appears between 3 and 12 months of age, occasionally later in mentally retarded children.

Complications. Death from malnutrition; frustration of caretakers, sometimes alienating them from the child.

Differential diagnosis. Congenital abnormalities, including pyloric stenosis, gastrointestinal infections.

Diagnostic criteria for Rumination Disorder of Infancy:

A. Repeated regurgitation, without nausea or associated gastrointestinal illness, for at least one month, following a period of normal functioning.
B. Weight loss or failure to achieve expected weight gain.

Eating Disorder Not Otherwise Specified (307.50)

This residual category is for clinically significant disorders that do not meet criteria for a specific eating disorder and are not subsumed by other psychiatric or medical diagnoses (e.g., self-induced vomiting for routine weight loss; features of Anorexia Nervosa in a female without absence of menses; features of Bulimia Nervosa without the required frequency of binge-eating episodes).

E. GENDER IDENTITY DISORDERS

The disorders in this subcategory are characterized by incongruity between one's clinically assigned sex and his or her gender identity. That is, the patient's sense of knowing the sex to which he or she belongs—the private experience of gender role (as the public expression of gender identity)—is distorted. These disturbances are quite rare and should not be confused with common feelings of inadequacy at fulfilling one's gender expectations. Patients may present at any age, but in the majority the onset can be traced to childhood.

Gender Identity Disorder of Childhood (302.60)

Essential features. Persistent and intense distress in a child about his or her assigned sex and the desire to be—or insistence that one is—the opposite sex. This feature does not imply mere sex role nonconformity, but rather a profound disturbance of the sense of maleness or femaleness. Boys with this disorder are either preoccupied with stereotypic female activities or persistently repudiate their male anatomy. In girls, there is persistent, marked aversion to normal feminine clothing or repudiation of female anatomical characteristics. The diagnosis is not made after onset of puberty.

Associated features. Other signs of psychopathology may be present; however, many patients, especially girls, show none. Social withdrawal, separation anxiety, or depression is common.

Complications. A small number of patients evolve into Transsexualism or Gender Identity Disorder of Adolescence or Adulthood, Nontranssexual Type. Impairment may vary from little to extreme, largely relative to peer and family behavior.

Predisposing factors. Effeminate physical features in boys, subtle or obvious reinforcement of opposite-sex behavior, unduly weak reinforcement of normal gender-role behavior, nonavailability of a father, physical and psychological seductiveness by the mother. In clinical populations, the disorder is considerably more common in boys.

Differential diagnosis. Children whose behavior merely does not fit cultural stereotypes, physical abnormalities of sex organs (which rarely are associated with this disorder, and should be noted on Axis III).

Diagnostic criteria for Gender Identity Disorder of Childhood:

For *females:*

A. Persistent and intense distress about being a girl, and a desire to be a boy or insistence that she is a boy (and not merely a voicing of perceived advantages of boyhood).

B. *One* of the following:
   1. persistent marked aversion to normal feminine clothing and insistence on wearing stereotypic masculine clothing
   2. persistent repudiation of female anatomy, as evidenced by at least *one* of the following:
      a. an assertion that she has, or will grow, a penis
      b. rejection of urinating in a sitting position
      c. assertion that she does not want to grow breasts or menstruate

C. Has not reached puberty.

For *males*:

A. Persistent, intense distress about being a boy, and an intense desire to be a girl or insistence that he is a girl.

B. *One* of the following:
   1. preoccupation with stereotypic female activities, including a preference for either cross-dressing or simulating female attire, or an intense desire to participate in the games and pastimes of girls with rejection of stereotypic male toys, games, and activities
   2. persistent repudiation of male anatomy, as indicated by at least one of the following:
      a. repeated assertions that he will grow up to become a woman
      b. repeated assertions that his penis or testicles is/are disgusting or will disappear
      c. repeated assertions that it would be better not to have a penis or testes

C. Has not yet reached puberty.

Transsexualism (302.50)

Essential features. Persistent discomfort and sense of inappropriateness about one's assigned sex, in a person who has reached puberty, with a

64 consistent preoccupation with ridding oneself of his or her primary and secondary sex characteristics and acquiring those of the opposite sex. This includes a wish to live as a member of the opposite sex.

Associated features. There is usually moderate to severe personality disturbance, with considerable anxiety and depression frequently present. The patient may attribute this discomfort to his or her inability to live in the role of the desired sex. Genetic or physical sexual abnormalities are occasionally present and should be coded on Axis III.

Predisposing factors. Gender Identity Disorder of Adolescence or Adulthood, Nontranssexual Type; Gender Identity Disorder of Childhood; or extensive, pervasive childhood femininity in a boy, masculinity in a girl. This disorder usually develops in a context of severely disturbed relationships with one or both parents.

Differential diagnosis. Transient disturbances of gender identity, usually related to stress (which may be diagnosed in some cases as Gender Identity Disorder Not Otherwise Specified), Schizophrenia, Transvestic Fetishism, Gender Identity Disorder of Adolescence of Adulthood, Nontranssexual Type, and some rare cultural conditions.

Diagnostic criteria for Transsexualism:

A. Persistent discomfort and sense of inappropriateness about one's assigned sex.
B. Persistent preoccupation for at least two years with being rid of one's primary and secondary sex characteristics and acquiring those of the opposite sex.
C. The person has reached puberty.

The history of sexual orientation (asexual, homosexual, heterosexual, or "unspecified") may be specified.

Gender Identity Disorder of Adolescence or Adulthood, Nontranssexual Type (GIDAANT) (302.85)

Essential features. Persistent or recurrent discomfort and sense of
65 inappropriateness about one's assigned sex, with persistent or recurrent

cross-dressing in the role of the opposite sex, either in fantasy or in actuality.

Associated features. Anxiety and depression are common and are often relieved during cross-dressing.

Complications. Evolvement to Transsexualism is the primary complication. In the absence of other diagnoses, impairment is generally restricted to conflicts with family members and other persons.

Predisposing factors. Similar to those for the other Gender Identity Disorders already described.

Differential diagnosis. GIDAANT differs from Transvestic Fetishism in that GIDAANT cross-dressing is not solely for the purpose of sexual excitement. It differs from Transsexualism in that in GIDAANT there is no persistent preoccupation with ridding oneself of current primary and secondary sex characteristics and acquiring those of the opposite sex.

Diagnostic criteria for GIDAANT:

A. Persistent or recurrent discomfort and sense of inappropriateness about one's assigned sex.
B. Persistent or recurrent cross-dressing, either in fantasy or in actuality, but not for the purpose of sexual excitement.
C. No two-year persistent preoccupation with ridding oneself of his or her primary and secondary sex characteristics and acquiring those of the other sex.
D. The person has reached puberty.

Specify: history of sexual orientation (asexual, homosexual, heterosexual, or "unspecified").

Gender Identity Disorder Not Otherwise Specified (302.85)
This residual category should be used for persons with clinically significant gender identity disorders not classifiable in the categories above, and not subsumed under other major psychiatric or physical disorders. Examples include children with persistent cross-dressing without other criteria of Gender Identity Disorder of Childhood, adults with transient, stress-

related cross-dressing, adults with clinical features of transsexualism that have lasted less than two years, or patients preoccupied with castration or penectomy without any desire to acquire characteristics of the other sex.

F. TIC DISORDERS

Tics are involuntary, sudden, rapid, recurrent, nonrhythmical, stereotyped motor movements or vocalizations, experienced as irresistible but **66** usually able to be suppressed for varying lengths of time. All forms of tics are frequently exacerbated by stress and usually markedly diminished during sleep (and sometimes during absorbing activities such as reading).

Tourette's Disorder (307.23)

Essential features. Multiple motor and one or more vocal tics, which may appear simultaneously or at different periods during the illness. They **67** occur frequently, often many times a day. The tics typically involve the head. The vocal tics are generally guttural and primitive and often include coprolalia. The first symptoms to appear are often single tics, perhaps eye blinking or tongue protrusion.

Associated features. Occasional intrusive, socially unacceptable or obscene thoughts, other disorders such as Attention-Deficit Hyperactivity Disorder or Obsessive Compulsive Disorder.

Differential diagnosis. The differential diagnosis of tics in general includes other movement disturbances (choreiform, dystonic, athetoid, myoclonic, and/or hemiballismic movements, as well as muscle spasms, synkinesis, dyskinesias, stereotyped movements [as seen in Stereotypy/ Habit Disorder] and compulsions). Other items in the differential diagnosis include amphetamine intoxication, a variety of neurological disorders, organic mental disorders, Schizophrenia, and tardive dyskinesia.

Diagnostic criteria for Tourette's Disorder:

A. Multiple motor and one or more vocal tics present at some time during the illness, not necessarily concurrently.
B. Tics occurring many times a day, almost every day or intermittently throughout a period of more than one year.
C. Anatomical location, number, frequency, complexity, and severity of the tics change over time.

D. Onset before age 21.

E. Occurrence not exclusively during psychoactive substance intoxication or known central nervous system (CNS) disease (e.g., Huntington's chorea, postviral encephalitis).

Chronic Motor or Vocal Tic Disorder (307.22)

Essential features. Either motor or vocal tics, but not both. Otherwise generally similar to Tourette's Disorder, except that the severity and functional impairment are usually much less.

Differential diagnosis. Transient Tic Disorder (see below), Tourette's Disorder. (See differential diagnosis of tics in general, under Tourette's Disorder, above.)

Diagnostic criteria for Chronic Motor or Vocal Tic Disorder:

A. Either motor or vocal tics, but not both, present at some time during the illness.

B. The tics occur many times a day, nearly every day, or intermittently throughout a period of more than one year.

C. Onset before age 21.

D. Occurrence not exclusively during psychoactive substance intoxication or known CNS disease.

Transient Tic Disorder (307.21)

Essential feature. Motor and/or vocal tic(s) that occur many times a day, nearly every day, for at least two weeks, but not longer than one year. Eye blinking or other facial tics are most common, but other parts of the body may be involved.

Differential diagnosis. Tourette's Disorder, Chronic Motor or Vocal Tic Disorder. (See differential diagnosis of tics in general, under Tourette's Disorder, above.)

Diagnostic criteria for Transient Tic Disorder:

A. Single or multiple motor and/or vocal tics.

B. The tics occur many times a day, nearly every day for at least two weeks, but for no longer than one year.

C. No history of Tourette's Disorder or Chronic Motor or Vocal Tic Disorder.

D. Onset before age 21.

E. Occurrence not exclusively during psychoactive substance intoxication or known CNS disease.

Specify: "single episode" or "recurrent."

Tic Disorder Not Otherwise Specified (307.20)

This is a residual category for tics that do not meet any of the above criteria for specific Tic Disorder. It should not be used for tics of very short duration (under two weeks), but may be a useful diagnosis for patients in whom the Tic Disorder begins in adulthood.

G. ELIMINATION DISORDERS

Functional Encopresis (307.70)

Essential feature. Repeated defecating in inappropriate places (e.g., clothing or floor).

Associated features. Shame and embarrassment, avoidance of situations such as school or camp which may lead to embarrassment, other psychopathology (especially when the incontinence is clearly deliberate). Adverse effects on the child's self-esteem, social ostracism, and adverse reactions by caretakers may be seen. A large percentage of such children also have Functional Enuresis. Smearing of feces should be differentiated from childish attempts to clean or hide feces accidentally passed. Intentional encopresis is often associated with conduct disorders and other psychopathology.

Predisposing factors. Inadequate, inconsistent toilet training and severe psychosocial stress (sometimes, however, as little as starting school or acquiring a sibling).

Differential diagnosis. Structural organic causes of encopresis (e.g., aganglionic megacolon).

Diagnostic criteria for Functional Encopresis:

A. Repeated passage of feces in places not appropriate for that purpose, whether voluntary or intentional (including overflow incontinence secondary to functional fecal retention).

B. At least one episode per month for at least six months.

C. Chronological and mental age at least four years.

D. Not due to physical disorder.

Specify:
Primary—disturbance not preceded by normal fecal continence for at least one year.

Secondary—disturbance preceded by at least one year of fecal continence.

Functional Enuresis (307.60)

Essential feature. Repeated involuntary or intentional urination, during day or night into bed or clothes, after an age at which continence is expected. An arbitrary definition of at least two events per month for children between ages five and six, and at least one per month for older children, is established in DSM-III-R.

Associated features. Shame and embarrassment, avoidance of situations such as school or camp which may lead to embarrassment. Most children do not have a coexisting mental disorder, although Functional Encopresis, Sleepwalking Disorder, and Sleep Terror Disorder may be seen. Adverse effects on the child's self-esteem, social ostracism, and adverse reactions by caretakers may be seen.

Predisposing factors. Delay in development of bladder musculature and other causes of lowered bladder volume threshold; delayed or lax toilet training; psychological stress such as early hospitalization, entering school, or the birth of a sibling.

Differential diagnosis. Organic causes (e.g., diabetes, seizure disorder, urinary tract infection).

Diagnostic criteria for Functional Enuresis:

A. Repeated voiding of urine during the day or night into bed or clothes, whether involuntary or intentional.
B. At least two such events per month for children between five and six, and at least one per month for older children.
C. Chronological age at least five; mental age at least four.
D. Not due to a physical disorder.

Specify:
Primary—disturbance not preceded by at least one year of urinary continence.

Secondary—disturbance preceded by at least one year of urinary continence.

Specify: "nocturnal only," "diurnal only," or "nocturnal and diurnal."

H. SPEECH DISORDERS NOT ELSEWHERE CLASSIFIED

Cluttering (307.00)

Essential feature. Disturbance of fluency involving an abnormally rapid rate and erratic rhythm of speech, impeding intelligibility. Faulty phrasing may include bursts of speech not related to the grammatical structure of the sentence. The affected person is usually unaware of any impairment.

Associated features. Articulation errors, expressive language errors, Academic Skills Disorder, Attention-Deficit Hyperactivity Disorder, auditory-perception or visual-motor impairments.

Differential diagnosis. Normal, transient childhood dysfluency (common around the age of two years). Stuttering and spastic dysphonia (in which the individual is aware of and distressed about the speech dysfluency).

Diagnostic criteria for Cluttering:

Disordered rate and rhythm of speech resulting in impaired speech intelligibility. Speech is erratic and dysrhythmic, consisting of rapid and jerking spurts that usually involve faulty phrasing patterns.

Stuttering (307.00)

Essential feature. Marked impairment in speech fluency characterized by frequent repetitions or prolongations of sounds or syllables. Other speech dysfluencies may be involved, and the disturbance is more severe when there is special pressure to communicate. Stuttering may be absent during oral reading, singing, or talking to nonhuman objects. Stammering is not distinguished from stuttering in the United States.

Associated features. The speaker is usually unaware of the problem initially, but later becomes quite aware and anticipates it fearfully. Anxiety, frustration, and low self-esteem may result, with limitations in adult social and occupational choice. Developmental Articulation Disorder, Developmental Expressive Language Disorder, Attention-Deficit Hyperactivity Disorder, and Anxiety Disorders are commonly associated in childhood.

Predisposing factors. Developmental Articulation Disorder or Developmental Expressive Language Disorder, or a family history of either. Stress and anxiety exacerbate stuttering, but are not thought to cause it.

Differential diagnosis. Normal childhood dysfluency, usually intermittent, and occurring around age two; Cluttering, spastic dysphonia (distinguished by abnormal breathing pattern).

Diagnostic criteria for Stuttering:

Frequent repetitions or prolongations of sounds or syllables that markedly impair the fluency of speech.

I. OTHER DISORDERS OF INFANCY, CHILDHOOD, OR ADOLESCENCE

Elective Mutism (313.23)

Essential feature. Persistent refusal to talk in one or more major social situations, including school, despite physical and intellectual ability to speak. Not a symptom of Social Phobia, Major Depression, or Psychotic Disorder. Communication may be by gestures or short utterances. The child commonly will not speak at school, but will talk normally at home.

Associated features. Some children have delayed language development or abnormalities of articulation. Speech disorders may be present,
as well as excessive shyness, social isolation or withdrawal, clinging,
school refusal, compulsiveness, or controlling or oppositional behavior
(including tantrums). School and social functioning may be severely
impaired.

Predisposing factors. Maternal overprotection, language and speech
disorders, Mental Retardation, immigration, and hospitalization or trauma
before age three.

Differential diagnosis. Severe or profound Mental Retardation, Pervasive Developmental Disorder, Developmental Expressive Language Disorder (in which there may be inability to speak rather than refusal to do
so). Children who have immigrated to a country with a different language
may refuse to speak the new language. Elective Mutism should only be
diagnosed when comprehension of the new language is known to be
adequate and refusal to speak persists.

Diagnostic criteria for Elective Mutism:

A. Persistent refusal to talk in one or more major social situations
   (including school).
B. Ability to comprehend spoken language and to speak.

Identity Disorder (313.82)

Essential feature. Inability to integrate various aspects of the self into
a coherent and acceptable sense of self, causing considerable subjective
distress. The patient may express his or her feelings with a plaintive "Who
am I?"

68

Associated features. Mild anxiety or depression, self-doubt, transient
experimenting with various roles.

Differential diagnosis. Normal maturation conflict (e.g., in adoles-
cence or middle age); Schizophrenia, Schizophreniform Disorder, Mood
Disorder (all of which preempt this diagnosis); Borderline Personality
Disorder.

Diagnostic criteria for Identity Disorder:

A. Severe subjective distress regarding uncertainty about one or more issues related to identity, including at least *three* of the following:
   1. long-term goals
   2. career choice
   3. friendship patterns
   4. sexual orientation and behavior
   5. religious identification
   6. moral value systems
   7. group loyalties
B. Impairment in social or occupational (including academic) function as a result of the above symptoms.
C. Duration of at least three months.
D. Does not occur exclusively during the course of a Mood Disorder or a Psychotic Disorder.
E. Not sufficiently pervasive and persistent to warrant a diagnosis of Borderline Personality Disorder.

Reactive Attachment Disorder of Infancy or Early Childhood (313.89)

Essential feature. Marked disturbance of social relatedness in most or all social/interpersonal contexts, related to grossly inadequate or pathogenic care by the primary caregivers. The disturbance may be manifested by either persistent failure to initiate or respond to social interactions in an age-expected manner or (in an older child) indiscriminate familiarity with others. Some severe forms of the disorder are often called "failure to thrive" or "hospitalism."

Infants with this disorder present with poor social responsiveness. They may exhibit little (or late-to-develop) visual tracking of others' eyes and faces or little response to the voice of the parent or caregiver (both of which should be developed by two months of age). In order to confirm or rule out the diagnosis, the examiner may have to observe the caregiver and child together extensively, perhaps in their home environment.

Adequate infant or child care, whether in or out of the hospital, leads to substantial improvement, unless the neglect has been so extreme that physical complications (e.g., starvation, dehydration) have reached severe proportions.

Associated features. Feeding disturbances (e.g., rumination, regurgitation, vomiting), sleep disturbances, sensory hypersensitivity. Infants or children may be apathetic, with weak cries and weak or ineffectual motor responses. Many sleep excessively and are uninterested in the environment.

Differential diagnosis. Mental Retardation and Pervasive Developmental Disorders are overriding diagnoses. Some severe neurologic deficits or chronic physical illnesses may partially mimic this disorder; however, the marked disturbance in social relatedness found in Reactive Attachment Disorder is generally absent. Psychosocial dwarfism may resemble this disorder, with the problems in social relatedness disappearing upon hospitalization, but the grossly pathogenic care found in Reactive Attachment Disorder is usually absent.

Diagnostic criteria for Reactive Attachment Disorder of Infancy or Early Childhood:

A. Markedly disturbed social relatedness in most contexts beginning before the age of five and evidenced by *one* of the following:
   1. persistent failure to initiate or respond to most social interactions (e.g., in infants, absence of visual tracking and reciprocal play; at later ages, lack of curiosity or social interests)
   2. indiscriminate sociability (e.g., excessive familiarity or affection with strangers)

B. The disturbance in "A" is not related to either Mental Retardation or any Pervasive Developmental Disorder.

C. Grossly pathogenic care by the primary caregivers, as evidenced by at least *one* of the following:
   1. persistent disregard for the child's basic emotional need for comfort, stimulation, and affection
   2. persistent disregard for the child's basic physical needs, including nutrition, housing, and protection
   3. repeated change of primary caregiver so that stable attachments are not possible (e.g., frequent changes of foster parents)

D. Presumption that the symptoms and behavior in "A" are caused by the pathogenic care described in "C."

Note: If physical failure to thrive is present, it should be coded on Axis III.

Stereotypy/Habit Disorder (307.30)

Essential features. Intentional and repetitive behaviors that serve no constructive or socially acceptable purpose except self-stimulation (e.g., rocking, other rhythmical behaviors, headbanging, picking at oneself, vocalizations).

Associated features. Mental Retardation, self-restraining behaviors (e.g., keeping one's hands inside his shirt).

Complications. Complications are usually related to self-injury, which may in rare cases (e.g., Lesch-Nyhan syndrome) be quite severe.

Predisposing factors. Mental Retardation, multiple handicaps, congenital blindness, neurological disorders. The disorder may be separately diagnosed if it coexists with severe psychiatric disorders or substance-induced Organic Mental Disorders (other than Pervasive Developmental Disorder or Tic Disorder).

Differential diagnosis. Normal self-stimulation, Pervasive Developmental Disorder, Tic Disorders.

Diagnostic criteria for Stereotypy/Habit Disorder:

A. Intentional, repetitive, nonfunctional behaviors, such as rocking, head-banging, thumb-sucking, or nail-biting.
B. The disturbance causes physical injury or markedly interferes with normal activities.
C. Does not meet criteria for either a Pervasive Developmental Disorder or a Tic Disorder.

Undifferentiated Attention-Deficit Disorder (314.00)

Essential feature. A persistent syndrome of marked and developmentally inappropriate inattention which is not part of another disorder or of a disorganized, chaotic environment. This code may be appropriate for some patients who would have been diagnosed as having Attention-Deficit Disorder without Hyperactivity in DSM-III.

DIFFERENCES BETWEEN DSM-III AND DSM-III-R DISORDERS USUALLY FIRST EVIDENT IN INFANCY, CHILDHOOD, OR ADOLESCENCE

- "Atypical" versions of the disorders are now referred to as *Not Otherwise Specified (NOS)*.
- *Mental Retardation* is now grouped with the Developmental Disorders.
- Attention Deficit Disorder with Hyperactivity is now renamed *Attention-Deficit Hyperactivity Disorder*, to reflect the frequency of hyperactivity in ADD, and grouped with the *Disruptive Behavior Disorders*.
- Attention Deficit Disorder, Residual Type is now deleted, and *Attention-Deficit Hyperactivity Disorder, Residual State* is used to indicate residua persisting into adulthood.
- Socialized, undersocialized, and atypical subtypes of *Conduct Disorder* were felt to lack clinical and research validity; Conduct Disorder has been redivided into *Isolated Aggressive, Group*, and *Undifferentiated* types.
- Criteria for *Separation Anxiety Disorder* have become more selective, to "raise the threshold for diagnosis."
- Criteria for *Reactive Attachment Disorder of Infancy or Early Childhood* have been revised to include older children and a broader range of grossly inadequate care.
- Schizoid Disorder of Childhood or Adolescence is deleted.
- Criteria for *Oppositional Defiant Disorder* (formerly "Oppositional Disorder") have been revised to better distinguish it from Conduct Disorder and improve clinical description.
- The criteria for *Anorexia Nervosa* now require less weight loss, but require amenorrhea in females.
- Bulimia is now named *Bulimia Nervosa*, and the criteria are more strictly related to eating behavior.

- Stereotyped Movement Disorders are now renamed and divided among the *Tic Disorders*, separate from Stereotypy/Habit Disorder.
- Chronic Motor Tic Disorder has been renamed *Chronic Motor or Vocal Tic Disorder.*
- Atypical Stereotyped Movement Disorder is now subsumed under *Stereotypy/Habit Disorder,* reflecting separation from the more pervasive disorders.
- *Stuttering* and the new diagnosis of *Cluttering* are classified under *Speech Disorders Not Elsewhere Classified.*
- *Functional Enuresis and Encopresis* are now classified as *Elimination Disorders.*
- *Sleepwalking and Sleep Terror Disorders* are now classified as *Sleep Disorders.*
- Infantile Autism and Childhood Onset Pervasive Developmental Disorder are now felt to represent a single category, called *Autistic Disorder* in DSM-III-R. The criteria have been revised extensively.
- *Specific Developmental Disorders* are now grouped under the *Developmental Disorders.*
- Developmental Language Disorder has been divided into *Developmental Expressive Language Disorder* and *Developmental Receptive Language Disorder.*
- *Developmental Expressive Writing Disorder, Developmental Coordination Disorder,* and *Cluttering* are new diagnoses.

CASE VIGNETTE 1

An 18-month-old girl is seen after reports by a neighbor that she is often left alone for several days in a backyard shed. When visited by a child protective agency, the parents are found to be former mental patients, both with schizophrenic diagnoses. They eventually admit leaving the child alone, saying that this is "God's way," and "Only the strong shall survive."

The child is thin, originally found in soiled diapers. She is grossly apathetic, does not respond (either positively or negatively) to the investigating social worker or child psychiatrist, does not follow objects with her eyes (although she will look at them), and shows no inclination or ability to play. The only affect she shows at first is some distress at the sounds of several dogs, which are kept in a pen beside the shed.

The child is removed from the parents' home and placed in foster care. Six months later, she has improved greatly, responds to her environment with interest and curiosity, and enjoys playing simple games with her foster parent.

Discussion

Autistic Disorder and other Developmental Disorders are ruled out by the presence of grossly pathogenic care by the parents and by the marked improvement following placement in a healthy environment. Although not apparent in this child, failure to thrive should be considered in the differential diagnosis and coded on Axis III if found.

Diagnosis

Axis I   313.89   Reactive Attachment Disorder of Infancy or Early Childhood

Axis II   V71.09   No diagnosis or condition

CASE VIGNETTE 2

For the past year, this 14-year-old boy has been irritable, vindictive, and seems to deliberately annoy others. For example, he taunts his siblings and classmates, even when parents or teachers are present, in apparent defiance of their authority. He argues, often hotly, with his parents and teachers and has such an unreasonable temper that he has been thrown off the baseball team (one of the activities he enjoys most) for fighting and talking back to the coach. Everyone agrees that his behavior is well outside the range of adolescent turmoil and annoyance seen in other boys of his age and development.

He seems uncomfortable at times, but does not meet criteria for any mood disorder. His school performance is good when he applies himself, and there are no prodromal signs of a psychotic disorder. He is not particularly cruel (except verbally) and has not run away from home; broken into, stolen, or destroyed property; or used weapons in any of his several fights.

Discussion

The symptoms are clearly outside the normal range for adolescents of similar developmental stages, but nevertheless do not include major abridgment of the rights of others (e.g., stealing, cruelty) or other severely antisocial behavior (running away, truancy, use of weapons), thus differentiating them from Conduct Disorder. Neither behavioral nor age criteria are met for Antisocial Personality. There is no mention of evidence for Dysthymia or other Mood Disorder which, in children and adolescents, can be reflected in behavioral symptoms. There is no mention of family instability or short duration of symptoms, which might suggest a situational or adjustment disorder.

Diagnosis

> Axis I   313.81 Oppositional Defiant Disorder, probably "Moderate"
> Axis II V71.09 No diagnosis or condition

CASE VIGNETTE 3

A seven-year-old has refused to go to first-grade classes for several weeks. She had some trouble tolerating kindergarten, which was alleviated when her mother was allowed to sit in the back of the classroom. Her parents were briefly separated when she was four, when her military father was transferred to a different city and left the family for a few weeks to find housing. For several months thereafter she needed frequent reassurance that the family wasn't going to move again soon. She often clings to both parents and cries bitterly when either is gone overnight. She says she is afraid there will be a war while they are gone, and one of them—either the child or the parent—will be killed in an atomic blast. She has no apparent Developmental Disorders.

Discussion

The symptoms are outside the expected range even for a first-grader. There is no evidence for a more serious disorder.

Diagnosis

> Axis I   309.21 Separation Anxiety Disorder
> Axis II V71.09 No diagnosis or condition

CASE VIGNETTE 4

An 11-year-old child has not mastered basic reading skills and reads at about a second-grade level despite normal scores on individually administered IQ tests. She has been held back twice because of her reading problems and is now in the fourth grade. She is from a stable home and has been in the same public school since first grade. Physical examination, including vision and hearing tests, is normal.

Discussion

There is no evidence of mental retardation on careful (perhaps oral or nonverbal) testing and no evidence of neurological, hearing, or vision defect. The educational environment seems adequate (although it may not recognize the patient's Specific Developmental Disorder) for most children.

Diagnosis

Axis I   V71.09 No diagnosis or condition
Axis II 315.00 Developmental Reading Disorder

Chapter 11

Organic Mental Syndromes and Disorders

This chapter contains a discussion of both Organic Mental Syndromes and Organic Mental Disorders. The distinction in DSM-III-R between a syndrome and a disorder is as follows: A syndrome is an aggregate of psychological or behavioral signs and symptoms (e.g., Delirium), and a disorder is a syndrome that is caused by a known, or presumably known, etiology (e.g., Amphetamine Delirium). The clinician will usually recognize a syndrome by its clinical features, and then, through history, physical exam, and laboratory tests try to identify a specific Organic Mental Disorder. Note that Organic Mental Syndromes do not have diagnostic codes, whereas specific Organic Mental Disorders do. 70

A. ORGANIC MENTAL SYNDROMES

The essential feature of an Organic Mental Syndrome is brain dysfunction. This dysfunction manifests itself by psychological and/or behavioral 71 abnormalities. The clinical presentation may be multifaceted, as seen in Delirium or Dementia, or the clinical abnormalities may be limited to certain areas of cognitive function, as seen in Amnestic Syndrome or Organic Hallucinosis.

Delirium

Essential features. Brain dysfunction in Delirium is global; therefore, clinical manifestations of Delirium are widespread. Delirious patients 72 have difficulty maintaining and shifting attention and also manifest disorganized thinking. The onset of symptoms is usually rapid, and the severity of dysfunction may fluctuate widely over the course of a day.

Associated features. Concomitant emotional disturbances, such as fear, anxiety, depression, anger, and apathy, are common. Neurological signs such as dysgraphia (difficulty writing), constructional apraxia (difficulty drawing), and dysnomia (difficulty naming objects) are often present. Tremor, symmetrical increase or decrease in reflexes, and signs of autonomic hyperactivity (sweating, flushed face, increased heart rate and blood pressure, and dilated pupils) may also be seen.

Predisposing factors. Advanced age (>60 years), young age (children), drug dependence, cardiotomy, and preexisting brain injury increase the risk for developing Delirium.

Differential diagnosis. Schizophrenia, Schizophreniform Disorder, other Psychotic Disorders, Dementia (often coexists with Delirium), and Factitious Disorder with Psychological Symptoms are considered in the differential diagnosis.

Diagnostic criteria for Delirium:

A. Reduced ability to maintain and shift attention.
B. Disorganized thinking.
C. At least *two* of the following:
   1. reduced level of consciousness
   2. perceptual disturbances (hallucinations, delusions)
   3. sleep-wake cycle disturbance
   4. increased or decreased psychomotor activity
   5. disorientation
   6. impairment of recent memory
D. Syndrome develops abruptly (hours to days) and fluctuates in severity during the course of a day.
E. A specific organic etiology is identified or organic cause is presumed because nonorganic mental disorders cannot account for disturbance.

Dementia

Essential features. Dementia, like Delirium, has signs and symptoms 73
that indicate global brain dysfunction. There is impairment of both recent
and remote memory and impairment of other brain functions. The cumu-
lative effects of these impairments must interfere with work, social activities,
or relationships.

Associated features. Awareness of cognitive deficits varies among
individuals. Early in a progressive dementing illness the individual may be
very aware of deficits; however, that awareness usually fades if the Dementia progresses. Anxiety or depression may accompany Dementia. Increased
stress may aggravate deficits.

Differential diagnosis. Normal aging, Delirium, Schizophrenia, Major
Depressive Disorder ("depressive pseudodementia"), and Factitious Disorder with Psychological Symptoms are considered in the differential
diagnosis.

Diagnostic criteria for Dementia:

A. Impairment in short- and long-term memory.
B. At least *one* of the following:
   1. impairment in abstract thinking
   2. impaired judgment
   3. impairment in higher cortical functions (e.g., aphasia, agnosia,
      apraxia)
   4. personality change
C. "A" and "B" significantly interfere with work, usual social activities,
   or relationships.
D. Not due to Delirium.
E. A specific organic etiology is identified or organic cause is presumed because nonorganic mental disorders cannot account for
   disturbance.

Criteria for severity:
Mild—capacity for independent living remains.
Moderate—independent living is hazardous.
Severe—independent living is impossible.

Amnestic Syndrome

Essential features. Impairment is limited to short- and long-term memory. Immediate memory, measured by the ability to immediately repeat a series of digits, is unimpaired. The memory deficits are not part of a Delirium or a Dementia.

74

Associated features. Since an individual with Amnestic Disorder cannot form memory for recent events, disorientation and amnesia are nearly always present. Confabulation, or fabrication of events that are not remembered, is common, particularly early in the syndrome. Individuals with Amnestic Syndrome often are unconcerned about these deficits and may exhibit lack of initiative, apathy, disinterest, and emotional blandness.

Predisposing factors. Chronic alcohol use that results in thiamine deficiency is commonly associated with Amnestic Syndrome.

Differential diagnosis. Delirium, Dementia, and Factitious Disorder with Psychological Symptoms are considered in the differential diagnosis.

Diagnostic criteria for Amnestic Syndrome:

A. Impairment in both long- and short-term memory.
B. Not a part of a Delirium or Dementia.
C. Evidence of a specific organic factor exists.

Organic Delusional Syndrome

Essential features. Delusions must be the prominent part of the individual's presentation. In addition, a specific organic factor must be identified that, in all likelihood, caused the syndrome. The clinician must also ensure that the delusions are not part of another diagnosis, such as a Delirium.

Associated features. Mild cognitive impairment may be present, dysphoric mood is common, and hallucinations, although not a prominent feature, may also be present. According to DSM-III-R, almost any other symptom may be associated with this syndrome.

75 **Predisposing factors.** Certain psychoactive substances, such as amphetamines, cocaine, cannabis, and hallucinogens, may cause this syndrome.

Other medical disorders that have been associated with Organic Delusional Syndrome are temporal-lobe epilepsy, Huntington's chorea, and right-hemisphere cerebral lesions.

Differential diagnosis. Delirium, Schizophrenia, Organic Hallucinosis, Organic Mood Syndrome, and Delusional Disorder are considered in the differential diagnosis.

Diagnostic criteria for Organic Delusional Syndrome:

A. Prominent delusions.
B. Evidence of a specific causative organic factor.
C. Not part of a Delirium.

Organic Hallucinosis

Essential features. Hallucinations with an organic etiology are a prominent and persistent part of this syndrome. The clinician must also be sure that the hallucinations are not part of a Delirium.

76

Associated features. The emotional response to the hallucinations can vary and includes pleasure, anxiety, depression, or other dysphoric affects. Individual responses depend on surroundings and preexisting psychopathology. Certain psychoactive substances (e.g., alcohol), are more likely to cause auditory hallucinations, whereas hallucinogens usually cause visual hallucinations.

Predisposing factors. Hallucinogen use, prolonged alcohol use, and sensory deprivation (blindness, deafness) place an individual at increased risk of Organic Hallucinosis.

Differential diagnosis. Delirium, Dementia, Organic Delusional Syndrome, Schizophrenia, Mood Disorders, hypnogogic and hypnopompic hallucinations are considered in the differential diagnosis.

Diagnostic criteria for Organic Hallucinosis:

A. Prominent and persistent hallucinations.
B. Evidence of a specific causative organic factor.
C. Not part of a Delirium.

Organic Mood Syndrome

Essential features. A manic episode or a major depressive episode that is caused by a specific organic factor is necessary for the diagnosis. The clinician must also be sure that the mood abnormalities are not part of a Delirium.

Associated features. Mild cognitive impairment is often observed. The individual may experience any symptoms normally associated with a Mood Disorder.

Predisposing factors. This syndrome can be caused by medications (e.g., reserpine-induced depression or steroid-induced mania), endocrine dysfunction, hallucinogens, or disease (depression associated with pancreatic carcinoma).

Differential diagnosis. Mood Disorders are considered in the differential diagnosis.

Diagnostic criteria for Organic Mood Syndrome:

A. Prominent and persistent depressed, elevated, or expansive mood.
B. Evidence of a specific causative organic factor.
C. Not part of a Delirium.

Specify: manic, depressed, or mixed.

Organic Anxiety Syndrome

Essential features. Prominent anxiety, such as recurrent panic attacks or generalized anxiety, caused by a specific organic factor, is necessary for the diagnosis.

Associated features. Mild cognitive impairment with problems in maintaining attention is often seen.

Predisposing factors. This syndrome can be caused by endocrine disorders, psychoactive substances, stimulant intoxication, withdrawal syndromes, brain tumors, and medical diseases.

Differential diagnosis. Anxiety Disorders, Organic Mood Syndrome, Delirium, Dementia, Organic Personality Syndrome are considered in the differential diagnosis. Anxiety is also a common symptom of many other mental and medical disorders.

Diagnostic criteria for Organic Anxiety Syndrome:

A. Prominent recurrent panic attacks or generalized anxiety.
B. Evidence of a specific causative organic factor.
C. Not part of a Delirium.

Organic Personality Syndrome

Essential features. A persistent personality disturbance caused by a specific organic factor is necessary for the diagnosis. Organic Personality Syndrome is not diagnosed in a child or adolescent if the clinical presentation is solely due to Attention-Deficit Hyperactivity Disorder.

Associated features. Irritability and mild cognitive impairment may be present.

Predisposing factors. Brain injury, such as that caused by neoplasms, head trauma, and strokes are common predisposing factors.

Differential diagnosis. Dementia, Schizophrenia, Delusional Disorders, Mood Disorders, and Impulse Control Disorders Not Otherwise Specified are considered in the differential diagnosis.

Diagnostic criteria for Organic Personality Syndrome:

A. Persistent personality disturbance involving at least *one* of the following:
   1. affective instability
   2. recurrent outbursts of aggression or rage
   3. markedly impaired social judgment
   4. marked apathy or indifference
   5. suspiciousness or paranoid ideation

B. Evidence of a specific causative organic factor.

C. If an adolescent or child, symptoms not are consistent with Attention-Deficit Hyperactivity Disorder.

Intoxication

Essential features. Intoxication requires recent use of a psychoactive substance, development of a specific syndrome known to result from that substance, and the presence of maladaptive behavior. Note that this definition does not include recreational drug use unless maladaptive behavior results.

Associated features. Disturbances may occur in perception, attention, clarity of thought, judgment, and emotion. An individual's particular response to a psychoactive substance depends on the substance, environment, premorbid personality, medical condition, and the individual's expectations.

Differential diagnosis. Intoxication is treated as a residual diagnostic category. Therefore, all other Organic Mental Syndromes are considered in the differential diagnosis prior to this diagnosis. Neurological diseases can sometimes result in symptoms that resemble an intoxicated state (e.g., slurred speech, uncoordinated gait).

Diagnostic criteria for Intoxication:

A. A substance-specific syndrome caused by recent use of a psycho-active substance.

B. Maladaptive behavior due to "A."

C. Clinical features are not consistent with any of the other Organic Mental Syndromes.

Withdrawal

Essential features. Withdrawal symptoms develop after recent cessation, or decreased intake, of a regularly used psychoactive substance.

Associated features. The particular withdrawal syndrome that develops will depend on the psychoactive substance. For example, symptoms associated with Opioid Withdrawal resemble a viral influenza (e.g., nausea and vomiting, muscle aches, diarrhea, and fever).

Differential diagnosis. Withdrawal does not resemble any of the other Organic Mental Syndromes, but can be superimposed on them. Symptoms of withdrawal resemble symptoms of physical disorders (e.g., Opioid Withdrawal and influenza).   **79**

Diagnostic criteria for Withdrawal:

A. Development of a substance-specific syndrome following the cessation, or reduction, of that regularly used substance.
B. The clinical picture does not correspond to any other Organic Mental Syndrome.

Organic Mental Syndrome Not Otherwise Specified

Essential features. This category is used for any Organic Mental Syndrome that is caused by a specific organic factor and does not meet diagnostic criteria for the other Organic Mental Syndromes: for example, unusual disturbances of consciousness that are sometimes associated with partial complex seizures.

B. ORGANIC MENTAL DISORDERS

Organic Mental Disorders include Dementias Arising in the Senium and Presenium, Psychoactive Substance-Induced Organic Mental Disorders and Organic Mental Disorders Associated with Axis III Physical Disorders, or Whose Etiology Is Unknown.

Dementias Arising in the Senium and Presenium

Historically, dementias were considered as either senile onset dementias when the person's age was greater than 65 years or presenile-onset dementias when the person's age was 65 or less. This distinction is maintained in DSM-III-R even though the pathological findings and clinical presentation of Alzheimer's Dementia is not age-specific.

Primary Degenerative Dementia of the Alzheimer Type (290.xx)

80   **Essential features.** A Dementia with a subtle onset and slowly progressive, deteriorating course. In addition, a complete evaluation fails to identify any other potential cause. The demented individual has multiple intellectual and higher cortical dysfunctions (i.e., meets diagnostic criteria for Dementia).

Associated features. Awareness of cognitive deficits varies among individuals. Early in a progressive dementing illness the individual may be very aware of deficits; however, awareness usually fades if the Dementia progresses. Anxiety or depression may accompany Dementia. Increased stress may aggravate deficits.

Predisposing factors. Down's syndrome and, rarely, dominant genetic transmission of Alzheimer's disease.

Differential diagnosis. Normal aging, "reversible dementias" (e.g., subdural hematomas, normal-pressure hydrocephalus, endocrine dysfunction, neoplasms), Multi-infarct Dementia, Psychoactive Susbstance Intoxication, Major Depressive Disorder ("depressive pseudodementia"), and Factitious Disorder with Psychological Symptoms are considered in the differential diagnosis.

TABLE 5
Diagnostic Codes and Subtypes

	For Presenile Onset	For Senile Onset
Uncomplicated	290.10	290.00
With delirium	290.11	290.30
With delusions	290.12	290.20
With depression	290.13	290.21

Diagnostic criteria for Primary Degenerative Dementia of the Alzheimer Type:

A. Dementia.

B. Subtle onset and generally progressive deteriorating course.

C. Exclusion of all other specific causes of Dementia.

Onset: Age 65 or less = Presenile; over 65 years = Senile.

Subtypes: The clinical picture is occasionally complicated by Delirium, delusions, or depression.

Multi-infarct Dementia (290.4x)

Essential features. A Dementia caused by multiple strokes due to cerebrovascular disease, vascular disease, or cardiac disease. Multi-infarct Dementia usually presents with abrupt onset, stepwise deterioration, "patchy" intellectual deficits, and focal neurologic signs and symptoms.

Associated features. A variety of neurologic signs may present, including limb weakness, reflex asymmetry, extensor plantar response, gait abnormalities, and pseudobulbar palsy (affective incontinence and lability), dysarthria (difficulty talking), dysphagia (difficulty swallowing).

Predisposing factors. Arterial hypertension, carotid vascular disease, and valvular disease of the heart are risk factors.

Differential diagnosis. Primary Degenerative Dementia of the Alzheimer Type and a solitary stroke are considered in the differential diagnosis.

Diagnostic criteria for Multi-infarct Dementia:

A. Dementia

B. Stepwise deterioration and a "patchy" pattern of deficits.

C. Focal neurologic signs and symptoms.

D. Presence of significant cerebrovascular/vascular/cardiac disease judged to be causative.

Specify fifth digit as in Table 5, Presenile Onset.

Senile Dementia Not Otherwise Specified (290.00)

Essential features. Dementia arising after age 65 that is caused by an organic factor and cannot be otherwise classified (e.g., cannot be classified as Dementia Associated with Alcoholism, Primary Degenerative Dementia of the Alzheimer Type, or Multi-infarct Dementia). List etiology on Axis III when known.

Presenile Dementia Not Otherwise Specified (290.10)

Essential features. Dementia arising before age 66 that is caused by an organic factor and cannot be otherwise classified (e.g., cannot be classified as Presenile Primary Degenerative Dementia of the Alzheimer Type or Multi-infarct Dementia). List etiology on Axis III when known.

Psychoactive Substance-Induced Organic Mental Disorders

Essential features. Table 6 lists the Organic Mental Syndromes caused by direct central nervous system action of psychoactive substances. The appropriate diagnostic code is also listed. Note that some diagnoses share code numbers (e.g., 305.90 is used for phencyclidine, inhalant, and caffeine intoxication). Toxicologic tests are often required to ensure proper diagnosis and treatment of substance use. The section in this chapter titled "Organic Mental Syndrome" outlines the diagnostic criteria for each syndrome.

When an Organic Mental Disorder is caused by either a psychoactive substance not classified in the 11 categories listed in Table 6 (e.g., Steroid Mood Disorder), or when an Organic Mental Disorder is caused by ingestion of an unknown substance, use one of the following diagnoses.

Other or Unspecified Psychoactive Substance-Induced:

305.90	Intoxication
292.00	Withdrawal
292.81	Delirium
292.82	Dementia
292.83	Amnestic Disorder
292.11	Delusional Disorder
292.12	Hallucinosis
292.84	Mood Disorder

TABLE 6
Organic Mental Syndromes Caused by Direct CNS Action of Psychoactive Substances

	Intoxication	Withdrawal	Delirium	Delusional Disorder	Mood Disorder	Hallucinosis	Amnestic Disorder	Dementia
Alcohol*	303.00	291.80	291.00†			291.30	291.10	291.20
Amphetamines and related substances	305.70	292.00	292.81	292.11				
Caffeine	305.90							
Cannabis	305.20			292.11				
Cocaine	305.60	292.00	292.81	292.11				
Hallucinogens‡				292.11	292.84	305.30		
Inhalants	305.90							
Nicotine		292.00						
Opioids	305.50	292.00						
Phencyclidine (PCP)§ and related substances	305.90		292.81	292.11	292.84			
Sedatives, hypnotics, or anxiolytics	305.40	292.00	292.00†				292.83	

*Also Alcohol Idiosyncratic Intoxication (291.40).
†Delirium only during withdrawal.
‡Also Posthallucinogen Perception Disorder (292.89).
§Also Phencyclidine (PCP) or Similarly Acting Arylcyclohexylamine Organic Mental Disorder Not Otherwise Specified (292.90).

292.89   Anxiety Disorder
292.89   Personality Disorder
292.90   Organic Mental Disorder Not Otherwise Specified

Organic Mental Disorders Associated with Axis III Physical Disorders, or Whose Etiology Is Unknown

Essential features. Physical disorders may cause any of the following Axis I Organic Mental Disorders. The specific physical disorder present should be listed on Axis III.

293.00   Delirium
294.10   Dementia
294.00   Amnestic Disorder
293.81   Organic Delusional Disorder
293.82   Organic Hallucinosis
293.83   Organic Mood Disorder. Specify: manic, depressed, or mixed
294.80   Organic Anxiety Disorder
310.10   Organic Personality Disorder. Specify: explosive type, if appropriate
294.80   Organic Mental Disorder Not Otherwise Specified

DIFFERENCES BETWEEN DSM-III AND DSM-III-R ORGANIC MENTAL SYNDROMES AND DISORDERS

- Substance-Induced Organic Mental Disorders are now referred to as *Psychoactive Substance-Induced Organic Mental Disorders.*
- *Posthallucinogen Perception Disorder* is new in DSM-III-R and is used for the diagnosis of "flashbacks" following hallucinogen ingestion.
- Barbiturate or similarly acting sedative or hypnotic drugs, as a group of substances, is now referred to as *sedative, hypnotic, or anxiolytic* drugs.
- New diagnoses secondary to cocaine use include *Cocaine Withdrawal, Cocaine Delirium*, and *Cocaine Delusional Disorder.*

- New diagnoses secondary to *Amphetamine or Similarly Acting Sympathomimetic* use include *Withdrawal* and *Delusional Disorder.*
- New diagnoses secondary to *Phencyclidine (PCP) or Similarly Acting Arylcyclohexylamine* use include *Delusional Disorder* and *Mood Disorder.*
- New diagnoses secondary to *Hallucinogen* use include *Delirium* and *Posthallucinogen Perception Disorder.*
- *Inhalant Intoxication* is a new category in DSM-III-R.
- *Organic Anxiety Disorders* are now a specific diagnostic category in DSM-III-R.

CASE VIGNETTE

The family of a 70-year-old man (Mr. A.) brings him to you for evaluation because he has had increasing difficulty caring for himself. His memory is poor and he has gotten lost several times in his own neighborhood. Police assistance was needed to find him. Mr. A. believes that his neighbors are stealing things from his house. Further history reveals that Mr. A.'s memory problems first began about two years ago. His memory dysfunction has slowly progressed, and he has gotten more irritable and suspicious over the last six months. According to his children, "He acts like a different person." His four married children have alternated staying with him for the last month, but are unable to continue this effort. He has been in good physical health, is on no medication, and has no history of mental disorder or psychoactive substance use.

Mr. A. appears disheveled and is somewhat hostile. He is alert and does not cooperate with the examiner. When asked to perform memory tasks, he says, "I'm not going to answer your dumb questions." He believes his wife, who died five years ago, is alive and is being held captive. His handwriting is unreadable and he is unable to copy even simple designs. Physical examination, laboratory results, and radiographic findings are all normal.

Discussion

Mr. A. presents with short- and long-term memory impairment, impaired judgment, dysgraphia, constructional apraxia, delusional thinking, and a personality change. The clinical course is one of slow deterioration and increasing impairment. A thorough medical evaluation failed to reveal a specific cause for his declining cognitive function. There is no history of affective illness, and he does not appear depressed. The most likely diagnosis is dementia, specifically Primary Degenerative Dementia of the Alzheimer Type. The onset was approximately two years ago, when the patient was 68, and the Dementia is complicated by delusions.

Diagnosis

> Axis I   290.20   Primary Degenerative Dementia of the Alzheimer
> Type, Senile Onset, with delusions
> Axis II   V71.09   No diagnosis
> Axis III   Alzheimer's Dementia

Chapter 12

Psychoactive Substance Use Disorders

The use of certain psychoactive substances is considered normal in our society. For example, taking prescribed medication to relieve insomnia or pain is a generally accepted practice. The recreational use of alcohol and the consumption of coffee, except among a few groups within our society, are also accepted behaviors. These practices lack the key elements that distinguish the Psychoactive Substance Use Disorders. To qualify as a disorder, the regular use of a psychoactive substance must lead to *cultur-* **81** *ally undesirable symptoms and maladaptive behaviors.*

Psychoactive Substance Use Disorders lead to substance-induced maladaptive behaviors, whereas Psychoactive Substance-Induced Organic Mental Disorders refer to the direct or chronic effects of these substances on the central nervous system. Most individuals who regularly ingest psychoactive substances will have both a Psychoactive Substance Use Disorder and a Psychoactive Substance-Induced Organic Mental Disorder (particularly intoxication or withdrawal). Nine classes of psychoactive substances are associated with both dependence and abuse, and nicotine is associated with Dependence but not Abuse. Psychoactive Substance Dependence and Psychoactive Substance Abuse will be defined before specific coded disorders are discussed.

A. PSYCHOACTIVE SUBSTANCE DEPENDENCE

Essential features. As a result of regular psychoactive substance use, the individual develops impaired control of substance use and continues **82**

97

to use the substance in spite of adverse consequences. Dependence usually, but not always, includes the development of tolerance (i.e., one must increase the dose to maintain the same effects) and the development of withdrawal symptoms upon discontinuation or dosage reduction. In order to meet the diagnostic criteria for Psychoactive Substance Dependence, some of the cognitive, behavioral, and/or physiologic symptoms from use of the chemical must persist for at least one month or occur repeatedly over a longer period of time.

Associated features. Repeated bouts of Psychoactive Substance-Induced Intoxication are almost always present in the history. Personality and mood disturbances are often present. In chronic abuse or dependence, mood lability, suspiciousness, and violent behavior may be seen.

Differential diagnosis. Nonpathological psychoactive substance use for recreational or medical purposes, and repeated episodes of Psychoactive Substance Intoxication are considered in the differential diagnosis.

Diagnostic criteria for Psychoactive Substance Dependence:

A. At least *three* of the following:
    1. substance often taken in larger amounts, or over a longer period of time, than the individual intended
    2. persistent desire to cut down or one or more unsuccessful efforts to control substance use
    3. a great deal of time spent getting the substance, taking the substance, or recovering from the substance
    4. frequent intoxication or withdrawal symptoms when expected to fulfill major obligations at work, school, or home, or when substance use is hazardous
    5. important social, occupational, or recreational activities given up or reduced because of substance use
    6. continued substance use despite persistent or recurrent social, psychological, or physical problems caused by the substance
    7. marked tolerance: at least 50% increase in amount needed to achieve intoxication or desired effect, or markedly diminished effect with continued use of the same amount (NOTE: May not apply to cannabis, hallucinogens, or phencyclidine [PCP])

8. characteristic withdrawal symptoms upon discontinuation or reduced consumption of the substance

9. substance taken to relieve or avoid symptoms of withdrawal from the same substance

B. Some of the symptoms in "A" have persisted for at least one month or have occurred repeatedly over a longer period of time.

Specify severity:
Mild—Few, if any, symptoms and mild impairment in occupation, or social activities, or relationships
Moderate—Symptoms or functional impairment between mild and severe
Severe—Many symptoms which markedly interfere with occupation, or social activities, or relationships
In partial remission—During the last six months, some substance use and some symptoms of dependence
In full remission—During the last six months, either no substance use, or if substance is used there are no symptoms of dependence

Polysubstance Dependence (304.90)

Essential feature. When an individual uses at least three categories of psychoactive substances (excluding nicotine and caffeine) for at least six months, no single substance predominates, and the criteria for dependence have been met, this diagnosis is appropriate. If the person meets diagnostic criteria for one or more Psychoactive Substance Use Disorders, specific diagnoses should be made. **83**

Psychoactive Substance Dependence Not Otherwise Specified (304.90)

Essential features. This residual diagnostic category is used to classify individuals with Psychoactive Substance Dependence when other drugs are taken (e.g., anticholinergic dependence). In addition, this diagnosis can be used until the specific drug(s) of dependence is (are) identified.

B. PSYCHOACTIVE SUBSTANCE ABUSE

Essential features. This is basically a residual diagnostic category. In other words, the individual has maladaptive behavior as a result of **84**

psychoactive substance use, but does not meet the diagnostic criteria for Psychoactive Substance Dependence. The maladaptive behavior may be either continued substance use despite occupational, psychological, or physical problems, or recurrent use in physically hazardous situations (e.g., operating a punch press while intoxicated).

Associated features. Repeated bouts of Psychoactive Substance-Induced Intoxication are almost always present in the history. Personality and mood disturbances are often present. In chronic abuse or dependence, mood lability, suspiciousness, and violent behavior may be seen.

Differential diagnosis. Nonpathologic psychoactive substance use for recreational or medical purposes and repeated episodes of Psychoactive Substance Intoxication are considered in the differential diagnosis.

Diagnostic criteria for Psychoactive Substance Abuse:

A. Maladaptive pattern of psychoactive substance use as indicated by at least _one_ of the following:
   1. continued substance use despite persistent or recurrent social, psychological, or physical problems caused by the substance
   2. recurrent substance use in situations that are physically hazardous
B. Some symptoms persist over at least one month, or symptoms occurred repeatedly over a longer period of time.
C. Has never met the criteria for Psychoactive Substance Dependence for this substance.

Psychoactive Substance Abuse Not Otherwise Specified (305.90)

Essential features. This residual diagnostic category is used to classify individuals with Psychoactive Substance Abuse where other drugs are taken (e.g., anticholinergic abuse). In addition, this diagnosis can be used until the specific drug(s) of dependence or abuse is(are) identified.

DIFFERENCES BETWEEN DSM-III AND DSM-III-R PSYCHOACTIVE SUBSTANCE USE DISORDERS

• In DSM-III, Substance Dependence required evidence of physiological dependence, specifically the presence of either tolerance or withdrawal. DSM-III-R *Psychoactive Substance Dependence* now includes clinically significant behaviors, cognition, and other symptoms that signify loss of control of substance use and continued use of the substance despite adverse consequences.

- New diagnoses in DSM-III-R are *Cocaine Dependence, Hallucinogen Dependence, Inhalant Abuse,* and *Inhalant Dependence.*
- Dependence on combinations of substances are now classified as *Polysubstance Dependence.*

CASE VIGNETTE
Mr. T. is a 20-year-old who is brought by his wife to the emergency room for evaluation. According to the wife, he has been very agitated for the last few hours. She suspects he is using drugs and reports that he has spent all of their savings. She also states that his behavior has changed over the last four months, in that he is frequently absent from home and has been taking money from her wallet.

His vital signs show a tachycardia (rate 120), mild blood pressure elevation (150/95), and a slight fever (Temp=100.3° F). On examination, Mr. T. is quite anxious, has a gross tremor, is pacing the floor and sweating, and complains of severe muscle pain. His pupils are enlarged (mydriasis) and he has rhinorrhea (runny nose). He is anxious to leave the emergency room and keeps saying, "I'll be O.K. Just let me out of here." He denies regular psychoactive substance use, but states that he has tried marijuana, cocaine, and heroin. The physical examination reveals recent needle marks on both arms. Toxic screen is positive for opioids.

Discussion
The clinical picture resembles a viral influenza and is typical of Opioid Withdrawal (Other symptoms may include lacrimation, diarrhea, yawning, and insomnia.) The individual, as is often the case, did not reveal the reason for his symptoms and only wants to get another "fix" to relieve his intense discomfort. Laboratory tests for general drug screening and more specific tests for identification of specific substances are very helpful in the clinical evaluation of possible Psychoactive Substance Use.

Mr. T. meets the criteria for Psychoactive Substance Dependence. He has withdrawal symptoms, no longer spends time with his family, but instead spends time in drug-related activities, has spent the family savings, and is taking money from his wife. Because insufficient information is available about Mr. T.'s personality prior to the time of his opioid use, Axis II diagnosis is deferred.

Diagnosis

Axis I   292.00 Opioid Withdrawal
         304.00 Opioid Dependence
Axis II   799.90 Diagnosis deferred
Axis III   No known medical conditions

Chapter 13

Schizophrenia

Essential features. All patients with Schizophrenia exhibit characteristic symptoms during the acute phase of the illness, functioning below the highest level previously achieved (and/or failing to achieve expected levels 85 of social development). There must be, either at present or in the past, delusions, hallucinations, or characteristic disturbances in affect or form of thought (see below). DSM-III-R criteria consider both duration of illness and characteristic symptom pattern (i.e., tendencies toward onset in early adulthood, recurring symptoms, and social and occupational deterioration).

Associated features. Almost any psychiatric symptom may be associated with Schizophrenia. Poor or eccentric grooming, dress, or behavior; psychomotor abnormalities; stereotypic movements; and a perplexed appearance are common. Concreteness and poverty of speech, ritualistic behavior, magical thinking, and dysphoric mood (e.g., depression, anxiety, anger) are not unusual. Dissociative symptoms, ideas of reference, hypochondriasis and other symptoms of somatization, and illusions may be present as well. Disturbance of the sensorium is unusual (and may mitigate toward other diagnoses), although during exacerbation of the illness the patient may be confused or disoriented.

Course. The course of Schizophrenia is quite relevant to the diagnosis. The disorder should not be diagnosed in the absence of at least six months 86 of symptoms, in which at least some active or positive symptoms (see below) have been present. There is usually a *prodromal phase* (see definition below), which is often noticed only in retrospect once acute symptoms or prolonged social deterioration has occurred. After an *active phase* has remitted somewhat, there is usually a *residual phase*. Return to full premorbid functioning is uncommon. The diagnosis should be reconsidered if the patient is able to remain in full remission without treatment for more than a few months.

Predisposing factors. Familial patterns of Schizophrenia or schizophreniform illness are relatively predisposing and become much more predictive if an affected relative is a parent or sibling. Predisposing factors related to socioeconomic or parenting theories are as yet unproved.

Differential diagnosis. Organic Mental Disorders that can account for most or all of the diagnostic criteria, including Organic Delusional Syndromes. Moderate, severe, or profound Mental Retardation; psychotic forms of Mood Disorders (particularly Bipolar) or Schizoaffective Disorder (q.v.). Psychotic Disorder Not Otherwise Specified (NOS) may be diagnosed if not all of the diagnostic criteria listed below are present. Schizophreniform Disorder, which may otherwise be indistinguishable from Schizophrenia, should be diagnosed only when the duration of illness is under six months. Delusional Disorder, Autistic Disorder (in which the additional diagnosis of Schizophrenia may be made if prominent delusions or hallucinations are also present). Note that Schizophrenia in a child preempts the residual disorder Pervasive Developmental Disorder NOS.

Several other psychiatric disorders may present with one or more schizophreniform symptoms, but not the complete diagnostic pattern. In some Personality Disorders, psychotic symptoms may occasionally appear, but are transient, and the patient generally returns to his or her prior level of functioning. It is difficult, however, to differentiate the prodromal phase of Schizophrenia from some Personality Disorders. Finally, unusual or eccentric cultural beliefs, such as those associated with particular religions, when shared and accepted by a cultural group, should not be considered evidence of Schizophrenia.

Diagnostic criteria for Schizophrenia (295.xx) (for subtype criteria, coded in the fourth digit, see Types of Schizophrenia, below):

A. Presence of characteristic psychotic symptoms in the active phase, for at least one week (unless successfully treated), as illustrated by at least *one* of the following:

1. *two* of the following:
   a. delusions
   b. prominent hallucinations lasting more than a few moments
   c. incoherence or marked loosening of associations
   d. catatonic behavior
   e. flat or grossly inappropriate affect
2. bizarre delusions, lasting more than a few moments, involving totally implausible beliefs
3. prominent hallucinations (as defined in "1b") of a voice, with content not apparently related to depression or elation, or a voice that appears to be either frequently commenting about the patient or conversing with the patient or another voice

B. During the course of the disturbance, functioning in such areas as work, social relations, and self-care is markedly below the highest level achieved before onset of the disturbance (when onset is in childhood or adolescence, the expected level of social development is not reached).

C. Schizoaffective Disorder and Mood Disorder with Psychotic Features have been ruled out.

D. There have been continuous signs of the disturbance for at least six months, such signs to include an active phase of at least one week (provided symptoms have not been successfully treated), during which the symptoms in "A" were present. This may occur with or without a prodromal or residual phase, as defined below.

E. It cannot be established that an organic factor initiated and maintained the disturbance.

F. If there is a history of Autistic Disorder, the additional disorder of Schizophrenia is made only if prominent delusions or hallucinations are also present.

Specify *Prodromal Phase* to describe a clear deterioration in functioning *before the active phase*, not due to a mood disturbance or a Substance Use Disorder, and involving at least *two* of the symptoms listed after the next paragraph.

87

Specify *Residual Phase* to describe persistence of at least *two* of the symptoms listed below, *after the active phase*, and not due to Mood Disturbance or Substance Use Disorder.

Prodromal or residual symptoms of Schizophrenia:

1. Marked social isolation or withdrawal
2. Marked impairment in functioning as a wage earner, student, or homemaker
3. Markedly peculiar behavior
4. Marked impairment in personal hygiene and grooming
5. Blunted or inappropriate affect
6. Digressive, vague, circumstantial, or overly elaborate speech or poverty of speech or its content
7. Odd beliefs or magical thinking, which influence(s) the patient's behavior and is/are inconsistent with cultural norms
8. Unusual perceptions (e.g., recurrent illusions or sensing something not actually present)
9. Marked lack of initiative, interests, or energy

TYPES OF SCHIZOPHRENIA
The types below, diagnosed phenomenologically, refer to characteristics currently presenting or, for patients with subchronic, chronic, or "in remission" illness, seen during the last exacerbation.

Catatonic Type (295.2x)

Essential feature. Marked psychomotor disturbance, sometimes rapidly alternating between extremes, and sometimes associated with stereotypies, mannerisms, and waxy flexibility (*cerea flexibilitas*).

Diagnostic criteria for Catatonic Type:

Schizophrenia in which the acute clinical picture is dominated by at least *one* of the following:
A. Catatonic stupor or mutism
B. Catatonic negativism
C. Catatonic rigidity
D. Catatonic excitement
E. Catatonic posturing

Disorganized Type (295.1x)

Essential features. Incoherence, marked loosening of associations, or grossly disorganized behavior, and, in addition, flat or grossly inappropriate affect. Fragmentary delusions or hallucinations are common, but the delusions are not systematized (as in Paranoid Type). There may be associated grimaces, mannerisms, hypochondriasis, social withdrawal, or other oddities. Social impairment is usually extreme. Onset is frequently early and insidious, with poor premorbid personality functioning, and the course is often chronic without significant remission. This type has also been called "hebephrenic" in other classifications, although "hebephrenic" sometimes refers to other syndromes in the literature.

Diagnostic criteria for Disorganized Type:

Schizophrenia, with the following:
A. Incoherence, marked loosening of associations, or grossly disorganized behavior.
B. Flat or grossly inappropriate affect.
C. Does not meet criteria for Catatonic Type.

Paranoid Type (295.3x)

Essential feature. Preoccupation with one or more systematized delusions or with frequent auditory hallucinations related to a single theme.

Associated features. Vague anxiety, anger, proneness to argument, and violence. Many patients have a stilted, formal demeanor, with markedly intense interactions with others.

Diagnostic criteria for Paranoid Type:

Schizophrenia, with the following:
A. Preoccupation with one or more systematized delusions, or with frequent auditory hallucinations of a single theme.
B. *None* of the following: incoherence, marked loosening of associations, flat or grossly inappropriate affect, catatonic behavior, grossly disorganized behavior.

Specify "stable type" if the above criteria have been met during all past and present exacerbations of the illness.

Undifferentiated Type (295.9x)

Essential features. Prominent psychotic symptoms that cannot be classified in any schizophrenic type previously listed *or* that meet the criteria for more than one type.

Diagnostic criteria for Undifferentiated Type:

Schizophrenia, with the following:
A. Prominent delusions, hallucinations, incoherence, or grossly disorganized behavior
B. Does not meet criteria for paranoid, catatonic, or disorganized type

Residual Type (295.6x)

Essential features. History of at least one episode of Schizophrenia, with persisting signs of the illness in the absence of currently prominent psychotic symptoms. Emotional blunting, social withdrawal, eccentric behavior, illogical thinking, and mild loosening of associations are common. Delusions or hallucinations may be present, but are not prominent and are not accompanied by strong affect. This diagnosis should be reserved for patients with either chronic or subchronic Schizophrenia, since acute exacerbation of active illness implies prominent psychosis, and "in remission" implies virtually no signs of the illness.

Diagnostic criteria for Residual Type:

Schizophrenia, with the following:
A. Absence of prominent delusions, hallucinations, incoherence, or grossly disorganized behavior.
B. Continuing evidence of the disturbance, as indicated by *two* or more of the residual symptoms in *Criterion D* of Schizophrenia (see p. 194 of DSM-III-R).

Specify *Fifth-Digit Coding, Course of Illness* in Schizophrenia: **88**

1 = subchronic. More than six months, but less than two years, have elapsed since the first signs of continuous disturbance.

2 = chronic. Above, for more than two years.

3 = subchronic with acute exacerbation. Reemergence of prominent psychosis in a person with subchronic illness, residual phase.

4 = chronic with acute exacerbation. Reemergence of prominent psychotic symptoms in a person with chronic illness, residual phase.

5 = in remission. Free of virtually all signs of the disturbance, with or without medication. (The DSM-III-R "No Mental Disorder" code; should not be used if medication or other treatment is required to continue the remission.)

0 = unspecified.

DIFFERENCES BETWEEN DSM-III AND DSM-III-R SCHIZOPHRENIA

- "Schizophrenic Disorders" has been renamed *Schizophrenia* and the criteria made more specific (and to some extent simpler). The age criterion has been deleted.
- Criteria for *Paranoid Type* have been revised and a "Stable" Paranoid Type delineated.

CASE VIGNETTE

A 46-year-old man has a long history of psychiatric and social problems. He enlisted in the Army at age 19, after dropping out of college. He scored very well on military intelligence tests, but was unable to complete basic training because of apparent confusion under stress and difficulty concentrating on training tasks. After an early discharge, he tried to return to school and was referred to the mental health center after being found wandering around campus in a heavy trenchcoat on a hot day.

A few weeks later, he was committed to a state mental hospital after starting a fire in his dormitory room "to help me stay warm so I can study." He was found to have delusions that he was unable to control his body temperature and would freeze to death if he weren't careful. He responded to treatment with neuroleptic medication, but discontinued it

after discharge from the hospital. Over the next 25 years he was hospitalized on many occasions, each time with delusions of body deterioration
of some sort and of persecution by vaguely described "dark angels."
The delusions were often accompanied by the voices of the "dark angels"
or of reassuring "white angels." He did not adapt well socially, never
married, has not been able to work, and has never had serious problems
with the law.

    At this time, the patient is living semiautonomously in a boarding
home, where he spends his days watching television or walking about a
nearby park. He scrupulously avoids illicit drugs and alcohol, although
he smokes 20 to 30 hand-rolled cigarettes a day. He takes antipsychotic
medication daily. He has not been completely free of his symptoms since
they first appeared. They remain prominent, but they don't trouble him
very much.

Discussion

The patient meets the criteria for Schizophrenia, with no indication that
his symptoms have been caused by organic factors or mood disorder. He
meets the duration criteria for chronicity and continues to have residual
symptoms. His schizophrenic symptoms are characterized by systematized delusions with accompanying hallucinations related to the delusional theme. The prominence of the hallucinations is one factor
differentiating his diagnosis from Delusional Disorder. There is no mention of incoherence, catatonia, or gross disorganization in any of the
exacerbations ("active phases") of his illness, implying "Stable Type." He
appears not to have exhibited a premorbid personality disorder; his poor
functioning early in life is best interpreted as prodromal signs of
Schizophrenia.

Diagnosis

> Axis I   295.32   Schizophrenia, Paranoid Type, Chronic, probably
>   "Stable Type"
> Axis II   V71.09   No diagnosis or condition

Chapter 14

Delusional (Paranoid) Disorder

Delusional (Paranoid) Disorder (297.10)

Essential feature. A persistent, nonbizarre delusion or system of delusions not due to any other mental disorder or organic factor. Except when associated with delusions, the person's behavior is not particularly odd, and hallucinations are not prominent.

Associated features. Five delusional themes or "types" are commonly seen:

A. *Erotomanic Type*, in which one has a delusion of being loved— usually secretly, romantically, and/or spiritually, and usually by a person of higher status or public prominence. The patient may attempt to monitor or contact the other person.

B. *Grandiose Type*, in which the delusion is one of great talent, insight, power, or spiritual leadership.   89

C. *Jealous Type*, in which one is convinced that his or her spouse or lover is unfaithful, in spite of a lack of any real evidence (although imaginary or trivial pseudo-"evidence" is often cited by the patient).

D. *Persecutory Type*, in which the delusional theme has to do with being persecuted (conspired against, cheated, followed, maligned, harassed, etc.). This is the most common type in many patient populations and may lead to elaborate, even dangerous behavior by the patient in order to "protect" himself or herself from harm.

E. *Somatic Type*, which is manifested by delusions of physical problems, usually bizarre ones such as foul odors, parasitic infestations, or malfunctioning body parts.

Predisposing factors. Symptoms of this disorder are disproportionately seen in persons who have emigrated to a new culture (e.g., Asian emigrants in America) and sometimes remit upon return to the familiar culture. Deafness and other severe stresses may predispose one as well, as may certain Personality Disorders (e.g., Paranoid, Schizoid, Avoidant).

Differential diagnosis. Any Organic Mental Disorder, including substance-related syndromes, which can be established to have initiated and maintained the disturbance preempts the diagnosis of Delusional Disorder. Schizophrenia and Schizophreniform Disorder also preempt the diagnosis and have a broader range of symptoms and impairments. Mood Disorder with Psychotic Features may be difficult to differentiate from Delusional Disorder; the clinician should attempt to draw an association between the mood disturbance and the appearance of delusions and other psychotic symptoms. Body Dysmorphic Disorder is differentiated from Delusional Disorder by the lack of delusional intensity involved in the somatic preoccupation. Paranoid Personality Disorder does not contain delusions.

Diagnostic criteria for Delusional Disorder:

A. Nonbizarre delusion(s) involving situations that occur in real life (e.g., being followed, having a disease), of at least one month's duration.

B. Auditory or visual hallucinations, if present, are not prominent (see definition under Schizophrenia, "A, 1, b").

C. Apart from the delusions or their ramifications, behavior is not obviously odd or bizarre.

D. If a Major Depressive or Manic Syndrome has been present during the delusional disturbance, the total duration of any episodes of Mood Disorder has been brief, relative to the total duration of the delusional disturbance.

E. Has never met criterion "A" for Schizophrenia, and it cannot be established that an organic factor initiated and maintained the disturbance.

Specify type, as outlined above. If a type cannot be specified, "Unspecified Type" may be specified.

DIFFERENCES BETWEEN DSM-III AND DSM-III-R DELUSIONAL DISORDER

- "Paranoid Disorders" in DSM-III are broadened into *Delusional Disorders* and are no longer limited to suspiciousness and jealousy. Several types are defined.
- Shared Paranoid Disorder is now called *Induced Psychotic Disorder* because its delusions need not be paranoid and is listed under *Psychotic Disorders Not Elsewhere Classified.*
- Acute Paranoid Disorder is deleted and its symptoms subsumed under *Psychotic Disorders Not Otherwise Specified.*

CASE VIGNETTE

A 44-year-old woman was arrested after harrassing a local television newscaster with telephone calls and letters asserting that he fathered, then absconded with, her child. She denied any wish to harm him, but steadfastly pursued him with demands that he give her "visitation rights" to "their" child. She said she understood that he would be unable to marry her, or even to outwardly acknowledge his love for her, because of his delicate public position.

There was no indication that the newscaster had ever had a relationship with the woman, although evidence from his files and the woman's apartment indicated that her fantasied relationship with him had existed for several years. There was no indication of hallucinations, disturbance of affect, significant mood disorder, or organic illness, and the woman had never been treated for a psychiatric disorder.

Discussion
The disorder appears limited to the delusions, which meet criteria for Erotomanic Type. There is no mention of organic or affective symptoms and

no indication that criterion "A" for Schizophrenia has ever been met. The delusions eliminate a diagnosis of Paranoid Personality Disorder, and there is no mention of any other symptoms of premorbid personality disorder.

Diagnosis

>   Axis I   297.10 Delusional Disorder, Erotomanic Type
>   Axis II 799.90 Diagnosis deferred

Chapter 15

Psychotic Disorders
Not Elsewhere Classified

The disorders in this category cannot be classified as Organic Mental Disorders, Schizophrenia, Delusional Disorder, or Mood Disorder with Psychotic Features.

Brief Reactive Psychosis (298.80)

Essential feature. Sudden onset of psychotic features of brief duration, with eventual full return to the premorbid functioning level. The symptoms are related to severe stress. Brief Reactive Psychosis should not be diagnosed in the presence of symptoms (including prodromal symptoms) or organic, schizophrenic, delusional, or mood disorder. 90

Associated features. Behavior may be quite bizarre, with marked disturbance of speech or affect. Hallucinations or delusions are common; disorientation and temporary memory impairment frequently occur.

Predisposing factors. Preexisting psychopathology, especially Personality Disorders, may predispose the patient to Brief Reactive Psychosis, although one should not automatically infer the preexistence of a Personality Disorder.

Differential diagnosis. Any of the Organic Mental Disorders, including Substance Abuse Disorders, and notably Delirium Organic Delusional Syndrome and various intoxications. Schizophreniform Disorder,

115

Delusional Disorder, Mood Disorder, Psychotic Disorder Not Otherwise Specified (all of which persist longer than one month). Manic and Major Depressive episodes. Factitious Disorder with psychological symptoms, malingering. All of the above diagnoses preempt a diagnosis of Brief Reactive Psychosis. The Personality Disorders may coexist with this disorder.

Diagnostic criteria for Brief Reactive Psychosis:

A. Presence of at least *one* of the following indications of impaired reality testing, which is not culturally sanctioned:
   1. incoherence or marked loosening of associations
   2. delusions
   3. hallucinations
   4. catatonic or disorganized behavior
B. Emotional turmoil, with rapid shifts from one intense affect to another, or overwhelming perplexity or confusion.
C. The symptoms described in "A" and "B" appear shortly after, and apparently in response to, one or more events that, singly or together, would be markedly stressful to almost anyone in similar circumstances in the person's culture.
D. Absence of the prodromal symptoms of Schizophrenia and failure to meet criteria for Schizotypal Personality Disorder before the onset of the disturbance.
E. Duration of a few hours to one month, with eventual full return to premorbid functioning. If the diagnosis must be made before the expected recovery, it should be listed as "provisional."
F. Not due to a psychotic Mood Disorder, and it cannot be established that an organic factor initiated and maintained the disturbance.

Schizophreniform Disorder (295.40)

Essential features, except for duration, are identical to those of Schizophrenia. If the patient has not recovered at the time of diagnosis, then the diagnosis should be qualified as "provisional." Change to Schizophrenia if the clinical syndrome persists beyond six months.

Differential diagnosis, is largely the same as that for Schizophrenia (q. v.). Brief Reactive Psychosis usually does not present with the complete schizophreniform syndrome.

Diagnostic criteria for Schizophreniform Disorder:

A. Meets criteria "A" and "C" for Schizophrenia.
B. All related symptoms, including prodromal, active, and residual phases, have a total duration of under six months.
C. Does not meet the criteria for Brief Reactive Psychosis, and it cannot be established that an organic factor initiated and maintained the disturbance.

Specify "with" or "without" good prognostic features, as indicated by the presence or absence, respectively, of at least *two* of the following:

1. Onset of prominent psychotic symptoms within four weeks of the first noticeable change in behavior or functioning.
2. Confusion, disorientation, or perplexity at the height of the psychotic episode.
3. Good premorbid social and occupational functioning.
4. Absence of blunted or flat affect.

Schizoaffective Disorder (295.70)

Essential features. Symptoms that reflect, at different times, both schizophrenic psychosis and mood disturbance. Schizoaffective Disorder is no longer considered a subtype of Schizophrenia, although it continues to be a somewhat confusing concept. DSM-III-R emphasizes the temporal relationship between schizophrenic and mood symptoms and notes that this diagnosis should not be considered if the patient meets full criteria for either Schizophrenia or Mood Disorder.

Differential diagnosis. Organic Mental Disorders, Schizophrenia, Mood Disorder with Psychotic Features, Delusional Disorder.

Diagnostic criteria for Schizoaffective Disorder:

A. Disturbance during which, at some time, there is either a Major Depressive or a Manic Syndrome concurrent with symptoms that meet the "A" criteria for Schizophrenia.
B. During at least one episode of the disturbance, there have been delusions or hallucinations for at least two weeks, but no prominent mood symptoms.

C. Schizophrenia has been ruled out (for example, because the duration of all episodes of a mood syndrome has been substantial relative to the total duration of the psychotic disturbance).
D. It cannot be established that an organic factor initiated and maintained the disturbance.

Specify type: *bipolar* (with current or prior Manic Syndrome) or *depressive* (without current or prior Manic Syndrome).

Induced Psychotic Disorder (297.30)

Essential feature. A delusional system that develops as a result of a close relationship with a dominant psychotic person. The delusions are at least partly shared by both persons. The content of the delusion is usually within the realm of possibility and often is specific to the two people, who usually have lived together and may be isolated from others.

Associated features. Interruption of the relationship with the "primary case" person usually decreases the delusional beliefs in the second person. Cases have been reported involving many people, although most commonly there are two (*folie à deux*).

Differential diagnosis. Delusional Disorder, Schizophrenia, Schizoaffective Disorder, none with the requisite close relationship with a dominant person who has a Psychotic Disorder, with whom the delusions are shared.

Diagnostic criteria for Induced Psychotic Disorder:

A. A delusion develops in the context of a close relationship with another person or persons (the "primary case") who has/have an already established delusion.
B. The delusion in the second person is similar in content to that in the "primary case."
C. Immediately before onset of the induced delusion, the second person did not have a Psychotic Disorder or prodromal symptoms of Schizophrenia.

Psychotic Disorder Not Otherwise Specified (Atypical Psychosis) (298.90)

Essential feature. Clearly psychotic symptoms that do not meet the criteria for any other organic or nonorganic DSM-III-R psychotic disorder.

The category should also be used for patients about whom there is not adequate information to make a specific diagnosis. It is preferred over the phrase "diagnosis deferred."

DIFFERENCES BETWEEN DSM-III AND DSM-III-R PSYCHOTIC DISORDERS NOT ELSEWHERE CLASSIFIED

- *Induced Psychotic Disorder* includes disorders previously diagnosed Shared Paranoid Disorder.
- Coding of *Schizophreniform Disorder* now addresses prognostic features, and its criteria have been revised to delete the minimum duration or symptoms.
- *Schizoaffective Disorder* now has specific criteria and can be subclassified *Bipolar* or *Depressive Type*.
- Criteria for *Brief Reactive Psychosis* have been clarified.

CASE VIGNETTE
A 20-year-old apprentice electrician was hospitalized one month ago with acute confusion and psychosis, including looseness of associations and statements that God had spoken to him and given him great powers. He showed no severe blunting of affect. He was doing well, in his training and socially, until about three months ago, when he began to show deterioration in productivity and ability to concentrate. He drinks socially and has used marijuana occasionally, but there is no evidence of continuous abuse or other drug use.

The patient has not recently been physically ill, is taking no prescribed medications, has a normal physical examination, and apparently has not been exposed to industrial or environmental toxins. At present, he has responded to hospitalization and medication, but is still delusional.

Discussion
The patient meets criteria "A" and "C" for Schizophrenia, but does not meet the duration criteria for either Schizophrenia or Brief Reactive Psychosis. Although his grandiosity may suggest a manic or hypomanic episode, there is no mention of other criteria for any Mood Disorder. Environmental (e.g., industrial) toxins and substance abuse have both been considered as sources of the psychosis, but have not been established as causative. The patient has not recovered fully, mandating a "Provi-

sional" notation until either recovery occurs, duration and other criteria for Schizophrenia are met, or other diagnostic information comes to light. His good premorbid functioning, confusion during psychosis, and absence of blunt or flattened affect are "good prognostic features" in DSM-III-R.

Diagnosis

> Axis I 295.40 Schizophreniform Disorder, Provisional, with good prognostic features
> Axis II 799.90 Diagnosis deferred

Chapter 16

Mood Disorders

"Mood" describes a prolonged, pervasive emotion, such as a depressed mood or an elated mood, that colors an individual's perception of the world. The Mood Disorders have in common a disturbance of mood and symptoms of a partial or full manic or depressive syndrome. In addition, the mood disturbance cannot be caused by an organic etiology, such as medication or a physical disorder. Mood Disorders are divided into Bipolar Disorders and Depressive Disorders.

Before the coded disorders in this diagnostic category are discussed, the reader must understand the definitions of Manic Episode, Hypomanic Episode, and Major Depressive Episode.

Manic Episode

Essential features. The individual experiences a distinct period of elated, expansive, or irritable mood, and symptoms such as grandiosity, decreased need for sleep, talkativeness, flight of ideas, distractibility, increase in activity, and involvement in risky activity. This disturbance must result in marked dysfunction on the job or in school, in social activities, or in relationships with others. Delusions and/or hallucinations may accompany the mood disturbance, but the delusion or hallucination does not exist without the accompanying mood disturbance for longer than two weeks. In other words, the mood disturbance is not part of another psychotic disorder (i.e., Schizophrenia, Schizophreniform Disorder, Delusional Disorder, or Psychotic Disorder Not Otherwise Specified). In addition, there should be no evidence that organic factors either initiated or sustained the disturbance.

Associated features. An individual with Manic Episodes frequently resists treatment. Clinical features include mood lability (e.g., rapid shifts from anger to depression) and depressive symptoms that may last moments, minutes, or, more rarely, days. When delusions and hallucination occur, they are usually mood-congruent. For example, the individual with an elated mood may believe he is endowed with special powers. Catatonic symptoms may also be seen.

Predisposing factors. Psychosocial stress, antidepressants, electro-convulsive therapy, and childbirth may precipitate a Manic Episode. When an organic factor, such as psychoactive medication (e.g., amphetamines), causes a Manic Episode, it is considered an Organic Mood Syndrome. (Note: By definition in DSM-III-R, somatic antidepressant treatments, such as antidepressant drugs or electroconvulsive therapy, and childbirth are not considered organic factors.)

Differential diagnosis. Organic Mood Disorders, Attention-Deficit Hyperactivity Disorder, and Schizophrenia (Paranoid Type) are considered in the differential diagnosis.

Diagnostic criteria for Manic Episode:

A. A distinct period of an abnormal, persistently elevated, expansive, or irritable mood.

B. During the mood disturbance, at least *three* (four if the mood is irritable) of the following symptoms have persisted and have been present to a significant degree:
   1. inflated self-esteem or grandiosity
   2. decreased need for sleep
   3. more talkative than usual
   4. flight of ideas or subjective experience that thoughts are racing
   5. distractibility
   6. increase in activity (socially, sexually, or vocationally) or psychomotor agitation

7. excessive involvement in pleasurable activities that are potentially risky (e.g., buying sprees, driving at a high rate of speed,
foolish investments)

C. Mood disturbance is severe enough to cause marked impairment
in occupational function, social activities, or relationships, or
severe enough to necessitate hospitalization to prevent harm to
self or to others.

D. At no time have delusions or hallucinations been present for two
weeks in the absence of prominent mood symptoms.

E. Not superimposed on Schizophrenia, Schizophreniform Disorder,
Delusional Disorder, or Psychotic Disorder Not Otherwise
Specified.

F. No organic factor is known that initiated or maintained the
disturbance. Note: According to DSM-III-R, somatic antidepressant treatments (e.g., antidepressant medications, electroconvulsive treatment) and childbirth that apparently precipitate a
mood disturbance are not considered organic factors.

Specify severity (digit codes fifth digit of Bipolar Disorder, below):
Mild = 1: Minimum symptoms present for a Manic Episode.

Moderate = 2: Extreme hyperactivity or impaired judgment.

Severe, without psychotic features = 3: Almost continual supervision necessary to prevent harm to self or to others.

Severe, with psychotic features = 4: Delusions, hallucinations, or
catatonic symptoms are present; specify whether psychotic features
are mood-congruent or are mood-incongruent.

In partial remission = 5: Previously met the full criteria does not
although some symptoms persist.

In full remission = 6: Previously met the full criteria but has been
without manic symptoms for at least six months.

Unspecified = 0.

Hypomanic Episode

Essential features. As in a Manic Episode, the predominant mood is
either elevated, expansive, or irritable, and there are similar associated 94
symptoms. However, the disturbance is not severe enough to cause marked
impairment (in job, social activities, or relationships) or require hospitalization. Delusions or hallucinations are never present.

Diagnostic criteria for Hypomanic Episode:

Using the diagnostic criteria for Manic Episode, a Hypomanic Episode includes "A" and "B," but not "C" (marked impairment) or "D" (delusions or hallucinations).

Major Depressive Episode

Essential features. The person must have for at least a two-week period either a depressed mood (in children or adolescents the mood may be irritable) or loss of pleasure or interest in almost all activities (sometimes referred to as anhedonia). In addition, at least four other depressive symptoms are present. The Major Depressive Episode is not initiated or maintained by an organic etiology, is not secondary to Uncomplicated Bereavement, and is not superimposed on a psychotic disorder. Delusions and/or hallucinations may accompany the mood disturbance, but the delusion or hallucination cannot exist without the accompanying mood disturbance for longer than two weeks.

Associated features. Accompanying clinical features may include tearfulness, anxiety, obsessive ruminations, panic attacks, phobias, and excessive health concerns. When delusions and hallucinations occur, they are usually mood-congruent. For example, the individual may believe that his bowels are rotting in spite of normal medical evaluations.

Predisposing factors. Chronic medical illness, Psychoactive Substance Dependence (particularly Alcohol and Cocaine Dependence), psychosocial stress, and childbirth.

Differential diagnosis. Organic Mood Disorder, Primary Degenerative Dementia of the Alzheimer's Type, Multi-infarct Dementia, Dementia with depression, depressive pseudodementia, Adjustment Disorder with depressed mood, Schizophrenia, Schizoaffective Disorder, and Uncomplicated Bereavement are considered in the differential diagnosis.

Diagnostic criteria for Major Depressive Episode:

A. At least *five* of the following symptoms must be present simultaneously for a two-week period or more. This represents a change from previous levels of functioning, and one symptom must be either depressed mood or anhedonia.

1. depressed mood or, in children or adolescents, an irritable mood

2. anhedonia
3. significant weight loss (not due to a voluntary diet), or weight gain, or chronic decrease or increase in appetite.
4. insomnia or hypersomnia nearly every day
5. observable psychomotor agitation or retardation nearly every day
6. loss of energy or fatigue almost every day
7. feeling of worthlessness, or excessive or inappropriate guilt almost every day
8. decrease in ability to concentrate, or indecisiveness almost every day
9. recurrent thoughts of death, or recurrent suicidal ideation

B. The disturbance is not caused or maintained by an organic factor or Uncomplicated Bereavement. Note: Bereavement can be complicated by a Major Depressive Episode. This is suggested when the bereaved reports morbid preoccupation with worthlessness, suicidal ideation, marked functional impairment, psychomotor retardation, or prolonged duration.
C. At no time have delusions or hallucinations been present for two weeks in the absence of prominent mood symptoms.
D. Not superimposed on Schizophrenia, Schizophreniform Disorder, Delusional Disorder, or Psychotic Disorder Not Otherwise Specified.

Specify severity (coded in fifth digit of Bipolar Disorder or Major Depression, below):

Mild = 1: Few symptoms in excess of the minimum criteria for the diagnosis of a Major Depressive Episode.

Moderate = 2: Impairment between mild and severe.

Severe, without psychotic features = 3: Several symptoms in excess of minimum criteria for the diagnosis, and symptoms markedly interfere with occupation, social activities, or relationships.

With psychotic features = 4: Delusions or hallucinations are present. When possible, specify whether psychotic features are mood-congruent or are mood-incongruent.

In partial remission = 5: Previously met the full criteria but currently has symptoms intermediate between "Mild" and "In full remission." In addition, there is no previous Dysthymia. Note: If Major Depressive Disorder is superimposed on Dysthymia (i.e., Dysthymia is the individual's usual baseline), the diagnosis of Dysthymia is again given once the person does not meet the full criteria for Major Depressive Episode.

In full remission = 6: Once met the full criteria but has been without signs or symptoms of the disturbance for at least six months.

Unspecified = 0.

Subtypes of Major Depressive Episode

There are two subtypes of Major Depressive Episode that are sometimes seen by the clinician: *chronic* and *melancholic*.

Chronic. The current Major Depressive Episode has lasted for two years or more with no more than a two-month period of symptom remission during that time.

Melancholic. A severe form of Major Depressive Episode that seems to be quite responsive to somatic treatments. The diagnostic criteria include at least *five* of the following depressive symptoms: (1) anhedonia; (2) lack of response to pleasurable stimuli; (3) depression is regularly worse in the morning; (4) early-morning awakening, at least two hours before usual time; (5) observable psychomotor agitation or retardation; (6) significant anorexia or weight loss (for example, more than 5% of body weight in a month); (7) no significant personality disturbance prior to first Major Depressive Episode; (8) one or more previous Major Depressive Episodes followed by full, or nearly full, remissions; (9) previous good response to specific and adequate somatic therapy (polycyclic antidepressant, electroconvulsive therapy, lithium).

A. BIPOLAR DISORDERS

Essential features. In Bipolar Disorders, one or more Manic or Hypomanic Episodes are usually associated with one or more Depressive Episodes. Bipolar Disorders are subclassified as either mixed, manic, or depressed according to the clinical features of the current or most recent episode.

Associated features. An individual with Bipolar Disorder frequently resists treatment. Clinical features include mood lability (e.g., rapid shifts from anger to depression) and depressive symptoms that may last moments, minutes, or days. Depressive and Manic symptoms may occur simultaneously or may alternate. Patients with two or more complete cycles (a manic and a major depressive episode that follow each other without a period of remission) within a year have been referred to as "rapid cyclers."

Predisposing factors. A family history of Bipolar Disorder.

Differential diagnosis. Cyclothymia is considered in the differential diagnosis.

Diagnostic criteria for Bipolar Disorders (specify if seasonal pattern):

Bipolar Disorder, Mixed (296.6x)
A. Current or most recent episode involves the intermixed or alternating (every few days) clinical features of both Manic and Major Depressive Disorder (except for the two-week duration requirement).
B. Prominent depressive symptoms that last at least a full day.

Bipolar Disorder, Manic (296.4x)
A. Current or most recent disturbance is a Manic Episode. Note: To make this diagnosis, the current disturbance does not have to meet the full diagnostic criteria if the individual has had a previous Manic Episode.

Bipolar Disorder, Depressed (296.5x)
A. Has had one or more Manic Episodes.
B. Current, or most recent, disturbance is a Major Depressive Disorder. If the individual had a previous Major Depressive Episode, the current disturbance does not have to meet the full diagnostic criteria.

Specify severity (coded in the fifth digit): Mild = 1, Moderate = 2, Severe without psychotic features = 3, Severe with psychotic features = 4, In partial remission = 5, In full remission = 6, or Unspecified = 0.   **96**

Classified as seasonal pattern if: (1) there is a regular temporal relationship between the onset of the Bipolar Disorder or Recurrent Major

Depression and a particular 60-day period of the year (exclude if there are seasonal psychosocial stressors); (2) full remission, or a change from depression to mania or hypomania, occurs within a particular 60-day period of the year; (3) at least three episodes of mood disturbance in three separate years demonstrate the temporal pattern in (1) and (2), *and* at least two years were consecutive; and (4) seasonal episodes outnumber the nonseasonal episodes by more than three to one.

Cyclothymia (301.13)

Essential features. Cyclothymia is a chronic mood disturbance involving frequent Hypomanic Episodes and frequent periods of depressive mood or anhedonia. During the first two years of the disturbance there is neither a Manic Episode nor a Major Depressive Episode. The diagnosis is not made if the disturbance is superimposed on a psychotic disorder, or if the disturbance is initiated or sustained by an organic etiology.

Associated features. There may be social, academic, interpersonal, or occupational difficulties caused by recurrent mood swings. However, there are no marked areas of functional impairment. Psychoactive Substance Abuse is common.

Differential diagnosis. Bipolar Disorder, Bipolar Disorder Not Otherwise Specified, and Borderline Personality Disorder are considered in the differential diagnosis.

Diagnostic criteria for Cyclothymia:

A. At least two years (or one year in children or adolescents) of numerous Hypomanic Episodes and numerous periods of depressed mood or anhedonia.

B. During a two-year period (or one year in children or adolescents) the individual is without "A" for no longer than two months.

C. During the first two years (or one year in children or adolescents) of the disturbance there is no clear evidence of a Manic or a Major Depressive Episode.

D. Not superimposed on a chronic psychotic disorder.

E. No organic etiology is established that either initiated or maintains the disturbance.

Bipolar Disorder Not Otherwise Specified (296.70)

Essential features. A disorder in which manic or hypomanic features exist but the disturbance does not meet the criteria for other Bipolar Disorders. An example would be a patient who has had one Major Depressive Episode in the past, as well as several Hypomanic Episodes (none meet the full diagnostic criteria for Manic Episode). This diagnosis is sometimes referred to as "Bipolar Type II" or "Bipolar II." The clinician specifies whether a seasonal pattern exists.

B. DEPRESSIVE DISORDERS

Major Depression, Single Episode (296.2x)

Major Depression, Recurrent (296.3x)

Essential features. The individual has had one or more Depressive Episodes without either a Manic or unequivocal Hypomanic Episode.

Associated features. A significant number of individuals, from 20% to 35% according to DSM-III-R, will follow a chronic course with considerable residual symptoms and impairment. Some persons who are diagnosed with Dysthymia will experience a superimposed Major Depressive Episode (so-called "double-depression").

Predisposing factors. Major Depression is twice as common in women as men. Presence of Major Depression in first-degree relations predisposes one to the diagnosis.

Differential diagnosis. Organic Mood Disorder, Primary Degenerative Dementia of the Alzheimer Type, Multi-infarct Dementia, Dementia with depression, depressive pseudodementia, Adjustment Disorder with depressed mood, Dysthymia, Bipolar Disorders, Cyclothymia, Schizophrenia, Schizoaffective Disorder, and Uncomplicated Bereavement are considered in the differential diagnosis.

Diagnostic criteria for Major Depression:

Major Depression, Single Episode
A. A single Major Depressive Episode.
B. Has had neither a Manic Episode nor an unequivocal Hypomanic Episode.

Major Depression, Recurrent

A. Two or more Major Depressive Episodes, separated by at least two months of full or partial remission of symptoms. If a prior Major Depressive Episode occurred, the present depressive episode does not have to meet the full criteria for Major Depressive Episode.

B. Has had neither a Manic Episode nor an unequivocal Hypomanic Episode.

Specify severity (coded in fifth digit): Mild = 1, Moderate = 2, Severe without psychotic features = 3, Severe with psychotic features = 4, In partial remission = 5, In full remission = 6, or Unspecified = 0.

Specify if seasonal pattern (see criteria under bipolar disorders).

Dysthymia (or Depressive Neurosis) (300.40)

97   **Essential features.** Dysthymia is a chronic mood disturbance involving frequent periods of depressive mood or anhedonia. Specifically, during a two-year period (1) depressive symptoms are absent for no more than two months, and (2) no Major Depressive Episode occurs. The diagnosis is not made if the disturbance is superimposed on a psychotic disorder, or if the disturbance is initiated or sustained by an organic etiology.

    Associated features. There are no delusions or hallucinations. Individuals with Dysthymia often also have an Axis II Personality Disorder. Major Depressive Episodes are superimposed on this disorder ("double-depression"). Depressed children and adolescents often show deterioration in school performance and behavior.

    Predisposing factors. Secondary-type Dysthymias result from non-mood Axis I disorders and/or Axis III medical disorders. In children and adolescents, Attention-Deficit Hyperactivity Disorder, Conduct Disorder, Mental Retardation, a severe Specific Developmental Disorder, or a chaotic environment may predispose to Dysthymia.

    Differential diagnosis. Major Depressive Disorder, normal fluctuation in mood, Adjustment Disorder with depressed mood, and Cyclothymia are considered in the differential diagnosis.

Diagnostic criteria for Dysthymia:

A. Depressed mood (or can be an irritable mood in children and adolescents) for at least two years (one year for children and adolescents).

B. Presence, while depressed, of at least *two* of the following:

   1. poor appetite or overeating

   2. insomnia or hypersomnia

   3. low energy or fatigue

   4. low self-esteem

   5. poor concentration or difficulty making decisions

   6. feelings of hopelessness

C. During a two-year period (or one year in children or adolescents) the individual is without symptoms in "A" for no longer than two months.

D. During the first two years of the disturbance (or one year in children or adolescents) there is no clear evidence of a Major Depressive Episode.

E. Has never had a Manic or unequivocal Hypomanic Episode.

F. Not superimposed on a chronic psychotic disorder.

G. No organic etiology is established that either initiated or maintains the disturbance.

Specify:

Primary type if Dysthymia is not related to preexisting, chronic Axis I non-mood disorder or Axis III medical disorder.

Secondary type if the Dysthymia is apparently related to the preexisting, chronic Axis I non-mood disorder or Axis III medical disorder.

Early onset if the disturbance begins before age 21.

Late onset if the disturbance begins at age 21 or older.

Depressive Disorder Not Otherwise Specified (311.00)

Essential features. A disorder with depressive features that does not meet the criteria for a Mood Disorder or Adjustment Disorder with Depressed Mood. The clinician specifies whether a seasonal pattern exists.

DIFFERENCES BETWEEN DSM-III AND
DSM-III-R MOOD DISORDERS

- The DSM-III diagnostic category "Affective Disorders" is replaced in DSM-III-R by the term *Mood Disorders*.
- The diagnostic criteria for a Manic Episode now require marked social or occupational impairment.
- The fifth-digit code for Manic and Depressive Episodes in DSM-III-R indicates symptom severity.
- The criteria for melancholia have been revised.
- In *Dysthymia*, the clinician now specifies *primary* or *secondary type* and the onset as either *early* or *late*.
- The clinician now indicates when a *seasonal pattern* exists between the Mood Disorder and a particular 60-day period of the year.
- "Bipolar II" is classified in DSM-III-R as a *Bipolar Disorder Not Otherwise Specified*.

CASE VIGNETTE

Ms. C. is a 34-year-old bank executive who is brought for evaluation by her husband. According to the husband, she has been in excellent health until two weeks ago, when she began staying up later and later at night. He was initially not too concerned, until she began awakening him to talk about the "revolutionary" new ideas she had about creating an international bank cartel. He notes she was "full of energy" and talked rapidly about the many ideas that she had. He became quite concerned when at 3 A.M. she telephoned the president of the bank where she works to discuss her ideas. She then began telephoning European banks in an attempt to find partners for her business venture. When her husband confronted her about the inappropriateness of her phone calls, she became enraged and accused him of purposefully attempting to sabotage her venture. She was brought to the emergency room by the husband and two friends.

Ms. C.'s speech is quite rapid and she jumps quickly from one subject to another. She states that she is about to revolutionize banking and control the world currency market. When questioned about the likelihood of achieving this goal, she becomes irritable and threatens to leave. She admits to auditory hallucinations that are telling her how to corner the market on gold and other precious metals. The patient is on no medications, has no prior psychiatric history (including absence of Depressive Episodes), and denies drug abuse. Family history is positive for Mood Disorders. Her younger brother had a severe depression two years ago that required hospitalization, and her mother was diagnosed as "Manic-Depressive" many years ago. Her physical examination is normal and toxic screen is negative.

Discussion
Ms. C.'s symptoms and behavior are typical of a Manic Episode. Her mood is expansive. She is grandiose, talkative, has flight of ideas, and is having mood-congruent hallucinations. She also has a markedly decreased need for sleep. Her impairment in function is severe. There is no evidence of an organic factor. There is no evidence of any preexisting psychotic disorder, and Ms. C.'s hallucinations appear concurrently with the Mood Disorder.

Diagnosis

    Axis I   296.44   Bipolar Disorder, Manic, Severe, with mood-congruent psychotic features
    Axis II V71.09 No diagnosis
    Axis III   No known medical conditions

Chapter 17

Anxiety Disorders
(Anxiety and Phobic Neuroses)

98 The characteristic features of the Anxiety Disorders are anxiety and avoidance behavior. Note that some Anxiety Disorders are not classified here. Separation Anxiety Disorder, related to separation from parental figures, is classified under Disorders Usually First Evident in Infancy, Childhood, or Adolescence. Sexual Aversion Disorder, listed under Sexual Disorders, is characterized by phobic avoidance which is limited to sexual activities.

Panic Disorder with Agoraphobia (300.21)

Panic Disorder without Agoraphobia (300.01)

Essential features. These disorders, considered subtypes of Panic
99 Disorder, are characterized by recurrent panic attacks which are described below. The attacks usually last minutes, and rarely last more than an hour. They are usually unexpected (i.e., not immediately associated with a known stressful or phobic setting) and are different from those described in the other Anxiety Disorders below. The "unexpected" aspect is essential to the diagnosis of either type of Panic Disorder.

Associated features. The patient is often apprehensive between attacks, usually in fear of having another attack. Some Depressive Disorder is often present. Agoraphobia is very common.

134

Predisposing factors. Separation Anxiety Disorder, sudden loss of social support, disruption of important interpersonal relationships.

Differential diagnosis. Anxiety or panic related to organic factors, including medications, substance abuse, and any of a large number of physical disorders (see Organic Anxiety Syndrome). Withdrawal of (prescribed or nonprescribed) substances, including medications or caffeine. Major Depressive Episode and Somatization Disorder should be differentiated from Panic Disorder, although each can coexist with it. An additional diagnosis of Generalized Anxiety Disorder should *not* be made when the patient's anxiety between panic attacks is focused on the fear of having another attack. Simple Phobia and Social Phobia should be differentiated according to their diagnostic criteria, listed below.

Diagnostic criteria for Panic Disorder, with or without agoraphobia (see below for agoraphobic criteria):

A. At some time during the disturbance, one or more panic attacks have occurred that were (1) unexpected *and* (2) not triggered by situations in which the person was the focus of others' attention.

B. Either four attacks (defined above) have occurred within four weeks, *or* one or more attacks have been followed by periods of at least a month of persistent fear of having another attack.

C. At least *four* of the following symptoms developed during at least one of the attacks:
   1. shortness of breath or a smothering sensation
   2. dizziness, unsteady feelings, faintness
   3. palpitations or accelerated heart rate
   4. trembling or shaking
   5. sweating
   6. choking
   7. nausea or abdominal distress
   8. depersonalization or derealization
   9. numbness or tingling sensations
   10. flushes, "hot flashes," or chills
   11. chest pain or discomfort

12. fear of dying

13. fear of going crazy or becoming out of control

100   **Note** that patients whose attacks involve fewer than four symptoms may have "limited symptom attacks" (see Agoraphobia Without History of Panic Disorder).

D. During at least some of the attacks, at least four of the symptoms in "C" developed suddenly and increased in intensity within 10 minutes of the first "C" symptom noticed in the attack.

E. It cannot be established that an organic factor (including medication or other substance use) initiated and maintained the disturbance.

Note: Mitral valve prolapse may be an associated condition, coded on Axis III, but does not preclude the diagnosis of Panic Disorder.

Diagnostic criteria for Panic Disorder, *with* Agoraphobia:

A. Meets the criteria for Panic Disorder (above).

B. Agoraphobia.

Specify: current severity of *agoraphobia:*

1. **Mild**—some avoidance, but relatively normal lifestyle.

2. **Moderate**—avoidance creates a constricted lifestyle.

3. **Severe**—avoidance results in being nearly or completely homebound or unable to leave unaccompanied.

4. **In partial remission**—no current agoraphobic avoidance, but some during the past six months.

5. **In full remission**—no agoraphobic avoidance for six months or more.

Specify: current severity of *panic attacks:*

1. **Mild**—for the past month, either all attacks have been "limited symptom attacks" (fewer than four symptoms of criterion "C" above), or there has been no more than one panic attack.

2. **Moderate**—during the past month attacks have been intermediate between mild and severe.

3. **Severe**—during the past month there have been at least eight panic attacks.

4. **In partial remission**—intermediate between "in full remission" and "mild."

5. **In full remission**—no panic attacks or limited symptom attacks for at least six months.

Diagnostic criteria for Panic Disorder *without* Agoraphobia:

A. Meets the criteria for Panic Disorder.
B. Absence of agoraphobia.

Specify: current severity of panic attacks, defined above.

Agoraphobia without History of Panic Disorder (300.22)

Essential feature. Agoraphobia without a known history of Panic Disorder. The person may be afraid of having a limited symptom attack (see criteria for Panic Disorder), such as becoming dizzy or falling, depersonalization, or cardiac distress. Such symptoms may have occurred in the past, and the patient may be preoccupied with fears of recurrence.

Associated features. Personality disturbance, particularly symptoms of Avoidant Personality Disorder.

Complications. Some patient subsequently develop Panic Disorder.

Differential diagnosis. Avoidant behavior may be seen in some Psychotic or Delusional Disorders with Persecutory Features, and in major depressive episodes. Panic Disorder with Agoraphobia precludes this diagnosis. Extreme cases of Social Phobia may cause similar avoidance patterns.

Diagnostic criteria for Agoraphobia without History of Panic Disorder:

A. Agoraphobia.
B. Has never met the criteria for Panic Disorder.

Specify: *with* or *without* limited symptom attacks (see criteria for Panic Disorder, above).

Social Phobia (300.23)

Essential feature. A persistent fear of one or more situations in which the patient is exposed to possible scrutiny by others, and fears that he or she may do something or act in a way that will be humiliating or embarrassing. The Social Phobia may be circumscribed or may be "quite general." It must be unrelated to fears of panic attack, stuttering, trembling, or symptoms of other Axis I or Axis II disorders. Marked anticipatory anxiety when one must enter the situation that generates the phobia is the rule. The diagnosis should be made only if avoidant behavior interferes with social or vocational functioning, or if the patient has marked distress about the fear.

Associated features. Frequently coexists with Panic Disorder and Simple Phobia (but should not be related to the same phobic objects or situations).

Complications. People with this and other anxiety disorders are often predisposed to episodic abuse of alcohol or other anxiety-reducing substances. Impaired functioning may lead to depression.

Differential diagnosis. Simple avoidance of social situations that normally are a source of some distress (e.g., "normal" fear of public speaking), Avoidant Personality Disorder (which may coexist with it), Simple Phobia, Panic Disorder with Agoraphobia.

Diagnostic criteria for Social Phobia:

A. A persistent fear of one or more situations ("social phobic situations") in which the person is exposed to possible scrutiny by others and fears that he or she may do something or act in a way that will be humiliating or embarrassing.

B. If an Axis III or another Axis I disorder is present, the fear in "A" is not related to it.

C. During some phase of the disturbance, exposure to the specific social phobic stimulus almost invariably provokes an immediate anxiety response.

D. The phobic situation is avoided or is endured with intense anxiety.

E. The avoidant behavior interferes with occupational or social functioning or relationships with others, or there is marked distress about having the fear.

F. The person recognizes that the fear is excessive or unreasonable.

G. If the person is under 18, the disturbance does not meet criteria for Avoidant Disorder of Childhood or Adolescence.

Specify: "Generalized Type" if the phobic situation includes most social situations (i.e., is not well circumscribed) and consider coexisting Avoidant Personality Disorder.

Simple Phobia (300.29)

Essential feature. This disorder is characterized by a persistent fear of a *circumscribed* stimulus, which may be an object or a situation, *other than* fear of having a panic attack or a social phobic situation. During some phase of the disturbance, exposure to the simple phobic stimulus almost invariably provokes an immediate anxiety response, and marked anticipatory anxiety occurs if exposure is imminent. The diagnosis is made only if the avoidant behavior interferes with the person's normal routine, social activities, or relationships, or if there is marked distress about having the fear.

Associated features. Unrelated Social Phobia and Panic Disorder with or without Agoraphobia are often present.

Differential diagnosis. In Schizophrenia and other Psychotic Disorders, certain activities may be avoided, but the fear is not recognized by the patient as excessive or unreasonable. In Post-traumatic Stress Disorder, the phobic stimulus can be associated, in reality or symbolically, with the trauma. Simple Phobia should not be diagnosed in cases of Post-traumatic Stress Disorder unless the phobic stimulus cannot be related, symbolically or in reality, to the trauma. In Obsessive Compulsive Disorder, anxiety about dirt or contamination should not be diagnosed as Simple Phobia.

Diagnostic criteria for Simple Phobia:

A. Persistent fear of a circumscribed stimulus (object or situation) other than fears of having a panic attack or of humiliation or embarrassment in certain social situations.

   Note: Do not include fears that are part of Panic Disorder with Agoraphobia or Agoraphobia without History of Panic Disorder.

B. During some phase of the disturbance, exposure to the specific phobic stimulus almost invariably provokes an immediate anxiety response.

C. The object or situation is avoided or endured with intense anxiety.

D. The fear or avoidant behavior significantly interferes with the patient's normal routine, usual social activities, or relationships, or there is marked distress about having the fear.

E. The person recognizes that the fear is excessive or unreasonable.

F. The phobic stimulus is unrelated to the content of the obsessions of Obsessive Compulsive Disorder or the trauma of Post-traumatic Stress Disorder.

Obsessive Compulsive Disorder (or Obsessive Compulsive Neurosis) (300.30)

Essential feature. The essential feature of this disorder is recurrent obsessions or compulsions sufficiently severe to cause marked distress, consume considerable time, and/or significantly interfere with the patient's normal routine and/or occupational, social, or interpersonal functioning. The obsessions (or at least the energy consumed by them) are dysphoric. Attempts to resist the compulsions lead to a sense of mounting tension that can be immediately relieved by yielding to the compulsion.

Associated features. Depression, anxiety, phobic avoidance of situations related to obsessions (e.g., dirt, contamination).

Differential diagnosis. Many activities in which patients engage excessively, such as those associated with eating disorders, Paraphilias, gambling, or substance abuse, may be confused with compulsions; however, in true compulsions the activity itself is not usually pleasurable. Depressive Disorders are frequently associated with obsessiveness (especially obsessive guilt); however, the subjects of the obsessions are usually meaningful and rarely associated with compulsions. The obsessions and compulsions do not reach the level of delusion, which differentiates them from Schizophrenia or schizophreniform illness, or Delusional Disorder. The disorder should be differentiated from the stereotypic behavior of Tourette's Disorder and some other disorders, although it may coexist with them.

Diagnostic criteria for Obsessive Compulsive Disorder:

A. Either obsessions *or* compulsions, as defined below:
    Obsessions, containing *all four* of the following:
    1. Recurrent and persistent ideas, thoughts, impulses, or images that are experienced, at least initially, as intrusive and senseless.

2. The patient attempts to ignore or suppress such thoughts or impulses, or to neutralize them with some other thought or action.

3. The patient recognizes that the obsessions are the product of his or her own mind, not imposed from without (as in thought insertion).

4. If another Axis I disorder is present, the content of the obsession is unrelated to it.

Compulsions, characterized by *all three* of the following:

1. Repetitive, purposeful, and intentional behaviors that are performed in response to an obsession, or according to certain rules, or in a stereotyped fashion.

2. The behavior is designed to neutralize or prevent discomfort or some dreaded event or situation; however, either the activity is not connected in a realistic way with that which it is designed to neutralize and prevent, or it is clearly excessive.

3. The person recognizes that his or her behavior is excessive or unreasonable, except in young children or patients whose obsessions have evolved into "overvalued ideas."

B. The obsessions or compulsions cause marked distress, are time-consuming (taking more than an hour per day), and/or significantly interfere with the person's normal routine, occupational functioning, social activities, or relationships.

Post-traumatic Stress Disorder (309.89)

Essential feature. Characteristic symptoms following a psychologically distressing event that is outside the range of usual human experience. The original stressor is usually experienced with intense fear, terror, and/or helplessness.

The precipitating stressor must not be one which is usually well tolerated by most other members of the cultural group (e.g., death of a loved one, ordinary traffic accident). Post-traumatic Stress Disorder need not develop in every victim. Traumas may be experienced alone (e.g., rape, severe physical assault) or in groups (e.g., military combat, unusually serious automobile accidents). The stressor may arise from natural, accidental, or purposeful events.

101

Age-specific features. The disorder in children may present differently (see below).

Associated features. Depression and anxiety are common and may be diagnosed as separate disorders. Compulsive behavior or changes of routine or lifestyle may occur. Pseudo-"organic" symptoms, such as memory problems, difficulty in concentrating, or emotional lability, may occur and may be confused with Somatoform Disorders. "Survivor's guilt" may occur, particularly if others were killed in the traumatic event. Impairment may be mild or severe and may affect almost any aspect of life. Phobic avoidance of real or symbolic reminders of the trauma may occur.

Differential diagnosis: If criteria for Anxiety Disorders, Depressive Disorders, or Organic Mental Disorders are fully met, these diagnoses should also be made. "Adjustment Disorder" implies a less severe trauma, and the patient does not meet all of the criteria listed below.

Diagnostic criteria for Post-Traumatic Stress Disorder:

A. The person has experienced an event that is outside the range of usual human experience and that would be markedly distressing to almost anyone.

B. The traumatic event is persistently reexperienced in at least *one* of the following ways:
   1. recurrent and intrusive, distressing recollections of the event (in young children, repetitive play in which themes or aspects of the trauma are expressed)
   2. recurrent distressing dreams of the event
   3. sudden acting or feeling as if the traumatic event were recurring (including "flashback" or dissociative episodes, whether or not intoxicated)
   4. intense psychological distress at exposure to events that symbolize or resemble an aspect of the traumatic event, including anniversaries

C. Persistent avoidance of stimuli associated with the trauma or numbing of general responsiveness, as indicated by at least *three* of the following:
   1. efforts to avoid thoughts or feeling associated with the trauma
   2. efforts to avoid activities or situations that arouse recollections of the trauma

3. inability to recall an important aspect of the trauma (psychogenic amnesia)

4. markedly diminished interest in significant activities (in young children, loss of recently acquired developmental skills such as toilet training or language skills)

5. feeling of detachment or estrangement from others

6. restricted range of affect

7. sense of foreshortened future (e.g., the patient does not expect to live very long or to have a successful career)

D. Persistent symptoms of increased arousal (not present before the trauma), as indicated by at least *two* of the following:

1. difficulty falling or staying asleep

2. irritability or outbursts of anger

3. difficulty concentrating

4. hypervigilance

5. exaggerated startle response

6. physiological activity upon exposure to events that symbolize or resemble an aspect of the traumatic event

E. Duration of disturbance (symptoms in "B," "C," and "D") of at least one month.

Specify: "delayed onset" if symptom onset occurs at least six months after the traumatic event.

Generalized Anxiety Disorder (300.02)

Essential feature. The essential feature of this disorder is unrealistic or excessive anxiety which is pervasive, chronic, and not solely associated with panic attacks.

Associated features. Depressive symptoms, unrelated Panic Disorder or Depressive Disorder.

Differential diagnosis. Organic Disorders, including substance use and substance abuse disorders, covert or overt physical illness, or caffeine intoxication. Generalized anxiety occurring during the course of other disorders (e.g., Mood Disorder, Psychotic Disorder) should not be used to make this diagnosis. Adjustment Disorder with Anxious Mood rarely meets all the criteria of Generalized Anxiety Disorder, and a psychosocial stressor is present.

Diagnostic criteria for Generalized Anxiety Disorder:

A. Unrealistic or excessive anxiety and worry (apprehensive expectation) about two or more life circumstances, for a period of six months or longer, during which the person has been bothered by these concerns on most days. In children and adolescents, this may take the form of anxiety about academic, athletic, and social performance.

B. If another Axis I disorder is present, the focus of the anxiety and worry in "A" is not related to it.

C. The disturbance does not occur only during the course of a Mood Disorder or Psychotic Disorder.

D. At least *six* of the following 18 symptoms are often present (not only during panic attacks):

Motor tension:
   1. trembling, twitching, or a feeling of shakiness
   2. muscle tension, aches, or soreness
   3. restlessness
   4. easy fatigability

Autonomic hyperactivity:
   5. shortness of breath or smothering sensation
   6. palpitations/accelerated heart rate
   7. sweating or cold, clammy hands
   8. dry mouth
   9. dizziness or lightheadedness
   10. nausea, diarrhea, or other abdominal distress
   11. flushes (hot flashes) or chills
   12. frequent urination in the absence of urinary tract abnormality
   13. difficulty swallowing or "lump in throat"

Vigilance and scanning:
   14. feeling "keyed up" or "on edge"
   15. exaggerated startle response
   16. difficulty concentrating, or "going blank" because of anxiety
   17. trouble falling asleep or staying asleep
   18. irritability

E. It cannot be established that an organic factor initiated and maintained the disturbance.

Anxiety Disorder Not Otherwise Specified (300.00)
This diagnosis is used for disorders with prominent anxiety or phobic avoidance, not classifiable as a specific Anxiety Disorder, an Adjustment Disorder with Anxious Mood, or any other physical or mental disorder.

DIFFERENCES BETWEEN DSM-III AND DSM-III-R ANXIETY DISORDERS

- Anxiety Disorder diagnoses are no longer routinely preempted by diagnosis of other mental disorders (e.g., Major Depression, Schizophrenia).
- Agoraphobia with Panic Attacks is now seen as *Panic Attacks with Agoraphobia*, to reflect the finding that most agoraphobia is apparently a complication of Panic Disorder.
- Similarly, Phobic Disorders are divided into those which are agoraphobic, *Social Phobias*, and *Simple Phobias*.
- Agoraphobia without Panic Attacks, now called *Agoraphobia without History of Panic Disorder* and felt to be rare, may include "limited symptom attacks." These are similar to, but do not meet criteria for, panic attacks.
- *Social Phobia* may be subclassified as "Generalized Type," which implies a likelihood of Avoidant Personality Disorder.
- The required duration for *Generalized Anxiety Disorder* has been increased to six months, and the criteria expanded.
- The criteria for *Post-traumatic Stress Disorder* have been clarified and expanded, and childhood symptoms included. "Chronic" or "Delayed" is now reflected in the presence or absence of a specification of *Delayed Onset*.

CASE VIGNETTE
For the past six months, this 35-year-old woman has had increasing anxiety which is now associated with her work as a personnel director for a large corporation. When she goes to work, she often—sometimes more than once a day—has attacks of nausea, perspiring, a feeling of unreality and impending doom, trembling, and dyspnea. They become quite intense within a few minutes and last less than half an hour. The episodes are so uncomfortable that she occasionally stays at home to prevent them.

She has noticed that the episodes, which initially came randomly and unexpectedly, have become more specifically associated with certain responsibilities, such as board meetings and presentations to her superiors. She denies any discomfort from the meetings and presentations themselves, saying that she enjoys her position, handles it well, and feels very comfortable as a member of the management team. She is not affected when in ordinary social situations or while working with people in other settings. The patient has never had other psychiatric symptoms, enjoys a normal family life, and is in good health. She is taking no medications, has a low caffeine intake, and denies drug or alcohol abuse. Physical examination, including thyroid tests and echocardiogram, is normal.

Discussion
The patient has some agoraphobic symptoms, but there is really only one setting that precipitates the attacks. Her attacks meet the criteria for Panic Disorder, having at one time been unexpected, although they later became associated with specific work settings. They do not meet the criteria for Social Phobia or Generalized Anxiety Disorder because her fear is of the panic attacks, not (consciously at least) of a social or work situation itself. Adjustment Disorder with Anxious Mood should be considered, but there is no mention of any precipitating psychosocial stresssor and the criteria for Panic Disorder have been met, preempting a diagnosis of Adjustment Disorder. The symptoms do not meet the criteria for Avoidant Personality Disorder. Important organic considerations have been ruled out. She lacks any chronic or pervasive symptoms of Personality Disorder or other Axis II disorder. She apparently does not have mitral valve prolapse, which often coexists and is coded on Axis III.

Diagnosis

Axis I   300.01   Panic Disorder, without Agoraphobia
Axis II   V71.09   No diagnosis or condition

Chapter 18

Somatoform Disorders

Individuals with Somatoform Disorders have physical symptoms that suggest a physical illness. However, thorough evaluation of the patient's complaint either does not reveal organic pathology, or the organic pathology found cannot explain the degree of impairment present. There is usually strong evidence, or a strong presumption, that the physical symptoms are connected to psychological factors or conflicts. The symptom production in Somatoform Disorders is not intentional (or conscious), unlike the symptoms seen in Malingering or Factitious Disorder.

102

Body Dysmorphic Disorder (Dysmorphophobia) (300.70)

Essential features. There is marked preoccupation either with some imagined defect in appearance, or if a slight physical abnormality is present, the individual's concern is grossly exaggerated. Although exaggerated, the person's belief in this defect does not reach delusional proportions. The clinician must ensure that the somatic preoccupation is not part of another psychiatric disorder, such as Anorexia Nervosa or Transsexualism.

103

Associated features. Repeated visits to surgeons or dermatologists in an attempt to correct the defect are common. Depressive symptoms and obsessive compulsive personality traits are frequently found. Social or occupational situations where others might see the imagined defect may be avoided.

Differential diagnosis. Normal excessive concern of an adolescent about minor defects in appearance, Major Depression, Avoidant Personality Disorder, Social Phobia, Delusional Disorder (Somatic subtype), Anorexia Nervosa, and Transsexualism are considered in the differential diagnosis.

Diagnostic criteria for Body Dysmorphic Disorder:

A. Preoccupation with an imagined defect in appearance, or if a slight anomaly is present, the person's concern is grossly exaggerated.
B. The belief in the defect is not of delusional proportions.
C. Disturbance not due to Anorexia Nervosa or Transsexualism.

Conversion Disorder (or Hysterical Neurosis, Conversion Type) (300.11)

Essential features. The symptom is a loss of function, or a change in function, that implies a physical disorder. The symptom cannot be explained by any known pathophysiological mechanism or physical disorder and is not intentionally produced, as in Malingering or Factitious Disorder. The symptom is apparently an expression of a psychological conflict or need. By definition, the complaint is not limited to pain (Somatoform Pain Disorder), painful sexual dysfunction (Sexual Pain Disorders), or merely one of the plethora of symptoms of Somatization Disorder.

Associated features. The symptom usually appears suddenly, with onset during times of extreme psychosocial stress. Histrionic personality traits are sometimes seen.

Predisposing factors. Predisposing factors include extreme psychosocial stress and the presence of a model for physical illness. This model can be another person with a particular disorder or conversion symptom or a preexisting medical disorder in the patient (e.g., pseudoseizures in an individual with epilepsy).

Differential diagnosis. Undiagnosed physical disorder, Somatization Disorder, Schizophrenia, Hypochondriasis, Factitious Disorder with Physical Symptoms, and Malingering are considered in the differential diagnosis.

Diagnostic criteria for Conversion Disorder:

A. Loss of, or alteration of physical function suggesting a physical disorder.
B. Psychological factors are judged to be etiologically related to the symptom (i.e., a temporal relationship between a psychosocial stressor apparently related to a psychological conflict/need and the initiation or exacerbation of the symptom).
C. The person is not conscious of intentionally producing the symptom.
D. The symptom is not a culturally sanctioned response pattern and cannot, after appropriate investigation, be explained by a known physical disorder.
E. The symptom is not limited to pain or to sexual functioning.

Specify: single episode or recurrent.

Hypochondriasis (or Hypochondriacal Neurosis) (300.70)

Essential features. The person has an enduring (of at least six months' 105 duration), nondelusional belief or fear that he or she has a serious illness. The person is not reassured by appropriate clinical investigation that fails to confirm the illness. The clinician should be sure that the symptoms are not symptoms of a panic attack.

Associated features. The hypochondriacal individual usually presents his or her medical history in great detail. The person is often frustrated and angry with physicians. Doctor shopping and poor physician-patient relationships are common. Anxiety, depressed mood, and obsessive compulsive personality traits are frequently observed.

Predisposing factors. Past exposure to true disease and psychosocial stressors apparently predispose to this disorder.

Differential diagnosis. Organic disease, Schizophrenia, Major Depression with Psychotic Features, Dysthymia, Panic Disorder, General Anxiety Disorder, Obsessive Compulsive Disorder, and Somatization Disorder are considered in the differential diagnosis.

Diagnostic criteria for Hypochondriasis:

A. The fear or belief that one has a serious disease.

B. Appropriate physical evaluation does not support the diagnosis, and the symptoms in "A" are not due to panic attacks.

C. The fear or belief that one has a serious disease persists despite medical reassurance.

D. Duration of disturbance at least six months.

E. The fear or belief in "A" is not of delusional proportions.

Somatization Disorder (Briquet's Syndrome) (300.81)

Essential features. A long-standing pattern of multiple, recurrent medical complaints without an apparent physical disorder. Complaints are often present in a dramatic fashion, the medical history is complicated, and many physical diagnoses have been considered. This disorder begins before age 30, is extremely rare in men, and has a chronic, fluctuating course.

Associated features. Anxious and depressed mood are frequent. Antisocial behavior and occupational, interpersonal, and marital difficulties are common. Hallucinations are reported, usually hearing one's name called. Histrionic Personality Disorder, Antisocial Personality Disorder, and Psychoactive Substance Use Disorder can be seen.

Predisposing factors. Children whose natural parents have Antisocial Personality Disorder, Psychoactive Substance Use Disorders, or Somatization Disorder are at increased risk for developing Somatization Disorder.

Differential diagnosis. Undiagnosed physical disorder, Schizophrenia with multiple somatic delusions, Panic Disorder, Conversion Disorder, and Factitious Disorder are considered in the differential diagnosis.

Diagnostic criteria for Somatization Disorder:

A. History of multiple medical complaints that persists for several years, beginning before age 30.

B. At least 13 symptoms from the list below which meet the following criteria:

1. no organic pathology or pathophysiological mechanism to account for symptoms, or, when organic pathology is present,

the complaint or impairment is grossly in excess of what would be expected.

2. has not occurred only during a panic attack.
3. has caused the individual to take medication (other than over-the-counter pain medication), see a doctor, or alter lifestyle.

Symptom list:

Gastrointestinal symptoms:

1. vomiting* (other than during pregnancy)
2. abdominal pain (other than during menstruation)
3. nausea (other than motion sickness)
4. bloating (gassy)
5. diarrhea
6. intolerance to (gets sick from) several different foods

Pain symptoms:

7. pain in extremities*
8. back pain
9. joint pain
10. pain during urination
11. other pain (excluding headache)

Cardiopulmonary symptoms:

12. shortness of breath when not exerting oneself*
13. palpitations
14. chest pain
15. dizziness

Conversion or pseudoneurological symptoms:

16. amnesia*
17. difficulty swallowing*
18. loss of voice
19. deafness
20. double vision
21. blurred vision

---

*These seven symptoms (pp. 151–152) may be used to screen for the disorder. The presence of *two or more* indicates a high likelihood of the disorder.

22. blindness
23. fainting or loss of consciousness
24. seizure or convulsion
25. trouble walking
26. paralysis or muscle weakness
27. urinary retention or difficulty urinating

Sexual symptoms for the major portion of person's life after opportunities for sexual activity:

28. burning sensation in sexual organs or rectum (other than during intercourse)*
29. sexual indifference
30. pain during intercourse
31. impotence

Female reproductive symptoms judged by the person to occur more frequently or severely than in most women:

32. painful menstruation*
33. irregular menstrual periods
34. excessive menstrual bleeding
35. vomiting throughout pregnancy

Somatoform Pain Disorder (307.80)

Essential features. There is a preoccupation with pain of at least six months' duration, without physical findings or a pathophysiological mechanism, to explain either the pain or the pain's intensity. In some cases, evidence may exist that psychological factors are involved in the production of the pain.

Associated features. The individual frequently visits physicians, uses excessive pain medication, and assumes an invalid's role. Surgery may already have been performed or may be desired by the patient. The person denies that psychological factors have any role in symptom production. Depressed mood is common and an associated diagnosis of Major Depression is warranted in many cases.

Predisposing factors. Pain often develops following physical trauma. Some persons with Somatoform Pain Disorder began working at an early age, had physically stressful jobs, were "workaholics," and rarely took vacations. The disorder is twice as common in females.

Differential diagnosis. Exaggerated presentation of organic pain, Somatization Disorder, Depressive Disorders, Schizophrenia, and Malingering are considered in the differential diagnosis.

Diagnostic criteria for Somatoform Pain Disorder:

A. Preoccupation with pain for at least six months.
B. Either (1) appropriate evaluation fails to reveal an organic cause or pathophysiological mechanism, or (2) when organic pathology exists, the complaint of pain or the resulting impairment is grossly in excess of what would be expected.

Undifferentiated Somatoform Disorder (300.70)

Essential features. This is a residual diagnostic disorder. For at least a six-month period there is either a single symptom or, more commonly, multiple symptoms present that are not explainable by organic pathology or known pathophysiological mechanisms. Symptoms are apparently linked to psychological factors.

Associated features. Anxious and depressed mood are common.

Differential diagnosis. Somatization Disorder, Somatoform Pain Disorder, Sexual Pain Disorder, Mood Disorder, Anxiety Disorder, Sleep Disorder, Psychotic Disorder (e.g., Schizophrenia), Adjustment Disorder with Physical Complaints, and Psychological Factors Affecting Physical Condition are considered in the differential diagnosis.

Diagnostic criteria for Undifferentiated Somatoform Disorder:

A. One or more physical complaints.
B. *Either* (1) appropriate evaluation fails to reveal an organic cause or pathophysiological mechanism, *or* (2) when organic pathology exists, the complaint or the resulting impairment is grossly in excess of what would be expected.
C. Duration of at least six months.

D. Not exclusively during the course of another Somatoform Disorder, a Sexual Dysfunction, a Mood Disorder, an Anxiety Disorder, a Sleep Disorder, or a Psychotic Disorder.

Somatoform Disorder Not Otherwise Specified (300.70)

Essential features. Somatoform symptoms exist that do not meet the criteria for any specific Somatoform Disorder or Adjustment Disorder with Physical Complaints. An example would be a non-stress-related somatoform symptom of less than six months' duration.

DIFFERENCES BETWEEN DSM-III AND DSM-III-R SOMATOFORM DISORDERS

- The DSM-III-R symptom list for *Somatization Disorder* now has the same number of symptoms for both males and females. Seven of these symptoms (marked with an asterisk) can be used as a screening list. The presence of at least two of these seven symptoms suggests a strong likelihood of the disorder.
- The diagnostic criteria for *Conversion Disorder* have been revised to exclude culturally sanctioned response patterns.
- The DSM-III diagnosis "Psychogenic Pain Disorder" has been replaced by *Somatoform Pain Disorder.* The name change indicates that this disorder frequently appears without clear evidence of psychological factors.
- A diagnosis of *Hypochondriasis* now requires a symptom duration of at least six months.
- DSM-III-R has a new diagnosis, *Body Dysmorphic Disorder.*
- A new DSM-III-R diagnosis, *Undifferentiated Somatoform Disorder,* was added for persons with chronic, multiple, medically unsupported physical complaints who do not meet the criteria for any other Somatoform Disorder.
- Atypical Somatoform Disorder was renamed *Somatoform Disorder Not Otherwise Specified.*

CASE VIGNETTE

Ms. S. is a 32-year-old woman who is currently hospitalized on a general medical ward for evaluation of right-sided paralysis. The attending physician requested a consultation when no organic reason for the paralysis was found.

On examination, Ms. S. is initially quite upset that anyone doubts the medical nature of her complaints. She reports the sudden onset of right-sided problems while she and her boyfriend were talking with a lawyer. According to her, this complaint occurred once before, "and they thought I had a stroke." She is quite dramatic in her presentation and describes a long, complex medical history. She denies prior psychiatric hospitalizations or contact with other mental health professionals and denies drug or alcohol abuse or panic attacks. Her family history is positive for a father who was an alcoholic (she is unfamiliar with his recent whereabouts) and a brother who is currently in prison.

Review of Ms. S.'s medical record reveals numerous hospitalizations and medical evaluations for a variety of complaints. Complaints that resulted in past hospitalizations or medical evaluations include vomiting, chronic abdominal pain, dysuria (pain on urination), shortness of breath, amnesia, double vision, loss of consciousness, seizures, paralysis (on three different occasions), dyspareunia (painful intercourse), dysmenorrhea (painful menstruation), dysphagia (trouble swallowing), menometrorrhagia (excessive periods), and blindness. Despite extensive medical evaluations, no organic reasons have ever been found for any of the individual's complaints.

Discussion

Ms. S. presents in a dramatic fashion and has a long-standing, medically complex history. She has multiorgan complaints and no evidence of any organic etiology. There is no evidence of Panic Disorder.

Ms. S. has all the clinical features necessary for the diagnosis of one of the Somatoform Disorders. She meets the criteria for Somatization Disorder. She also meets the criteria for Conversion Disorder; however, this diagnosis is not made in the setting of a more pervasive disorder, such as Somatization Disorder (DSM-III-R, page 259). The Axis II diagnosis is deferred pending additional information and observation.

Diagnosis

Axis I   300.81   Somatization Disorder
Axis II   799.90   Diagnosis deferred
Axis III   No known medical diagnoses

Chapter 19

Dissociative Disorders (Hysterical Neuroses, Dissociative Type)

The Dissociative Disorders are all characterized by a disturbance or alteration in the normally integrative functions of identity, memory, or consciousness. Although Sleepwalking Disorder has this essential feature, it is classified as a Sleep Disorder.

Multiple Personality Disorder (300.14)

107   **Essential feature.** Two or more distinct personalities or personality states within one person. For the DSM-III-R diagnosis, "personality" is defined as a relatively enduring pattern of perceiving, relating to, and thinking about the environment and one's self that is exhibited in a wide range of important social and personal contexts. Personality "states" differ only in that the pattern is not exhibited in as wide a range of context. In classic cases, there are at least two fully developed personalities. In other cases, not universally accepted as true Multiple Personality, there may be one distinct personality and one or more "personality states." At least some of the personalities, at some time and recurrently, take full control of the patient's behavior. The transition is usually sudden.

The personalities may be aware of some or all of the others, to varying degrees, and may experience them as friends or adversaries. Most of the personalities are aware of lost periods of time or distortion in the experience of time. The individual personalities may be quite different or may differ only in alternating approaches to a major problem area (e.g., sexuality).

156

Associated features. One or more of the personalities may be dysfunctional or appear to have a specific mental disorder, while another appears relatively healthy. The patient has usually given each of the personalities a different first name, and occasionally a different last name, which may have some symbolic meaning.

Predisposing factors. The disorder is very often—perhaps almost always—preceded by child abuse (often sexual abuse) or other severe emotional trauma in childhood. Women outnumber men with the disorder by three to nine times.

Differential diagnosis. Other Dissociative Disorders, such as Psychogenic Fugue and Psychogenic Amnesia. Various psychotic disorders, including Schizophrenia or Psychotic Mood Disorder, both of which are far more common than Multiple Personality Disorder, may be considered. The belief that one is "possessed" by a person, spirit, or entity is not pathognomonic for Multiple Personality Disorder. Borderline Personality Disorder may coexist with Multiple Personality Disorder.

DSM-III-R cautions against underdiagnosis when the disorder is fused with Borderline Personality Disorder or other mental disorders; **108** however, other authorities feel that Multiple Personality Disorder is extremely rare, and that most presentations are actually subcategories of psychotic or borderline disorders. Malingering and Factitious Disorder with Psychological Features can be hard to differentiate from Multiple Personality Disorder.

Diagnostic criteria for Multiple Personality Disorder:

A. The existence of two or more distinct personalities or personality states within the person, each with its own relatively enduring pattern of perceiving, relating to, and thinking about the environment and the self.

B. At least two of these personalities or personality states recurrently alternate full control of the patient's behavior.

Psychogenic Fugue (300.13)

Essential features. Psychogenic Fugue is characterized by sudden, unexpected travel, assumption of a new identity, and inability to recall **109**

one's previous identity. Following recovery, there is no recollection of events that took place during the fugue. It may be manifested by the assumption of a completely new identity or less elaborately, with little more than brief, apparently purposeful travel.

Predisposing factors. Heavy alcohol use, severe psychosocial stress. The disorder is most common in wartime or in the wake of a natural disaster.

Differential diagnosis. Multiple Personality Disorder, Psychogenic Amnesia, Malingering, and factitious illness with psychological features. Organic Mental Disorders (such as temporal lobe epilepsy, often differentiated by dysphoria and lack of a precipitating stressor) preempt the diagnosis.

Diagnostic criteria for Psychogenic Fugue:

A. The predominant disturbance is sudden, unexpected travel away from home or one's customary place of work, with inability to recall one's past.
B. Assumption of a (partial or complete) new identity.
C. The disturbance is not due to Multiple Personality Disorder or to an organic mental disorder.

Psychogenic Amnesia (300.12)

Essential feature. Sudden, extensive loss of memory. The diagnosis is not made if the person travels to a new locale and assumes a new identity (see above) or if the amnesia is related to Multiple Personality Disorder.

110

Associated features. During the amnestic period there may be indifference toward memory disturbance (e.g., *belle indifférence*). There are four types of memory disturbance that may be associated: *localized* (circumscribed), in which there is failure to recall the events occurring during a specific period of time; *selective*, in which one recalls only some, not all, of the events occurring during a circumscribed period of time; *generalized*, in which one recalls nothing from his entire life; and *continuous*, in which the patient cannot recall events from a specific time through the present.

Predisposing factors. Severe psychosocial stress (especially severe physical threat or internal conflict). It is most common in wartime and natural disaster.

Differential diagnosis. Organic Mental Disorders, including Psycho-active Substance-Induced Intoxication or "blackouts," which are usually differentiated by incomplete return of memory. Other organic disorders associated with amnesia are Alcohol Amnestic Disorder, postconcussion amnesia, and ictal syndromes, all of whose forms often differ from Psychogenic Amnesia. Catatonic stupor sometimes suggests Psychogenic Amnesia. Malingering and factitious disorders must be differentiated as well.

Diagnostic criteria for Psychogenic Amnesia:

A. The predominant disturbance is an episode of sudden inability, too extensive to be explained by ordinary forgetfulness, to recall important personal information.
B. The disturbance is not due to Multiple Personality Disorder or to an Organic Mental Disorder.

Depersonalization Disorder (or Depersonalization Neurosis) (300.60)

Essential feature. Persistent or recurrent depersonalization severe enough to cause marked distress.

Associated features. Derealization, depression, rumination, somatic concerns, anxiety, disturbance of a sense of time.

Predisposing factor. Severe stress.

Differential diagnosis. Simple symptoms of depersonalization that do not cause social or occupational impairment, such as those seen frequently in young adults, must be distinguished from this disorder, even if they are recurrent. Depersonalization may be a symptom of Schizophrenia, Mood Disorders, Organic Mental Disorders (especially those related to substance use or abuse), Anxiety Disorders, Personality Disorders, and epilepsy. Depersonalization Disorder should *not* be diagnosed in these instances.

Diagnostic criteria for Depersonalization Disorder:

A. Persistent or recurrent experiences of depersonalization, as indicated by *one* of the following:
   1. an experience of feeling detached from, and as if one is an outside observer of, one's mental processes or body
   2. an experience of feeling like an automaton, or as if in a dream
B. During the depersonalization experience, reality testing remains intact.
C. The depersonalization is sufficiently severe and persistent to cause marked distress.
D. The depersonalization experience is the predominant disturbance and is not a symptom of another disorder.

Dissociative Disorder Not Otherwise Specified (NOS) (300.15)

These are disorders in which the predominant feature is a disturbance or alteration in the normally integrative functions of identity, memory, or consciousness, but which do not meet criteria for a specific Dissociative Disorder, and which do not meet criteria for superseding other DSM-III-R or physical diagnoses.

Examples include Ganser's syndrome, trance states (such as those which occur following abuse or trauma in children), and states related to brainwashing or indoctrination.

DIFFERENCES BETWEEN DSM-III AND DSM-III-R DISSOCIATIVE DISORDERS

• Atypical Dissociative Disorder is now *Dissociative Disorder NOS.*

CASE VIGNETTE

While checking into a motel on a fishing trip, a 36-year-old man was distressed to find that he apparently had someone else's wallet and credit cards and had inexplicably lost his own. While talking with the manager to arrange payment, it became apparent that he had no identifying cards or papers, he resembled the person whose picture was on the "other person's" driver's license, and—from documents in the glove box—he was driving the "other person's" car. Subsequently it was determined that he was actually the "other person" and had unexpectedly left his place of work that morning.

A detailed history revealed no prior serious psychiatric symptoms. He has had no episodes of unconsciousness or altered consciousness, to his knowledge, in the past. He has been a sales manager with the same firm for six years, is married, and has two adolescent children. There have been marital problems, and his 17-year old son was arrested for breaking and entering the day before the "fishing trip." He has a history of moderate alcohol intake, but was not intoxicated at the motel; indeed, he declined when the manager offered him a drink to help him "calm down while we figure this thing out." Physical examination is normal except for a mild heart murmur and increased cholesterol. An electroencephalogram with nasopharyngeal and sphenoidal leads is negative.

Discussion
There is an obvious dissociative disorder, apparently precipitated by severe psychosocial stress, with no sign of underlying psychotic disorder or neurological disease. The dissociative episode was not part of an alcoholic "blackout." Although another "person" was created, the condition does not meet criteria for Multiple Personality Disorder. The purposeful behavior and apparent creation of a new identity are inconsistent with Psychogenic Amnesia. There is no indication of Malingering. Although the condition is probably a reaction to psychosocial stressors, Adjustment Disorder is not an appropriate diagnosis, and in any event would be preempted once the criteria for Psychogenic Fugue are met. Available evidence does not suggest a Personality Disorder, although the code for Deferred Axis II Diagnosis or Condition (799.90) would also be correct.

Diagnosis

Axis I   300.13   Psychogenic Fugue
Axis II   V71.09   No diagnosis or condition

Chapter 20

Sexual Disorders

The Sexual Disorders are divided into two groups. The *Paraphilias* are characterized by arousal in response to sexual objects or situations not part of normal arousal-activity patterns, which may interfere with the capacity for reciprocal, affectionate sexual activity. The *Sexual Dysfunctions* are characterized by inhibitions in sexual desire or dysfunction of the psychophysiological changes that characterize the sexual response cycle.

A. PARAPHILIAS

All the paraphilic disorders are characterized by recurrent, intense sexual urges and sexually arousing fantasies generally involving nonhuman objects, suffering or humiliation, or nonconsenting persons (including children). The diagnosis is made only if the urges have been acted upon, or if the patient is markedly distressed by them. These disorders are sometimes referred to as "sexual deviations." The paraphilic impulses and behaviors, in order to be diagnosed, must be preferred avenues of sexual excitement and expression (whether or not there is opportunity to act on them), and not simply sexual experimentation.

Associated features. People with Paraphilias may have extreme guilt, shame, or depression or may overtly see their activities as normal. Sexual Dysfunctions may be present. Personality disturbances, often severe enough

111

to warrant an Axis II diagnosis, are common. The existence of other Paraphilias in the same patient is common.

Differential diagnosis. Normal variants of sexual activity and nonpathological sexual experimentation should be ruled out before diagnosing any Paraphilia. Paraphilic-like behaviors which are carried out for nonarousing purposes (e.g., collecting fetishistic items or earning money as a prostitute) should not be confused with Paraphilia, even if the purpose is to arouse someone else (as in the case of prostitution). Although the Paraphilias can be diagnosed in addition to other mental disorders, paraphilic behavior arising out of a psychosis or a hormonally related physical disorder should be considered a symptom of the underlying disorder, and not as a separate diagnosis.

Severity criteria for the specific Paraphilias listed below:
Mild—The patient is markedly distressed by the paraphilic urges, but has never acted on them.   112
Moderate—The patient has occasionally acted on the paraphilic urge.
Severe—The patient has repeatedly acted on the urge.

Exhibitionism (302.40)

Essential features. Recurrent, intense sexual urges and sexually arousing fantasies involving the exposure of one's genitals to a stranger. Masturbation during the exposure incident, or while fantasizing about exposing, is common. There is no significant attempt at further sexual activity with the stranger. DSM-III-R states that the condition apparently occurs only in males, almost always with female victims. Other authors feel that it does occur in females, but that forensic and clinical populations are almost entirely male.

Associated features. Symptoms of other Paraphilias, usually not involving physical contact with a victim, which may be diagnosed as well, are not unusual.

Differential diagnosis. Accidental exposure and exposure not related to sexual activity (both of which may be offered as explanations or rationalizations for Exhibitionism).

Diagnostic criteria for Exhibitionism:

A. Over a period of at least six months, recurrent, intense sexual urges and sexually arousing fantasies involving the exposure of one's genitals to an unsuspecting stranger.
B. The person has acted on these urges or is markedly distressed by them.

Fetishism (302.81)

Essential feature. Recurrent, intense sexual urges and sexually arousing fantasies involving the use of nonliving objects (fetishes). Women's apparel are common fetish objects. Some authors include nonsexual body parts ("partialism"). The diagnosis should not be made when the fetish is limited to articles of female clothing used in cross-dressing, or when the object has been specifically designed for a sexual purpose.

Differential diagnosis. Nonpathological sexual experimentation, Transvestic Fetishism.

Diagnostic criteria for Fetishism:

A. Over a period of at least six months, recurrent, intense sexual urges and sexually arousing fantasies involving the use of non-living objects by themselves (although at times they may be used with a sexual partner).
B. The person has acted on these urges or is markedly distressed by them.
C. The fetishes are not only articles of female clothing used in cross-dressing, or articles or devices specifically designed for genital stimulation (e.g., vibrators).

Frotteurism (302.89)

Essential feature. Recurrent, intense sexual urges and sexually arousing fantasies involving touching and rubbing against a nonconsenting person. DSM-III-R includes both Frotteurism (rubbing) and Toucherism (fondling) in this category. The frottage is usually committed in crowded places.

Associated features. The presence of other Paraphilias is common. Most persons identified with this diagnosis are male.

Differential diagnois. Normal sexual activity with a consenting person. Touching or fondling associated with poor judgment or impulse control (as in certain organic mental disorders, Mental Retardation, Schizophrenia, or some children who have been sexually abused).

Diagnostic criteria for Frotteurism:

A. Over a period of at least six months, recurrent, intense sexual urges and sexually arousing fantasies involving touching and/or rubbing against a nonconsenting person. It is the touching, not the coercive nature of the act, that is sexually exciting.

B. The person has acted on these urges or is markedly distressed by them.

Pedophilia (302.20)

Essential features. Recurrent, intense sexual urges and sexually arousing fantasies involving sexual activity with a prepubescent child. The age of the perpetrator is arbitrarily set at 16 years or older, and at least five years older than the child. Both the sexual maturity of the child and the age difference must be taken into account, particularly when evaluating adolescents.

Pedophiles may be attracted to both young girls and young boys. DSM-III-R states the attraction to girls is apparently twice as common; however, other authorities disagree. Actions related to pedophilic urges may be limited to relatively nonintrusive activities (e.g., exposing oneself, masturbating) or to touching and fondling, but may in other perpetrators involve genital contact or penetration, with varying degrees of force.

Associated features. Other Paraphilias are commonly associated with Pedophilia. Physical and mental conditions that affect judgment (e.g., Dementia, Mental Retardation, substance abuse) may be associated. Pedophilia should still be diagnosed if the criteria are met and the urges and behavior do not arise solely out of acute psychosis, significant organic disorder, or hormonally related physical illness.

Differential diagnosis. The disorder should not be rationalized as "educational" activity or "normal" sexual activity, in part because of the   113 child's lack of ability meaningfully to consent. As noted above, significant Mental Retardation, Organic Personality Syndrome, Substance Abuse Disorders, or psychotic disorders may be associated with isolated sexual activity with children (or activity in which the child is incidental to gratification, and not the primary focus or the preferred method of achieving sexual satisfaction). Exhibitionism and Voyeurism may involve children, but the separate diagnosis of Pedophilia should not be made unless children are clearly the preferred victims.

Diagnostic criteria for Pedophilia:

A. Over a period of at least six months, recurrent, intense sexual urges and sexually arousing fantasies involving sexual activity with a prepubescent child or children (generally age 13 or younger).

B. The person has acted on these urges or is markedly distressed by them.

C. The person is at least 16 years old *and* at least five years older than the victim(s) in "A." Late adolescents who are involved in ongoing sexual relationships with 12- or 13-year-old children should not be included in this disorder.

Specify: same sex, opposite sex, or both.

Specify: whether limited to incest or not.

Specify: "Exclusive Type" (solely attracted to children) or "Nonexclusive Type" (sometimes attracted to adults).

Sexual Masochism (302.83)

Essential feature. Recurrent, intense sexual urges and sexually arousing fantasies involving the real (not simulated) act of being humiliated, beaten, bound, or otherwise made to suffer. The masochistic fantasies may be invoked during intercourse or masturbation, but not otherwise acted upon (the fantasies are of real masochistic sex, not simulations). In some cases, the disorder can be quite dangerous.

Associated features. Other Paraphilias are common, particularly in men.

Differential diagnosis. Masochistic fantasies without marked distress or recurrent masochistic behavior. Transvestic Fetishism may be associated with Masochism, if the cross-dressing is humiliating and the humiliation is the sexually arousing feature (not the garments themselves). An accidental death during masochistic sexual acts must be differentiated from suicide and homicide. "Self-defeating" personality traits are distinguished from this disorder by their lack of association with sexual excitement.

Diagnostic criteria for Sexual Masochism:

A. Over a period of at least six months, recurrent, intense sexual urges and sexually arousing fantasies involving the act (real, not simulated) of being humiliated, beaten, bound, or otherwise made to suffer.
B. The person has acted on these urges or is markedly distressed by them.

Sexual Sadism (302.84)

Essential features. Recurrent, intense sexual urges and sexually arousing fantasies involving real (not simulated) acts in which the psychological or physical suffering (including humiliation) of the victim is sexually exciting. Some people with this disorder are bothered by their sadistic fantasies or actions; others are not. The fantasies usually involve having control over the victim, who is terrified. Other patients act with a consenting partner, who may have Sexual Masochism. The victim's suffering is the sexually arousing component.

Associated features. Cruel or sadistic fantasies or actions, with or without a sexual complement, have commonly been present since childhood. Other Paraphilias may be present, but are not as common as in some other paraphilic disorders.

Differential diagnosis. Rape or other sexual assault may or may not involve Sexual Sadism (and is often nonparaphilic in nature). Sadistic acts not repeatedly associated with sexual arousal should be differentiated from Sexual Sadism.

Diagnostic criteria for Sexual Sadism:

A. Over a period of at least six months, recurrent, intense sexual urges and sexually arousing fantasies involving acts (real, not simulated) in which the psychological or physical suffering (including humiliation) of the victim is sexually exciting to the person.

B. The person has acted on these urges or is markedly distressed by them.

Transvestic Fetishism (302.30)

Essential feature. Recurrent, intense sexual urges and sexually arousing fantasies involving cross-dressing. The person is virtually always male and usually keeps a collection of women's clothes used to cross-dress when alone (during which he generally masturbates and imagines other males as being attracted to him as a woman in his female attire). Some men wear only a single item of women's clothes; others dress up completely and may go out to public places. The basic sexual preference is heterosexual, although there may be sexual inadequacy or inexperience, and the patient may have engaged in occasional homosexual acts.

Associated features. Other Paraphilias, particularly Sexual Masochism, may be present.

Differential diagnosis. This disorder should not be diagnosed in the presence of Gender Identity Disorders or Transsexualism. Cross-dressing for relief of tension or gender discomfort, and not for specific sexual excitement, should not be diagnosed as Transvestic Fetishism. Masquerading as a female in a theatrical fashion should not be confused with this disorder, even if the cross-dresser is homosexual. Female impersonators, unless showing other signs of Transvestic Fetishism, should not receive this diagnosis. Persons with Sexual Masochism whose humiliation is associated with cross-dressing should not be given this diagnosis unless the garments themselves cause sexual arousal.

Diagnostic criteria for Transvestic Fetishism:

A. Over a period of at least six months, in a heterosexual male, recurrent, intense sexual urges and sexually arousing fantasies involving cross-dressing.

B. The person has acted on these urges or is markedly distressed by them.

C. Does not meet the criteria for Gender Identity Disorder of Adolescence or Adulthood, Nontranssexual Type, or Transsexualism.

Voyeurism (302.82)

Essential feature. Recurrent, obsessive observing of unsuspecting people, usually strangers, who are naked, in the process of undressing, and/or engaging in sexual activity. The act of looking itself, with no other sexual activity sought, is for the purpose of sexual excitement (although the patient may have fantasies of sexual experience with the observed person).

Associated features. Other Paraphilias, rarely ones that cause physical injury to others.

Differential diagnosis. Normal sexual activity which includes peeking or looking, but not with an unsuspecting, unconsenting partner, and not as the primary (often secretive) mode of excitement. The use of pornography, including observing live sexual entertainment, is not, by itself, sufficient for this diagnosis.

Diagnostic criteria for Voyeurism:

A. Over a period of at least six months, recurrent, intense sexual urges and sexually arousing fantasies involving the act of observing an unsuspecting person who is naked, in the process of disrobing, and/or engaging in sexual activity.

B. The person has acted on these urges or is markedly distressed by them.

Paraphilia Not Otherwise Specified (302.90)
This diagnostic code is reserved for syndromes that meet the criteria for Paraphilia, are not primarily due to psychotic or organic illness, and do not meet the criteria for any of the specific categories just discussed. Examples include necrophilia, zoophilia (bestiality), klismaphilia, and urophilia.

B. SEXUAL DYSFUNCTIONS
All the Sexual Dysfunctions listed below are characterized by inhibitions of appetitive or psychophysiological changes that characterize the complete "sexual response cycle." Sexual Dysfunction diagnoses are ordinarily applied only when the disturbance is a major part of the clinical

presentation (although it may not be part of the chief complaint). Sexual Dysfunction diagnoses should not be made if the disturbance is attributed entirely to organic factors (e.g., a physical disorder, medication, or substance abuse) or if it is due to another Axis I Mental Disorder. Multiple diagnoses within the broad category of Sexual Dysfunctions are sometimes appropriate. The Sexual Dysfunctions are divided into disorders related to sexual desire, sexual arousal, orgasm, and sexual pain. The first three of these correspond to the first three phases of the "sexual response cycle":

1. Appetitive (fantasies and desires).
2. Excitement (arousal, physiological changes such as erection or lubrication, sexual pleasure).
3. Orgasm (peaking of sexual pleasure, release of sexual tension, rhythmic muscle and genital contractions, ejaculation.
4. Resolution (general and muscular relaxation, feeling of well-being, physiological refractoriness to further sexual activity [especially in males; not necessarily seen in females]).

116

Associated features. Sexual Dysfunction complaints often outwardly focus on, or are associated with, problems in interpersonal relationships, depression, anxiety, or somatic symptoms.

Predisposing factors. Anxiety and excessively high subjective standards for sexual performance predispose one to the development of acquired Sexual Dysfunction. Negative attitudes toward sexuality, often due to particular past experiences, internal conflicts, inadequate education, or rigid cultural values, are predisposing, as are several mental disorders.

Differential diagnosis. Physical disorders (if both physical and functional factors contribute, both diagnoses may be given). If another Axis I mental disorder is the primary cause of the sexual problems, a Sexual Dysfunction should *not* be diagnosed. V-code conditions may be a primary cause of the disturbance, in which case both conditions should be diagnosed.

For each specific Sexual Dysfunction diagnosis, one may:

Specify: "Psychogenic Only" or "Psychogenic and Biogenic" (coding the Biogenic Disorder on Axis III).

Specify: "Lifelong" or "Acquired."
Specify: "Generalized" or "Situational."

Sexual Desire Disorders

Hypoactive Sexual Desire Disorder (302.71)
Diagnostic criteria:

A. Persistently or recurrently deficient or absent sexual fantasies and desire for sexual activity. The judgment of "deficiency" or "absence" should be made by the clinician, taking into account various factors that affect sexual functioning (e.g., age, sex, and the context of the person's life).
B. Occurrence not exclusively during the course of another Axis I disorder (other than another Sexual Dysfunction).

Sexual Aversion Disorder (302.79)
Diagnostic criteria:

A. Persistent or recurrent extreme aversion to, and avoidance of, all or almost all genital sexual contact with a sexual partner.
B. Occurrence not exclusively during the course of another Axis I disorder (other than another Sexual Dysfunction).

Sexual Arousal Disorders

Female Sexual Arousal Disorder (302.72)
Diagnostic criteria:

A. At least *one* of the following:
   1. persistent or recurrent partial or complete failure to obtain or maintain the lubrication-swelling response of sexual excitement until completion of the sexual activity
   2. persistent or recurrent lack of a subjective sense of sexual excitement and pleasure in a female during sexual activity
B. Occurrence not exclusively during the course of another Axis I disorder (other than another Sexual Dysfunction).

Male Erectile Disorder (302.72)
  Diagnostic criteria:

  A. At least *one* of the following:
      1. persistent or recurrent partial or complete failure to attain or maintain erection until completion of the sexual activity
      2. persistent or recurrent lack of a subjective sense of sexual excitement and pleasure in a male during sexual activity
  B. Occurrence not exclusively during the course of another Axis I disorder (other than another Sexual Dysfunction).

Orgasm Disorders

Inhibited Female Orgasm (302.73)
  Diagnostic criteria:

  A. Persistent or recurrent delay in, or absence of, orgasm following a normal sexual excitement phase, during sexual activity that the clinician judges to be adequate in focus, intensity, and duration. Orgasm that requires manual clitoral stimulation does not justify this diagnosis in most females, but may represent psychological inhibition that justifies the diagnosis in some.
  B. Occurrence not exclusively during the course of another Axis I disorder (other than another Sexual Dysfunction).

Inhibited Male Orgasm (302.74)
  Diagnostic criteria:

  A. Persistent or recurrent delay in orgasm in males following a normal sexual excitement phase, during sexual activity that the clinician believes to be adequate in focus, intensity, and duration. Orgasm may be possible with other types of stimulation, such as masturbation.
  B. Occurrence not exclusively during the course of another Axis I disorder (other than another Sexual Dysfunction).

Premature Ejaculation (302.75)
  Diagnostic criteria:

  A. Persistent or recurrent ejaculation with minimal sexual stimulation or before, upon, or shortly after penetration (and before the person wishes it). Factors that affect duration of the excitement phase (e.g., age, novelty, frequency of sexual activity) must be considered by the clinician.

Sexual Pain Disorders

Dyspareunia (302.76)
Diagnostic criteria:

A. Recurrent or persistent genital pain in either a male or female before, during, or after sexual intercourse.
B. The disturbance is not caused exclusively by lack of lubrication or by Vaginismus.

Vaginismus (306.51)
Diagnostic criteria:

A. Recurrent or persistent involuntary spasm of the musculature of the outer third of the vagina that interferes with coitus.
B. The disturbance is not caused exclusively by physical disorder and is not due to another Axis I disorder.

Sexual Dysfunction Not Otherwise Specified (302.70)
This residual category is reserved for Sexual Dysfunctions that do not meet any of the above specific sets of criteria, do not occur exclusively during the course of another Axis I disorder (other than another Sexual Dysfunction), and are not exclusively due to a physical disorder.

Other Sexual Disorders

Sexual Disorder Not Otherwise Specified (302.90)
This residual category is reserved for Sexual Disorders not classifiable in any of the previous categories, and not either occurring exclusively during or due to a nonsexual Axis I disorder or a physical disorder.

DIFFERENCES BETWEEN DSM-III AND DSM-III-R SEXUAL DISORDERS

- The entire Psychosexual Disorder category has been renamed *Sexual Disorders*.
- The Gender Identity Disorders are now listed under Disorders Usually First Evident in Infancy, Childhood, or Adolescence.

- *Gender Identity Disorder of Adolescence or Childhood, Non-transsexual Type,* has been added, connoting transsexual features without any preoccupation to be rid of one's sexual characteristics, under Disorders Usually First Evident in Infancy, Childhood, or Adolescence.
- "Atypical" disorders are now *"NOS."*
- The *Paraphilias* have been defined more consistently, to include both action and fantasy. Transvestism is now *Transvestic Fetishism.* Zoophilia is no longer separately coded. *Frotteurism* has been added.
- The *Sexual Dysfunctions,* formerly Psychosexual Dysfunctions, now specify "Psychogenic" vs. "Psychogenic and Biogenic"; "Life-long" vs. "Acquired"; and "Generalized" vs. "Situational."
- Inhibited Sexual Desire is now *Hypoactive Sexual Desire Disorder,* and *Sexual Aversion Disorder* has been added to connote extreme aversion to genital contact.
- Inhibited Sexual Excitement has been renamed and divided into *Female Sexual Arousal Disorder* and *Male Erectile Disorder.*
- The word "Functional" has been deleted from *Dyspareunia* and *Vaginismus.*
- Ego-dystonic Homosexuality has been deleted as a specifically defined disorder, but may be coded under *Sexual Disorder NOS.*

CASE VIGNETTES

Case Example 1
A 20-year-old college student is referred for counseling after being caught exposing himself and masturbating in a car outside a women's dormitory during "finals week." He is quite embarrassed and contrite. He is the first member of his family to attend college and feels great pressure to graduate, although he has had academic problems during the past semester. He thinks he did poorly on his exams. A careful, nonthreatening history reveals that since the tenth grade he has exposed himself to women and female children on many occasions and has also often peeked into bedroom windows. His masturbatory fantasies often center around these themes, sometimes involving children (always in settings of exposing himself to them). He lives in a rented room across the street from a sorority house.

He has never assaulted anyone and has no wish to do so. He had a girlfriend, with whom he had a sexual relationship, who left him after he was caught. Although he is sometimes depressed, he is not chronically dysphoric. He spends considerable time in his room, watching the sorority house through binoculars and studying, but goes to class regularly.

Discussion

The pedophilic parts of the patient's behavior and fantasies do not meet criteria for Pedophilia. His disorder is chronic and repetitive, and not merely an Adjustment Disorder related to the stress of college and family pressures. Although depression is a common symptom and might meet criteria for Adjustment Disorder with Depressed Mood based on his college and family stressors, there are insufficient data to diagnose a Mood Disorder. The V code for Academic Problem (V62.30) may be appropriate, but the low grades may be related to his time-consuming paraphilic behavior (and related disturbance of self-image), and not to separate factors. His relative social withdrawal does not meet criteria for either Avoidant Personality Disorder or Social Phobia. Available information mitigates against other Personality Disorders, but "Diagnosis Deferred on Axis II" (799.90) would also be correct.

Diagnosis

> Axis I 302.40 Exhibitionism
> 302.82 Voyeurism
> Axis II V71.09 No diagnosis or condition

Case Example 2

A 30-year-old woman presents to her female gynecologist two weeks after being married for the first time, with a request that the doctor "see if something's wrong with me." Upon interview and examination, it is found that the marriage has never been consummated and the patient is a virgin. She says that her husband has been gentle and understanding, but she is afraid he will be dissatisfied and leave her if she cannot overcome her persistent discomfort, to the point of marked disgust, regarding intercourse.

The patient has never been aroused by sexual situations or fantasies, either heterosexual or homosexual. She recounts blunt and frightening sex education by her mother, who warned her years ago that she would have to "do your husband's bidding no matter how repulsive it gets." There is some indication that an adult family member attempted to have intercourse with the patient when she was a small child, but details are sketchy.

The patient has been very shy since early adolescence. She has had few friends and no intimate relationships with people of either sex. She is successful in her job as a night supply clerk in a large factory, and at one time she turned down a promotion because it would mean changing to the day shift and working with others ("I like the quiet at night; nobody bothers you"). She rarely attends social activities, although she often wants to, offering excuses such as "it's too far for me to drive." She fears she wouldn't "fit in" and would be embarrassed. Her marriage, to a family friend 44 years old, occurred largely at her family's behest, to provide her with "security." She says her life was quite comfortable before she was married.

Discussion

The patient meets criteria for both Sexual Dysfunctions below and has an absence of other Axis I disorders. She meets the criteria, including chronicity and pervasiveness, for Avoidant Personality. No pattern of marked peculiarities of appearance, belief, or behavior are mentioned which might support a diagnosis of Schizotypal Personality Disorder. Her desire for social involvement and sensitivity to criticism mitigate against Schizoid Personality Disorder.

Diagnosis

> Axis I 302.79 Sexual Aversion Disorder
> 302.72 Female Sexual Arousal Disorder
> Axis II 301.82 Avoidant Personality Disorder

Chapter 21

Sleep Disorders

All of the Sleep Disorders described in this chapter are chronic (lasting more than one month). Those which last for only a few nights, often caused by psychosocial stressors, should not be diagnosed here. There are 117 two major subgroups of Sleep Disorders: the Dyssomnias and the Parasomnias.

Sleep Disorders should be diagnosed in addition to any mental or physical disorder that may be associated with them, including substance abuse and iatrogenic problems (e.g., side effects of some medications).

The criteria for the diagnoses presented here do not include data from laboratory procedures (such as polysomnograms). Such procedures may be necessary to establish the diagnosis firmly and are particularly helpful in establishing the relationship of the sleep disturbance to physical disorders (e.g., sleep apnea).

A. DYSSOMNIAS
All the Dyssomnias are characterized by a disturbance in the amount, 118 quality, or timing of sleep.

Insomnia Disorders (307.42, 780.50)

Essential feature. The essential feature of the insomnias is a predominant complaint of difficulty in initiating or maintaining sleep, or of not feeling rested after apparently adequate sleep ("nonrestorative" sleep).

Because of the great variability in the length of time it takes normal people to fall asleep, and the amount of sleep normally required, the clinician should be familiar with normal variations related to age and other factors.

Associated features. Nonspecific complaints are common, including disturbances in concentration or mood.

Complications are primarily related to treatment (including self-treatment) with pharmacological agents or other substances taken either to induce sleep or to increase alertness.

Differential diagnosis. Many mental and physical disorders give rise to insomnia. Insomnia Disorders should be diagnosed only when the sleep disturbance is the predominant complaint, as an additional disorder. Sleep-Wake Schedule Disorder is alleviated when the sleep-wake pattern is restored. The disorder should also be differentiated from Hypersomnia, in which the pattern of sleep is disturbed, the frequent awakenings of sleep apnea and narcolepsy, and normal decreases in sleep requirements.

Diagnostic criteria for Insomnia Disorders (all codes):

A. The predominant complaint is of difficulty in initiating or maintaining sleep, or of nonrestorative sleep.
B. The disturbance occurs at least three times a week, for at least one month, and is sufficiently severe to cause either complaints of significant daytime fatigue or the observation by others of some symptom attributable to the sleep disturbance (e.g., irritability, impaired daytime functioning).
C. Occurrence is not exclusively during the course of Sleep-Wake Schedule Disorder or a Parasomnia.

Types of Insomnia Disorders

**Insomnia Related to Another Mental Disorder (Nonorganic) (307.42)**
Diagnostic criteria:

Insomnia Disorder, as defined by criteria "A," "B," and "C" above, related to a nonorganic Axis I or Axis II mental disorder. The diagnosis is not used if the Insomnia Disorder is related to a known organic factor (including Psychoactive Substance Abuse Disorder).

Insomnia Related to a Known Organic Factor (780.50)
Diagnostic criteria:

Insomnia Disorder, as defined by criteria "A," "B," and "C" above, that is related to a known organic factor, such as a physical disorder, a substance use disorder, or a medication. The organic factor should be listed on Axis I or Axis III, as appropriate.

Primary Insomnia (307.42)
Diagnostic criteria:

Insomnia Disorder, as defined by criteria "A," "B," and "C" above, that apparently is not maintained by any other mental disorder or any known organic factor.

Hypersomnia Disorders (307.44, 780.50, 780.54)

Essential features. Either excessive daytime sleepiness or sleep attacks (not accounted for by an inadequate amount of sleep) or, more rarely, a prolonged transition to the fully awake state upon awakening ("sleep drunkenness"). Daytime sleepiness is defined as a tendency to fall asleep very easily at almost any time during the day, even following normal or prolonged sleep at night. The condition is usually present daily, such as when related to sleep apnea or narcolepsy. It is occasionally episodic, as in Kleine-Levin syndrome or some depressions.

Complications. Many patients with Hypersomnia Disorders become demoralized or depressed. Accidental injury is common, as are social and vocational problems. Patients often develop physiological tolerance to stimulant medication and may abuse it.

Differential diagnosis. Hypersomnia may be associated with many physical disorders, as well as Depressive Disorders, but it should not be diagnosed unless it is the predominant complaint. Certain forms of psychomotor epilepsy mimic narcoleptic sleep attacks.

Diagnostic criteria for Hypersomnia Disorders (all codes):

A. The predominant complaint is at least *one* of the following:
   1. excessive daytime sleepiness or sleep attacks not accounted for by an inadequate amount of sleep
   2. prolonged transition to the fully awake state upon awakening (sleep drunkenness)
B. The disturbance in "A" occurs almost every day for at least one month, or episodically for longer periods of time, and is sufficiently severe to result in impaired occupational functioning or impairment in usual social activities or relationships with others.
C. Occurrence not exclusively during the course of Sleep-Wake Schedule Disorder.

Types of Hypersomnia Disorders

Hypersomnia Related to Another Mental Disorder (Nonorganic) (307.44)
Diagnostic criteria:

Hypersomnia, as defined by criteria "A," "B," and "C" above, that is related to another Axis I or II mental disorder, such as Major Depression or Dysthymia, but not initiated or maintained by any organic factor (including substance abuse or medication).

Hypersomnia Related to a Known Organic Factor (780.50)

Associated features. Patients with narcolepsy often have other organic sleep signs and symptoms, such as cataplexy, hypnagogic or hypnopompic hallucinations, or sleep paralysis. People with obstructive sleep apnea are often obese and are subject to a number of serious cardiorespiratory problems. Other specific syndromes, such as Kleine-Levin syndrome, have other emotional and physical signs.

Predisposing factors. Marked obesity predisposes one to obstructive sleep apnea and some other organic Hypersomnia Disorders (e.g., "Pickwickian syndrome").

Diagnostic criteria for Hypersomnia Related to a Known Organic Factor:

Hypersomnia Disorder, as defined by criteria "A," "B," and "C" above, and related to a known organic factor, including physical disorders, psychoactive substance use disorders, or medications. The known organic factor should be listed on Axis I or Axis III, as appropriate.

Primary Hypersomnia (780.54)
Diagnostic criteria:

Hypersomnia, as defined in criteria "A," "B," and "C" above, that is apparently not maintained by any other mental disorder or any known organic factor (including physical disorder, Psychoactive Substance Abuse Disorder, or medication).

Sleep-Wake Schedule Disorder (307.45)

Essential feature. A mismatch between the normal sleep-wake schedule demanded by the person's environment and the individual's circadian rhythm. The usual result is either insomnia or hypersomnia, which disappears if, early in the development of the Sleep-Wake Schedule Disorder, the patient is allowed to follow his or her own sleep-wake schedule.

There are three types of Sleep-Wake Schedule Disorder. In *"Advanced or Delayed Type,"* there is a considerable advancement or delay of the onset of sleep, compared to one's desires or conventional schedule. When "advanced," most evening activity is preempted by a need to go to bed early, and the person may awaken several hours before daybreak. When "delayed," the opposite is the case (e.g., in "night people").

In *"Disorganized Type,"* there is a random or capricious pattern of sleep and wake times, in which there is no major daily sleep period. This is seen from time to time in elderly or bedridden people.

The *"Frequently Changing Type"* is apparently due to frequent changes in sleep and waking times, often associated with travel across time zones or changing shifts at work.

Associated features. Nonspecific dysphoria is common.

Predisposing factors. Lifestyles that include frequently changing or irregular patterns of sleep and wakefulness, whether related to erratic schedules or to frequent travel across several time zones.

Differential diagnosis. Insomnia Disorder, Hypersomnia Disorder. When the sleep-wake schedule problem is found within another mental disorder, the diagnosis is made only if disturbed sleep is the predominant complaint.

Diagnostic criteria for Sleep-Wake Schedule Disorder:

Mismatch between the normal sleep-wake schedule for a person's environment and his or her circadian sleep-wake pattern, resulting in a complaint of either insomnia (meeting criteria "A" and "B" for Insomnia Disorder, above) or hypersomnia (meeting criteria "A" and "B" for Hypersomnia Disorder, above).

Specify: "Advanced or Delayed," "Disorganized," or "Frequently Changing" Type.

Other Dyssomnias

Dyssomnia Not Otherwise Specified (307.40)
This is a residual category for insomnias, hypersomnias, or sleep-wake schedule disturbances that are the predominant complaint of the patient, but cannot be classified in any of the specific categories above.

B. PARASOMNIAS

119 The Parasomnias are characterized by one or more abnormal events that occur either during sleep or at the interface between wakefulness and sleep. The predominant complaint focuses on this disturbance, and not on its effects on sleep or wakefulness.

Some disorders (e.g., Functional Enuresis) meet these criteria, but are nevertheless classified elsewhere in DSM-III-R.

Dream Anxiety Disorder (Nightmare Disorder) (307.47)

Essential feature. Repeated awakenings from sleep with detailed recall of vivid, very frightening dreams. The dream anxiety episodes occur during REM sleep and thus involve little motor movement.

Associated features. Little pathology is usually associated with this disorder in children; however, in adults it may be associated with a number of other mental disorders. Sleeplessness after awakening from the nightmare is common.

Differential diagnosis. The diagnosis should not be made if the disturbance was initiated and maintained by a known organic factor, including medications or substance abuse. In such cases, a diagnosis of Parasomnia Not Otherwise Specified may be appropriate. Sleep Terror Disorder is differentiated by a number of factors.

Diagnostic criteria for Dream Anxiety Disorder (Nightmare Disorder):

A. Repeated awakenings from the sleep period or naps with detailed recall of extended and extremely frightening dreams, usually involving threats to survival, security, or self-esteem. The awakenings generally occur during the second half of the sleep period.
B. On awakening from frightening dreams, the person rapidly becomes oriented and alert.
C. The dream experience or resulting sleep disturbance causes significant distress.
D. It cannot be established that an organic factor initiated and maintained the disturbance (e.g., medications, substance abuse).

Sleep Terror Disorder (307.46)

Essential feature. Repeated episodes of abrupt awakening from sleep, with vague but intense anxiety. The disorder is associated with non-REM 120
sleep, stages III and IV. The patient typically sits up abruptly, with a frightened expression and both emotional and physiological signs of anxiety and confusion. The disorder is also called *"pavor nocturnus."*

Associated features. In children, there is no consistently associated psychopathology. In adults, situational stress, adjustment reactions, and Generalized Anxiety Disorder are sometimes found.

Predisposing factors. Many patients with this disorder have had a serious febrile illness in the past. Family history of the disorder is common in patients with Sleep Terrors.

Differential diagnosis. Dream Anxiety Disorder is distinguished by its appearance during REM sleep and concomitant differences in presentation. Hypnagogic hallucinations differ in that they occur at sleep onset and consist of vivid images at the transition period. Epileptic seizures during sleep may be similar to Sleep Terror Disorder and should be ruled out with neurological consultation and EEG or polysomnography.

Diagnostic criteria for Sleep Terror Disorder:

A. A predominant disturbance with recurrent episodes of abrupt awakening, lasting 1 to 10 minutes, usually occurring during the first third of the major sleep period and usually beginning with a panicky scream.
B. Intense anxiety and signs of autonomic arousal during each episode, but no detailed dream is recalled.
C. Relative nonresponsiveness to efforts of others to comfort the person during the episode and, almost invariably, at least several minutes of confusion, disorientation, and/or perseverative motor movements.
D. It cannot be established that an organic factor (including medication) initiated and maintained the disturbance.

Sleepwalking Disorder (307.46)

Essential features. Repeated episodes of complex dissociative behaviors, which usually include leaving the bed and walking about, associated with non-REM sleep stages III and IV and usually lasting less than 30 minutes. Perseverative movements are common, which may proceed to semipurposeful motor acts. The patient may engage in complex behaviors, rarely including leaving the house, driving a car, and so forth. Although outwardly seeming awake, the person is in an altered state of consciousness and cannot exercise the judgment or coordination expected during wakefulness. Fragments of dreams or memories of behaviors during sleepwalking may occur, but are commonly absent; the patient almost never recalls the entire episode.

Associated features. People with Sleepwalking Disorder have a higher-than-normal incidence of other non-REM Sleep Disorders. Children have not been observed to have any consistently associated psychopathology; however, adults frequently have situational stress, Adjustment Disorders, or Anxiety Disorders. DSM-III-R states that Personality Disorders are common; other authors feel that sleepwalking in adults is not consistently associated with serious psychopathology.

Predisposing factors. Febrile illness in childhood and family history of sleepwalking or other non-REM sleep disorders are common. In persons already predisposed, fatigue, external stress, and unconscious conflict increase its likelihood.

Differential diagnosis. Psychomotor epilepsy may manifest itself at night and should be ruled out in patients whose symptoms are especially troublesome and in those with neurological signs or symptoms. Psychogenic Fugue is distinguishable in a number of ways, notably by its lack of disturbed consciousness. Sleep drunkenness may resemble sleepwalking, but occurs after awakening and is often associated with aggressive behavior.

Diagnostic criteria for Sleepwalking Disorder:

A. Repeated episodes of arising from bed during sleep and walking about, usually occurring during the first third of the major sleep period, associated with non-REM sleep.

B. While sleepwalking, the person has a blank, staring face, is relatively unresponsive to others' efforts to influence the sleepwalking or to communicate, and can be awakened only with great difficulty.

C. On awakening, the person has amnesia for the episode (whether awakened from the sleepwalking episode or the next morning).

D. Within several minutes after awakening from the sleepwalking episode, there is no impairment of mental activity or behavior (although there may be a short period of initial confusion or disorientation).

E. It cannot be established that an organic factor initiated and maintained the disturbance.

Parasomnia Not Otherwise Specified (NOS) (307.40)

This residual category should be used for sleep disturbances that meet the basic criteria for Parasomnia, but cannot be classified in any of the specific categories noted above (e.g., sleep talking).

DIFFERENCES BETWEEN DSM-III AND DSM-III-R SLEEP DISORDERS

- *Sleep Disorders* are now defined and coded in the main body of the DSM, rather than in an Appendix. The current classification is much simpler than that compiled by the Association for the Psychophysiological Study of Sleep and is compatible with DSM-III-R's multiaxial system.

CASE VIGNETTE

A 19-year-old military recruit is referred to the psychiatrist after walking in his sleep in his barracks on three occasions. He walked in his sleep as a young child, as did one of his sisters, but has not done so since about age five. He says he is not aware of this behavior and does not recall any dream associated with it. There is no personal history of significant dysphoria, maladjustment, or other psychiatric symptoms, and no family history of psychiatric disorder (except for sleepwalking). He has been doing well in Basic Training and does not want a medical discharge. His physical examination, including neurological workup and EEG, is negative.

Discussion

Adjustment Disorder Not Otherwise Specified might be considered, but the patient does not perceive Basic Training as a severe psychosocial stressor, and there is an implication of personal and familial predisposition to sleepwalking. There is no indication of any other Axis I or Axis II disorder.

Diagnosis

Axis I   307.46   Sleepwalking Disorder
Axis II V71.09 No diagnosis or condition

Chapter 22

Factitious Disorders

Factitious Disorders are characterized by the intentional production of symptoms. The behavior is "voluntary" in the sense that the act is intentional. The behavior is not "voluntary" in the sense that it usually cannot be controlled by the individual. The presumed goal of this behavior is to assume the sick role, as opposed to Malingering, in which the goal is to accomplish an externally recognizable objective (e.g., obtain compensation, avoid jail, avoid military duty). The presence of factitious symptoms does not preclude true physical or psychological symptoms. The diagnosis of Factitious Disorder always implies psychopathology, frequently a severe personality disturbance.

Factitious Disorder with Physical Symptoms (301.51)

Essential features. The intentional production of physical symptoms without evidence of external incentives for the behavior. The presumed goal is the sick or "patient" role. The person may present in a variety of ways, including lying about symptoms, self-inflicted injury, medication ingestion to feign illness, exaggeration or purposeful exacerbation of a preexisting physical condition, or any combination of these deceptions.

In the chronic form, known as Munchausen syndrome, Factitious Disorder is associated with multiple hospitalizations, dramatic presentations, medical sophistication (often), pathological lying (*pseudologia fantastica*), frequent surgery ("gridiron abdomen"), and analgesic abuse (frequently). When confronted, the individual either denies the allegations or rapidly leaves the hospital against medical advice.

Associated features. Psychoactive Substance Abuse is common, and severe character pathology is invariably present.

Predisposing factors. True physical disorders during childhood or adolescence leading to extensive medical treatment and hospitalization; a grudge against the medical profession; employment in the medical field; underlying dependent, exploitative, or self-defeating personality traits; and an important past relationship with a physician are possible predisposing factors.

Differential diagnosis. True medical disorders, Somatoform Disorders, Malingering, Schizophrenia, and Antisocial Personality Disorder.

Diagnostic criteria for Factitious Disorder with Physical Symptoms:

A. Intentional production or feigning of physical, but not psychological, symptoms.
B. Psychological need to assume the sick role, in the absence of external incentives for the behavior (financial compensation, avoid jail, etc.).
C. Occurrence not exclusive during the course of another Axis I disorder.

Factitious Disorder with Psychological Symptoms (300.16)

Essential features. The intentional production of psychological symptoms, usually psychosis, without evidence of external incentives for the behavior. The presumed goal is the sick or "patient" role. The symptoms are typically worse when observed. The person may be extremely suggestible and admit to many additional symptoms when asked by the examiner or may be uncooperative and negativistic when questioned.

Associated features. Severe character pathology is almost always present, and the secret use of psychoactive substances may allow the individual to produce symptoms of a mental disorder.

Predisposing factors. Severe Personality Disorder.

Differential diagnosis. True mental disorders, Dementia, and Malingering are considered in the differential diagnosis.

Diagnostic criteria for Factitious Disorder with Psychological Symptoms:

A. Intentional production or feigning of psychological, but not physical, symptoms.
B. Psychological need to assume the sick role, in the absence of external incentives for the behavior (financial compensation, avoid jail, etc.).
C. Occurrence not exclusively during the course of another Axis I disorder, such as Schizophrenia.

Factitious Disorder Not Otherwise Specified (300.19)

Essential features. Factitious Disorders that cannot be elsewhere classified. For example, an individual who feigns both physical and psychological symptoms without evidence of external incentives.

DIFFERENCES BETWEEN DSM-III AND DSM-III-R FACTITIOUS DISORDERS

- The diagnostic criteria for Factitious Disorders in DSM-III emphasized that the disturbance was "voluntary." DSM-III-R revised the criteria to indicate that the behavior is "voluntary" in the sense that the act is intentional, but is not "voluntary" in the sense that it usually cannot be stopped by the individual.
- Atypical Factitious Disorder with Physical Symptoms has been renamed *Factitious Disorder Not Otherwise Specified.*

CASE VIGNETTE

Ms. B., a 28-year-old, never-married nurse currently hospitalized for evaluation of a bleeding disorder, is referred for consultation. According to the referring internist, Ms. B. has been evaluated on numerous occasions for a bleeding disorder, and no reasonable explanation, except intentional ingestion of an anticoagulant, is possible. The internist ordered a search of her hospital room, and a bottle of bishydroxycoumarin was found hidden in the bathroom.

During the evaluation, Ms. B. displays constant anger and adamantly denies taking any medications. She also denies a psychiatric history, illicit drug or alcohol abuse, or family history of psychiatric problems. She reports a very difficult childhood: "I was frequently severely beaten by both my mother and my father." She complains of a sense of chronic boredom and unhappiness with her career. Her relationships with significant others are chaotic, and she admits to threatening suicide on several occasions. Mental status examination reveals no evidence of psychosis.

Discussion

Ms. B. is intentionally feigning a bleeding disorder by ingestion of an anticoagulant. There is no evidence of personal gain, as in Malingering, and she is not psychotic. Her only obvious goal is to assume a sick role. Therefore, the diagnosis would be Factitious Disorder with Physical Symptoms. As is usually the case for persons with Factitious Disorders, this individual may also have a Personality Disorder. It is likely that she has a Borderline Personality Disorder. However, since the information in the case vignette is limited, either a deferred diagnosis or a (provisional) diagnosis would be appropriate.

Diagnosis

	Axis I	301.51	Factitious Disorder with Physical Symptoms
Either	Axis II	301.83	Borderline Personality Disorder (provisional)
or	Axis II	799.90	Diagnosis deferred
	Axis III		Bleeding disorder secondary to bishydroxycoumarin ingestion

Chapter 23

Impulse Control Disorders Not Elsewhere Classified

This is a residual diagnostic category for disorders of impulse control not elsewhere classified. The essential features include failure of the individual to resist performing a potentially harmful act, a sense of tension or arousal before committing the act, and a sense of relief or pleasure at the time the act is committed. Other features may or may not be present. These include conscious resistance to the impulse, preplanning, and guilt, or regret or self-reproach after committing the act.

Intermittent Explosive Disorder (312.34)

Essential features. The individual experiences several discrete episodes in which loss of control of aggressive impulse results in serious assaultive acts or destruction of property. The aggressiveness is grossly out of proportion to the precipitating events. Between aggressive episodes, there are no signs of impulsiveness or aggressiveness. Aggressiveness appears usually within minutes to hours and, regardless of duration, disappears quickly. The clinician must be sure that these episodes do not occur during the course of other mental disorders.

Associated features. Genuine regret may follow aggressive episodes.

Differential diagnosis. Psychotic disorders, Organic Personality Syndrome, Antisocial Personality Disorder, Borderline Personality Disorder, Conduct Disorder, and Psychoactive Substance-Induced Intoxication are considered in the differential diagnosis.

122

Diagnostic criteria for Intermittent Explosive Disorder:

A. Several discrete episodes of loss of control of aggressive impulses that result in serious assaultive acts or destruction of property.
B. Degree of aggressiveness is grossly out of proportion with precipitating events.
C. Between aggressive episodes, no signs of generalized impulsiveness or aggressiveness.
D. Episodes do not occur during the course of a psychotic disorder, Organic Personality Syndrome, Antisocial Personality Disorder, Borderline Personality Disorder, Conduct Disorder, or Psychoactive Substance-Induced Intoxication.

Kleptomania (312.32)

Essential features. The person cannot resist the impulse to steal objects. The object is not stolen for its monetary value, its utility, or to express anger or gain revenge. There is a sense of tension immediately before the theft and a sense of relief or pleasure afterward. The stealing is not due to a Conduct Disorder or Antisocial Personality Disorder.

Associated features. The person often has signs of depression, anxiety, guilt, and personality disturbance.

Differential diagnosis. Ordinary stealing, Malingering, Conduct Disorder, Antisocial Personality Disorder, Manic Episode, Schizophrenia, and Organic Mental Disorders are considered in the differential diagnosis.

Diagnostic criteria for Kleptomania:

A. Recurrent failure to resist impulses to steal objects not needed for personal use or monetary gain.
B. Increasing sense of tension immediately before the theft.
C. Pleasure or relief at the time of the theft.
D. Stealing is not motivated by anger or revenge.
E. Stealing is not due to Conduct Disorder or Antisocial Personality Disorder.

Pathological Gambling (312.31)

Essential features. A chronic, progressive failure to resist impulses to gamble. Gambling eventually disrupts and damages personal, family, or vocational pursuits. Characteristic problems include severe indebtedness, default on debts, family disruption, inattention to work, and illegal activities to finance gambling.

Associated features. As indebtedness from gambling activities increases, the individual is forced to lie, embezzle, steal, or perform other illegal acts. Pathological gamblers have been described as overconfident, very energetic, easily bored, and "big spenders." At times of increased stress, anxiety and depression may be seen.

Predisposing factors. Inappropriate parental discipline, exposure to gambling as an adolescent, high family value placed on material and financial symbols, and low family value placed on savings and budgeting are possible predisposing factors.

Differential diagnosis. Social gambling, Manic or Hypomanic Episode, and Antisocial Personality Disorder are considered in the differential diagnosis.

Diagnostic criteria for Pathological Gambling:

A. Maladaptive gambling behavior as indicated by at least *four* of the following:
1. frequent preoccupation with gambling or with obtaining money to gamble
2. frequent gambling with larger amounts of money or over a longer period of time than intended
3. need to increase the size or frequency of bets to achieve desired excitement
4. restless or irritable if unable to gamble
5. repeated loss of money by gambling and increased gambling to win back losses ("chasing")
6. repeated efforts to reduce or stop gambling
7. frequent gambling when expected to meet social or occupational obligations

8. sacrifice of some important social, occupational, or recreational activities in order to gamble
9. gambling continues despite inability to pay mounting debts, significant problems (social, occupational, or legal), and knowledge that gambling exacerbates the situation

Pyromania (312.33)

Essential features. Deliberate firesetting on more than one occasion, accompanied by increased tension prior to firesetting and intense pleasure or relief during firesetting or as a result of witnessing or participating in its aftermath. The firesetting is not motivated by monetary gain, sociopolitical ideology, anger or revenge, psychotic thinking (delusions or hallucinations), or to conceal criminal activity. There may be considerable advance preparation, and the person may leave clues.

Associated features. Persons with this disorder may be regular fire-watchers, set off false alarms, show interest in firefighting paraphernalia, seek employment as a firefighter, or work as a volunteer firefighter.

Differential diagnosis. A youngster's experimentation with fire, firesetting for gain, Schizophrenia, Bipolar Disorders, and Organic Mental Disorders are considered in the differential diagnosis.

Diagnostic criteria for Pyromania:

A. Deliberate firesetting on more than one occasion.
B. Tension or arousal before the act.
C. Fascination with, interest in, curiosity about, or attraction to fire and its situational context or associated characteristics.
D. Intense pleasure, gratification, or relief when firesetting, or when witnessing or participating in the fire's aftermath.
E. The firesetting is not motivated by monetary gain, sociopolitical ideology, anger or revenge, psychotic thinking (delusions or hallucinations), or to conceal criminal activity.

Trichotillomania (312.39)

Essential features. Recurrent failure to resist the impulse to pull out one's own hair. The individual experiences increased tension before the act, and gratification or relief during or immediately after the act. The scalp is the most common area involved. The affected scalp areas have an irregular "patchy" pattern of hair loss and hair of varying lengths within the patch. There is no evidence of scarring or pigmentary change. Other areas commonly involved are eyebrows, eyelashes, and beard. Other medical reasons for hair loss must be ruled out.

Associated features. Rituals may develop, such as mouthing the hair (trichophagy) or swallowing the hair. Denial of the behavior is common. When onset of the disorder occurs in adulthood, a psychotic disorder should be ruled out.

Predisposing factors. Psychosocial stress or Psychoactive Substance Abuse may predispose to the disorder.

Differential diagnosis. Medical disorders causing hair loss, Obsessive Compulsive Disorder, Factitious Disorder with Physical Symptoms, Psychological Factors Affecting Physical Condition, Stereotypy/Habit Disorder, and psychotic disorders are considers in the differential diagnosis.

Diagnostic criteria for Trichotillomania:

A. Recurrent failure to resist the urge to pull out one's own hair.
B. Increasing tension immediately before pulling out the hair.
C. Gratification or relief when pulling out the hair.
D. No association with preexisting inflammation of the skin, and not a response to a delusion or hallucination.

Impulse Control Disorder Not Otherwise Specified (312.39)

Essential features. Disorders of impulse control that do not meet the diagnostic criteria for other specific Impulse Control Disorders.

DIFFERENCES BETWEEN DSM-III AND DSM-III-R IMPULSE CONTROL DISORDERS NOT ELSEWHERE CLASSIFIED

- The diagnostic criteria for *Pathological Gambling* has been revised to stress its resemblance to *Psychoactive Substance Dependence.*
- Isolated Explosive Disorder was not retained in DSM-III-R.

- *Intermittent Explosive Disorder* has been retained in DSM-III-R despite reservations about its validity.
- *Trichotillomania* was added to this diagnostic category.

CASE VIGNETTE

Mr. M. is a 27-year-old house painter who is brought by his wife for evaluation. She states that he is unable to control his gambling, despite efforts by both to stop his behavior. He reports that his gambling began about three years ago during a vacation in Las Vegas. During that trip he spent increasing amounts of time gambling and reports that he was a big winner. Upon his return, he began placing bets, first on major league sports events and later on horse races. The amounts of his betting gradually grew from 5 or 10 dollars to several hundred dollars per bet. He spent more and more time either gambling or trying to obtain money to sustain his wagering. He states, "At this point I would bet on anything if the odds are right." About 12 months ago, he began having severe financial problems. He borrowed money from his relatives and friends to cover his debts. "The further behind I got, the more I would bet to try to cover my losses." He is now deeply in debt to his bookie, who is threatening harm if he doesn't at least pay the interest on the money.

Mr. M. denies prior psychiatric history, drug or alcohol abuse, and is in excellent health, except for mild hypertension. He is currently taking hydrochlorthiazide. He is unaware of his family's psychiatric history. His mother abandoned him when he was three. He reports going from foster home to foster home until he joined the Army at age 17. He has been employed as a house painter since his discharge from the Army.

Discussion

Mr. M. exhibits many of the symptoms of Pathological Gambling. These symptoms include preoccupation with gambling, increasing size and frequency of wagers, failure of repeated efforts to stop gambling, and continued, even increased, gambling despite mounting debts. There is no indication of an Axis II diagnosis from the history.

Diagnosis

Axis I	312.31	Pathological Gambling
Axis II	V71.09	No diagnosis
Axis III		Mild Hypertension

Chapter 24

Adjustment Disorder

Essential features. An Adjustment Disorder is a maladaptive reaction to a psychosocial stressor or stressors that manifests itself as impairment in occupational function, social activities, or interpersonal relationships. The symptoms are in excess of a normal or expected reaction to the   124
stressor(s) and are not part of a pattern of overreaction to stress (e.g., Histrionic Personality Disorder) or an exacerbation of a mental disorder. According to DSM-III-R, the disturbance must begin within three months after the onset of the psychosocial stress and last no longer than six months. When the diagnosis is made, it is assumed that the disturbance will cease shortly after discontinuation of the stressor or, in the face of a continuing stressor, that a new level of adaptation will be achieved.

The severity of the reaction is not altogether predictable from the intensity of the stressor. Certain individuals may have a severe disturbance with a seemingly mild stressor; others may have a mild reaction to a severe stressor. Stressors may be single, recurrent, or continuous.

Nine different types of Adjustment Disorder are listed in DSM-III-R. Disorders are classified according to the predominant symptoms. Note that Adjustment Disorders are partial syndromes of more specific disorders. For example, Adjustment Disorder with Depressed Mood is a depressive syndrome that does not meet the full criteria for a Major Depression and that develops after a psychosocial stressor.

Differential diagnosis. Conditions Not Attributed to a Mental Disorder That Are a Focus of Attention or Treatment (V codes), Personality

Disorders, and Psychological Factors Affecting Physical Condition are considered in the differential diagnosis.

Diagnostic criteria for Adjustment Disorder (all types):

A. A maladaptive reaction to an identifiable stressor, or stressors, that occurs within three months of the onset of the stressor(s).
B. The maladaptive reaction is manifested by *either:*
   1. impairment in occupational (or school) function, social activities, or interpersonal relationships, *or*
   2. symptoms in excess of a normal and expected reaction to the stressor(s)
C. Not merely one instance of a pattern of overreaction to stress or an exacerbation of a mental disorder.
D. The maladaptive reaction has persisted no longer than six months.
E. Disturbance does not meet criteria for a specific mental disorder and does not represent Uncomplicated Bereavement.

For coding, see diagnostic types below.

TYPES OF ADJUSTMENT DISORDER
(According to predominant symptoms)

• **Adjustment Disorder with Anxious Mood (309.24)**

Essential features. Predominant manifestations are symptoms such as nervousness, worry, and trouble falling asleep.

• **Adjustment Disorder with Depressed Mood (309.00)**

Essential features. Predominant manifestations are symptoms such as depressed mood, feelings of worthlessness, and decreased self-esteem.

• **Adjustment Disorder with Disturbance of Conduct (309.30)**

Essential features. There is violation of the rights of others or violation of age-appropriate norms and rules. The predominant manifestations are symptoms such as truancy, fighting, or reckless driving.

- **Adjustment Disorder with Mixed Disturbance of Emotions and Conduct (309.40)**

Essential features. The predominant manifestations are a combination of emotional symptoms, such as those found in Adjustment Disorder with Anxious or Depressed Mood, concurrent with behavior found in Adjustment Disorder with Disturbance of Conduct.

- **Adjustment Disorder with Mixed Emotional Features (309.28)**

Essential features. The predominant manifestations are a combination of emotional symptoms, such as those found in Adjustment Disorders with Anxious and Depressed Moods.

- **Adjustment Disorder with Physical Complaints (309.82)**

Essential features. The predominant manifestations are physical symptoms, such as headache, backache, and lethargy.

- **Adjustment Disorder with Withdrawal (309.83)**

Essential features. The predominant manifestation is social withdrawal without a significantly depressed or anxious mood.

- **Adjustment Disorder with Work (or Academic) Inhibition (309.23)**

Essential features. The predominant manifestation is inhibition of work or academic function that occurs in a person whose previous performance was adequate.

- **Adjustment Disorder Not Otherwise Specified (309.90)**

Essential features. A maladaptive reaction to psychosocial stress with a symptom or symptoms not classified by the other Adjustment Disorders. For example, a patient who is diagnosed with cancer but denies the diagnosis and is noncompliant with treatment recommendations.

DIFFERENCES BETWEEN DSM-III AND DSM-III-R ADJUSTMENT DISORDERS

- The maximum duration of an *Adjustment Disorder* is now six months. This eliminates classifying chronic reactions to psychosocial stress as transient adjustment reactions.
- A new diagnosis, *Adjustment Disorder with Physical Complaints*, was added to DSM-III-R since nearly all the Somatoform Disorders require a symptom duration of at least six months.

CASE VIGNETTE

Mr. B., a 44-year-old business executive with chest pains, was admitted to a coronary care unit (CCU) to rule out a myocardial infarction (MI). In the CCU he was anxious, jittery, and had marked nervousness. In spite of strict instructions to remain in bed, he paced at the bedside. He was taking no medications and had no past psychiatric impairment. Clinical evaluation revealed a nervous man who was puzzled by his own anxiety. His mental status, except for the aforementioned anxiety, was normal.

Discussion

The patient has a clear stressor in his admission to the CCU to rule out an MI. His behavior is maladaptive. His increased anxiety and pacing place him at higher risk of medical problems.

Since there is no evidence of any other mental disorder, the diagnosis of an Adjustment Disorder is appropriate. The predominant symptoms are anxiety related; therefore, the diagnosis would be Adjustment Disorder with Anxious Mood.

Diagnosis

Axis I	309.24	Adjustment Disorder with Anxious Mood
Axis II	V71.09	No diagnosis or condition
Axis III		Rule out myocardial infarction
Axis IV		Psychosocial stressors: Acute potentially serious medical illness
		Severity: 5 — Extreme (Acute event)

Psychological Factors
Affecting Physical Condition

Psychological Factors Affecting Physical Condition (316.00)

Essential features. This diagnosis is used when the clinician wishes to note that psychological factors contribute to the initiation or exacerbation of a physical condition. The physical disorder is recorded on Axis III, although in some instances it may be a physical *condition*, such as dizziness. This diagnosis implies that a temporal relationship exists between (1) an environmental stimulus and the meaning ascribed to the stimulus, and (2) the initiation or exacerbation of the physical condition. A repetitive pattern that demonstrates this temporal relationship strengthens diagnostic certainty. The physical condition involves either demonstrable organic pathology (e.g., peptic ulcer) or a known pathophysiological process (e.g., tension headache). Common examples of some of these physical conditions are obesity, tension headache, migraine headache, painful menstruation, gastric ulcer, nausea and vomiting, and frequency of urination. This diagnosis is *not* made in cases of Conversion Disorder 125 or other Somatoform Disorders.

Differential diagnosis. Somatoform Disorders, Adjustment Disorder with Physical Complaints, Factitious Disorder with Physical Symptoms, and Malingering are considered in the differential diagnosis.

Diagnostic criteria for Psychological Factors Affecting Physical Condition:

A. Psychologically meaningful environmental stimuli are temporally related to the initiation or exacerbation of a specific physical condition or disorder.

   Note: Record physical condition on Axis III.

B. The physical condition involves either demonstrable organic pathology (e.g., peptic ulcer) or a known pathophysiological process (e.g., tension headache).

C. The condition does not meet the diagnostic criteria for a Somatoform Disorder.

DIFFERENCES BETWEEN DSM-III AND DSM-III-R
PSYCHOLOGICAL FACTORS AFFECTING PHYSICAL CONDITION
No changes were made.

CASE VIGNETTE
Ms. A. is a 24-year-old woman referred for evaluation of the role of stress in her tension headaches. According to the patient, she began having headaches two years ago, shortly after she found out that her husband was having an affair. He discontinued the extramarital relationship when she discovered the affair. However, the headaches have continued. She reports the headaches are worse at nighttime upon going to bed and on weekends. The headaches are least bothersome during the day while the husband is at work.

She and her husband have not, and do not, discuss the affair that occurred. Ms. A. has no other medical or mental health problems. Ms. A. reports a difficult childhood in which her father abused alcohol and was unfaithful to her mother.

Discussion
Ms. A. has a psychologically meaningful stressor that seems to have initiated the headaches and has exacerbated her pain complaints. The temporal relationship is present, both with the onset of the headaches and with the variation in symptom severity according to her proximity to the husband. It is also likely that her childhood experience with a father who was unfaithful plays a meaningful role in her condition.

The condition, tension headaches, is a known pathophysiological process. Ms. A does not have a history consistent with a Somatoform Disorder. The diagnosis is Psychological Factor Affecting Physical Condition.

Diagnosis

Axis I   316.00   Psychological Factor Affecting Physical Condition
Axis II   V71.09   No diagnosis or condition
Axis III   Tension headaches

Chapter 26

Personality Disorders

According to DSM-III-R, Personality Disorders may be diagnosed when personality *traits* are inflexible and maladaptive and cause either significant functional impairment or subjective distress. These personality traits are enduring patterns of perceiving, relating to, and thinking about the environment and oneself. They are global in their presentation, rather than being limited to specific situations or times of life. Personality Disorders are often recognizable by adolescence (although some should not be diagnosed until the patient is an adult) and continue through most or all of adult life.

126

The diagnostic criteria for Personality Disorders refer to behaviors or traits that are characteristic of (1) recent functioning (e.g., during the past year) and (2) long-term functioning (i.e., since early adulthood).

Many features of the various Personality Disorders may be seen during episodes of other mental disorders (e.g., dependency in Major Depression). The diagnosis of a Personality Disorder should be made only when the characteristic features are typical of long-term functioning and are not limited to discrete episodes of illness.

Diagnosis of Personality Disorders in children and adolescents. Provided relevant specific criteria are met, Avoidant Personality Disorder and Borderline Personality Disorder may be diagnosed in children and adolescents, as well as in adults. Some other Personality Disorders should

127

Note: *All Personality Disorders are coded on Axis II.*

204

be diagnosed in younger persons only with caution, when the maladaptive personality traits appear to be quite stable. Antisocial Personality Disorder should not be diagnosed if the person is under 18 (see below). DSM-III-R relates Conduct Disorder in childhood or adolescence to a corresponding diagnosis in adults of Antisocial Personality Disorder. The clinician should be careful to apply this comparison only to the child's conduct, and not to imply that the child will develop Antisocial Personality Disorder.

Associated features. People with Personality Disorders rarely complain of the disorder themselves, although there may be a dissatisfaction with their ability to function effectively or to get along with others. Complaints of depression or anxiety are common.

When a person with a preexisting Personality Disorder develops a psychosis, then both the psychosis (Axis I) and the Personality Disorder (Axis II, "premorbid") should be diagnosed and coded. If the Personality Disorder has not existed in the absence of symptoms of an Axis I disorder, it should not be diagnosed or coded.

Personality Disorder Clusters. DSM-III-R groups the Personality Disorders as follows: "Cluster A" includes Paranoid, Schizoid, and Schizotypal Personality Disorders, characterized by odd or eccentric behaviors. "Cluster B" includes Antisocial, Borderline, Histrionic, and Narcissistic Personality Disorders, which have in common frequent dramatic, emotional, or erratic behaviors. "Cluster C" includes Avoidant, Dependent, Obsessive Compulsive, and Passive Aggressive Personality Disorders, all frequently characterized by anxiety and fearfulness.

CLUSTER A

Paranoid Personality Disorder (301.00)

Essential feature. This disorder is characterized by a pervasive and unwarranted tendency to interpret the actions of other people as deliberately demanding or threatening. There is a general expectation of being exploited or harmed by others in some way. When confronted with new situations, these persons search intensely for confirmation of their paranoid expectations and conclude what they expected all along.

These people have great difficulty with interpersonal relationships, being argumentative, usually very intense, and tending to counterattack when they perceive any threat. They are critical of others and often litigious, and they accept criticism only with great difficulty. They routinely lack any passive, sentimental, tender, or humorous feelings.

Associated features. During severe stress, transient psychotic symptoms may occur; however, these are usually only brief and do not warrant an additional diagnosis. The disorder may predispose one to the development of Axis I disorders such as Delusional Disorder and Schizophrenia, Paranoid Type.

Differential diagnosis. Delusional Disorder and Schizophrenia, Paranoid Type are differentiated by their persistent psychotic symptoms and other features. Antisocial Personality Disorder shares some symptoms with Paranoid Personality Disorder; however, the latter is not associated with a lifelong history of antisocial behavior. Schizoid Personality Disorder does not have prominent paranoid ideation.

Diagnostic criteria for Paranoid Personality Disorder:

A. A pervasive and unwarranted tendency, beginning in early adulthood and present in a variety of contexts, to interpret the actions of other people as deliberately demeaning or threatening, as indicated by at least *four* of the following:

1. expects, without sufficient basis, to be exploited or harmed by others

2. questions, without justification, the loyalty or trustworthiness of friends or associates

3. reads hidden demeaning or threatening meanings into benign remarks or events (e.g., suspects that a bank's bookkeeping error was on purpose)

4. bears grudges or is otherwise unforgiving of insults or slights

5. is reluctant to confide in others because of unwarranted fear that the information will be used against him or her

6. is easily slighted and quick to react with anger or to counterattack

7. questions, without justification, the fidelity of his or her spouse or sexual partner

B. Occurrence not exclusively during the course of Schizophrenia or Delusional Disorder.

Schizoid Personality Disorder (301.20)

Essential features. Pervasive indifference to social relationships and a restricted range of emotional experience and expression. These patients prefer to be "loners" and neither desire nor enjoy sexual or personal (even family) relationships. Their outward appearance may be aloof, without strong emotions. They are somewhat socially inadequate and appear self-absorbed. Although males are rarely assertive enough to date and marry, females may passively accept a marital relationship. The social impairment may not preclude intellectual or occupational achievement, provided the individual can maintain a comfortable isolation.

Differential diagnosis. Schizotypal Personality Disorder involves more eccentricity, with schizophreniform features. People with Avoidant Personality Disorder avoid, but desire, social relationships.

Diagnostic criteria for Schizoid Personality Disorder:

A. A pervasive pattern of indifference to social relationships and a restricted range of emotional experience and expression, beginning by early adulthood and presenting in a variety of contexts, as indicated by at least *four* of the following:

1. neither enjoys nor desires close relationships, including being part of a family

2. almost always chooses solitary activities over those involving other people

3. rarely, if ever, claims or appears to experience strong emotions

4. indicates little, if any, desire to have sexual experiences with another person

5. is indifferent to the praise or criticism of others

6. has no more than one close friend or confidant, other than first-degree relatives

7. displays constricted affect (e.g., seems aloof, rarely reciprocates the gestures or expressions of others)

B. Occurrence not exclusively during the course of Schizophrenia or a Delusional Disorder.

Schizotypal Personality Disorder (301.22)

Essential features. A pervasive pattern of peculiar ideation, appearance, and behavior, as well as deficits in interpersonal relatedness, none of which is severe enough to meet criteria for Schizophrenia.

Associated features. Patients with Schizotypal Personality Disorder commonly have thought content which includes paranoia, ideas of reference, odd beliefs, or magical thinking, which influence the person's behavior. Interpersonal relatedness is impaired, with inappropriate or constricted affect and rare reciprocation of the expressions or gestures of others (such as passing smiles or nods). Like persons with Schizoid Personality Disorder, they have very few close friends other than first-degree relatives and are quite anxious in unfamiliar social situations. Features of Borderline Personality Disorder are often present and may justify both diagnoses. Transient psychotic symptoms are not unusual during periods of internal or external stress.

Differential diagnosis. Schizophrenia implies a history of at least one active schizophrenic phase, with severe, usually nontransient psychotic symptoms. In Schizoid Personality Disorder and Avoidant Personality Disorder the eccentricities and oddities of Schizotypal Personality Disorder are absent. Borderline Personality Disorder may coexist with Schizotypal Personality Disorder. In Paranoid Personality Disorder, suspiciousness and paranoid ideation may be present, but the remaining criteria are not.

Diagnostic criteria for Schizotypal Personality Disorder:

A. A pervasive pattern of deficits in interpersonal relatedness and peculiarities of ideation, appearance, and behavior, beginning by early adulthood and present in a variety of contexts, as indicated by at least *five* of the following:
1. ideas of reference (excluding delusions of reference)
2. excessive social anxiety
3. odd beliefs or magical thinking, influencing behavior and inconsistent with cultural norms (in children and adolescents, this may take the form of bizarre fantasies or preoccupations)
4. unusual perceptual experiences (e.g., illusions, sensing the presence of things or people who aren't actually there)

    5. odd or eccentric behavior or appearance

    6. no more than one close friend or confidant, other than first-degree relatives

    7. odd speech (but not loosening of associations or incoherence)

    8. inappropriate or constricted affect

    9. suspiciousness or paranoid ideation

  B. Occurrence not exclusively during the course of Schizophrenia or a Pervasive Developmental Disorder.

CLUSTER B

Antisocial Personality Disorder (301.70)

Essential feature. A pervasive pattern of irresponsibility and antisocial behavior.   **130**

Associated features. Irritability and aggressiveness, including domestic aggression, are commonly associated with Antisocial Personality Disorder. Reckless behavior which does not consider the rights or safety of others is often seen. These individuals generally have little or no remorse about the effects of their behavior on others, but are rarely sadistic. Antisocial behavior often diminishes in midlife, although the other characteristics generally remain. Early-life substance abuse and sexual experience (not as a victim of sexual abuse) are common. There may be signs of personal distress, such as inability to tolerate dysphoric affects. There is almost invariably an inability to sustain close, responsible, warm relationships with others (including spouse and friends).

Predisposing factors. Attention-Deficit Hyperactivity Disorder and Conduct Disorder during childhood are predisposing factors, although one should never assume that the hyperactive or antisocial child will develop Antisocial Personality Disorder. Although DSM-III-R mentions child abuse, other authorities do not see clear correlations between physical, social, or socioeconomic environment and development of true Antisocial Personality. Serious antisocial behavior in the father, including criminality, may be predisposing.

Differential diagnosis. In children under the age of 18, diagnoses such as Conduct Disorder may be confused with Antisocial Personality; however, the latter diagnosis should not be made unless the patient is 18 or over. In addition, many authorities feel that people over 18 who still show characteristics of adolescence (e.g., some college students) should not receive the diagnosis until their adulthood is established. The V-code category "Adult Antisocial Behavior" should be considered when antisocial behavior cannot be attributed to any other mental disorder and the individual does not meet all the criteria for Antisocial Personality Disorder. Substance abuse and related disorders should not be equated with Antisocial Personality Disorder, although they may be associated with it and may be diagnosed concomitantly. Some patients who are mentally retarded, schizophrenic, or paranoid exhibit antisocial behavior; however, the criteria for an additional diagnosis of Antisocial Personality Disorder are rarely met. Manic episodes often have antisocial characteristics, but the nature and course of Bipolar Disorder are easy to differentiate; an additional diagnosis of Antisocial Personality Disorder is rarely indicated.

Diagnostic criteria for Antisocial Personality Disorder:

A. Current age at least 18.
B. Evidence of childhood or adolescent Conduct Disorder with onset *before age 15*, as indicated by a history of at least *three* of the following before age 15:
   1. was often truant
   2. ran away from home at least twice, overnight, while living in parental or parental surrogate home (or ran away once without returning)
   3. often initiated physical fights
   4. used a weapon in more than one fight
   5. forced someone into sexual activity with him or her
   6. was physically cruel to animals
   7. was physically cruel to other people
   8. deliberately destroyed others' property (other than by firesetting)
   9. deliberately engaged in firesetting
   10. often lied (other than to avoid physical or sexual abuse)
   11. has stolen without confronting a victim on more than one occasion (e.g., forgery, burglary, picking pockets)

12. has stolen with confrontation of a victim (e.g., mugging, purse snatching, robbery)

C. A pattern of irresponsible and antisocial behavior since the age of 15, as indicated by at least *four* of the following:

1. is unable to sustain consistent work behavior, as shown by *any* of the following (including similar behavior in academic settings while a student):

   a. significant unemployment for six months or more within five years, when expected to work and work was available

   b. repeated absences from work unexplained by significant illness in self or family

   c. abandonment of several jobs without realistic plans for others

2. fails to conform to social norms with respect to lawful behavior, as indicated by repeatedly performing antisocial acts that are grounds for arrest (whether or not arrested)

3. is irritable and aggressive, as indicated by repeated physical fights or assaults (not required by his or her job or to defend someone), including spouse or child beating

4. repeatedly fails to meet financial obligations, as indicated by defaulting on debts or failing to provide support for dependents on a regular basis

5. fails to plan ahead or is impulsive, as indicated by at least *one* of the following:

   a. traveling from place to place without a prearranged job or clear goal, or a clear idea about when the travel will terminate

   b. lack of a fixed address for one month or more

6. has no regard for the truth, as indicated by repeated lying, use of aliases, or "conning" others

7. is reckless regarding his or her, or others', personal safety (e.g., as indicated by driving recklessly or while intoxicated)

8. if a parent or guardian, the person lacks ability to function as a responsible parent, as indicated by at least *one* of the following:

   a. malnutrition in the child

   b. illness in the child as a result of inadequate hygiene, routine care, or nourishment

    c. failure to obtain medical care for a seriously ill child

    d. having a child dependent on neighbors or nonresident relatives for food or shelter

    e. failure to secure a proper caretaker for a young child when the parent is away from home

    f. repeated squandering of money required for household necessities or parental responsibilities

  9. has never sustained a totally monogamous relationship for more than one year

  10. lacks remorse or feels justified when having hurt, mistreated, stolen from, or significantly abridged the rights of another person

D. The antisocial behavior does not occur exclusively during the course of Schizophrenia, manic episodes, or substance abuse.

Borderline Personality Disorder (301.83)

131   **Essential feature.** A pervasive pattern of instability of self-image, interpersonal relationships, and mood. There is almost always a marked, persistent disturbance of identity, which is pervasive and frequently manifested by uncertainty about more than one important personal issue (e.g., self-image, sexual orientation, values, career).

    Associated features. Interpersonal relationships are usually unstable and intense, frequently characterized by extremes of idealization or devaluation. Although these persons may describe a wish to be alone, or left alone, they make physical and emotional efforts to avoid abandonment by others.

    Affective instability is often associated with Borderline Personality. There may be marked mood shifts, usually to depression, irritability, or anxiety. These are usually transient, but may be quite intense and may lead to impulsive activities (including self-destructive activities, substance abuse, illegal behavior, or inappropriate sexual behavior). Recurrent suicidal or self-mutilating behavior is fairly common when the disorder is severe. The self-destructive or aggressive behavior may appear to be "gesture" or trivial; however, impulsiveness, poor judgment, and transient intensity of affect make prediction of dangerousness to self or others difficult.

    The disorder is often accompanied by features of other Personality Disorders, and DSM-III-R suggests that more than one diagnosis is often warranted. Transient psychotic symptoms occur in many patients; however, they are rarely associated with complete criteria for additional diagnoses.

Differential diagnosis. Borderline Personality Disorder preempts the diagnosis of Identity Disorder, provided the Personality Disorder is pervasive and the symptoms are not limited to the patient's developmental stage. Cyclothymia is characterized by affective instability, but Borderline Personality Disorder is rarely associated with hypomania. Both disorders may be present in some patients.

Diagnostic criteria for Borderline Personality Disorder:

A. A pervasive pattern of instability of mood, interpersonal relationships, and self-image, beginning by early adulthood and present in a variety of contexts, as indicated by at least *five* of the following:

1. a pattern of unstable and intense interpersonal relationships characterized by alternating between extremes of idealization and devaluation

2. impulsiveness in at least two areas that are potentially self-damaging (e.g., spending money, sex, substance use, shoplifting, eating disturbance, recklessness), *not including* suicidal or self-mutilating behavior covered in "5," below

3. affective instability (i.e., marked shifts from baseline mood to depression, irritability, or anxiety), usually lasting only a few hours

4. inappropriate, intense anger or lack of control of anger

5. recurrent suicidal or self-mutilating threats, gestures, or behavior

6. marked and persistent identity disturbance manifested by uncertainty about at least *two* of the following:
   a. self-image
   b. sexual orientation
   c. long-term goals or career choice
   d. type of friends desired
   e. preferred values

7. chronic feelings of emptiness or boredom

8. frantic efforts to avoid real or imagined abandonment (*not including* the suicidal or self-mutilating behavior covered in "5," above)

Histrionic Personality Disorder (Hysterical Personality) (301.50)

Essential feature. A pervasive pattern of excessive emotionally and attention seeking. Emotions are often inappropriately exaggerated in response to minor stimuli. Patients are sometimes physically seductive and at other times more obviously attempting to gain the attention, caring, and regard that is the underlying object of their physical/pseudosexual seductive behavior.

132 When the phrase "attention seeking" is used in describing these individuals, one is not referring so much to a "look at me" wish as to a need for others to *attend to* and have regard for him or her.

Associated features. Attempts to control other persons while establishing a dependent relationship with them are common, as are expressions of romantic fantasy. The actual quality of emotional and sexual relationships is often somewhat immature. Somatization and occasional dissociation are not uncommon.

Differential diagnosis. In Somatization Disorder the physical complaints dominate the clinical picture. Some patients with Somatization Disorder or other Somatoform Disorders (e.g., Conversion Disorder) also meet the criteria for Histrionic Personality Disorder. The diagnosis may also be made concomitantly with Borderline Personality Disorder. In Dependent Personality Disorder, one sees similar excessive dependency and wishes for praise and guidance, but without the exaggerated emotional features of this disorder. Narcissistic Personality Disorder implies a similar self-centeredness, but grandiosity and intense envy are the rule.

Diagnostic criteria for Histrionic Personality Disorder:

A. A pervasive pattern of excessive emotionality and attention seeking, beginning by early adulthood and present in a variety of contexts, as indicated by at least *four* of the following:

1. constantly seeks or demands reassurance, approval, or praise
2. is inappropriately sexually seductive in appearance or behavior
3. is overly concerned with physical attractiveness
4. expresses emotion with inappropriate exaggeration
5. is uncomfortable in situations in which he or she is not the center of attention

6. displays rapidly shifting and shallow expression of emotions
7. is self-centered, with actions directed toward obtaining imme- diate satisfaction, and little or no tolerance for frustration/ delayed gratification
8. has a style of conversation that is excessively impressionistic and lacks detail (e.g., when asked to describe something the person can be no more specific than "it was fantastic" or "she was a lovely person")

Narcissistic Personality Disorder (301.81)

Essential feature. A pervasive pattern of grandiosity (in fantasy or in behavior), hypersensitivity to others' evaluations and criticisms of oneself, and lack of empathy. Feeling and professing grandiosity may alternate with (or lead to) an exaggerated feeling of failure when one does not live up to the expected perfection. Although there are fantasies of great success, brilliance, or beauty (with envy of those who are truly successful), reality is often quite different. Many such patients do attain significant achieve- ments; however, they rarely accept them as "enough" or derive genuine pleasure from them.

Self-esteem, while outwardly appearing high, is actually quite fragile, with a need for constant attention and admiration. Close relationships, including relationships with spouses or psychotherapists, invariably suffer, whether from lack of empathy, unreasonable expectations of continu- ously "special" treatment, or the unreasonable expectation that the other person will supply the patient's needs perfectly.

Associated features. Features of other Personality Disorders are often present, and sometimes more than one Personality Disorder diagnosis is warranted. Adjustment Disorders, generally associated with depression and frustration, are common. Psychotic Disorders, such as Brief Reactive Psychosis, occasionally occur, as do significant Mood Disorders as the person becomes older and narcissistic expectations are more often frustrated.

Differential diagnosis. Several of the Personality Disorders, such as Borderline, Histrionic, and Antisocial Personality Disorder, frequently present similar symptoms. Multiple diagnosis is occasionally indicated; at other times, careful attention to the diagnostic criteria will allow differentiation (or may suggest Personality Disorder Not Otherwise Specified, a category that includes the former DSM-III "Mixed Personality Disorder").

Diagnostic criteria for Narcissistic Personality Disorder:

133   A. Pervasive pattern of grandiosity (in fantasy or behavior), lack of empathy, and hypersensitivity to the evaluation of others, beginning by early adulthood and present in a variety of contexts, as indicated by at least *five* of the following:

    1. reacts to criticism with feelings of rage, shame, or humiliation (even if not expressed)

    2. is interpersonally exploitative (i.e., takes advantage of others to achieve his or her own ends)

    3. has a grandiose sense of self-importance (e.g., exaggerates achievements and talents, expects to be treated as "special" without appropriate achievement)

    4. believes that his or her problems are unique and can be understood only by other special people (or people who see his or her specialness)

    5. is preoccupied with fantasies of unlimited success, power, brilliance, beauty, or ideal love

    6. has a sense of entitlement (i.e., an unreasonable expectation of favorable treatment)

    7. requires constant attention and admiration to bolster self-esteem

    8. has a lack of empathy (i.e., inability to recognize and experience how others feel)

    9. is preoccupied with feelings of envy

CLUSTER C

Avoidant Personality Disorder (301.82)

Essential feature. A pervasive pattern of social discomfort, fear of negative evaluation, and timidness. These individuals are usually unwilling to enter into relationships without strong guarantees of unrelenting acceptance. Since this is difficult to attain, they often have very few close friends or confidants. Their social avoidance often prevents otherwise rewarding situations (e.g., job promotions).

Associated features. The patient may appear to have general or specific phobias and may exhibit depression, anxiety, or anger at himself or herself for what is perceived as a lack of social success.

Predisposing factors. Avoidant Disorder of Childhood or Adolescence is associated with later development of this disorder. Disfigurement related to congenital factors, injury, or physical illness may predispose one to avoidant behavior; however, the clinician should be careful to evaluate the patient on the basis of the specific diagnostic criteria below.

Differential diagnosis. Schizoid Personality Disorder is characterized by little desire for social involvement and an indifference to criticism. In Social Phobias, the phobic situation is usually specific, rather than involving personal relationships. Avoidant Personality Disorder preempts the diagnosis of Avoidant Disorder of Childhood or Adolescence, provided the criteria for the Personality Disorder are met, the disturbance is sufficiently pervasive and persistent, and it appears not to be limited to a specific developmental stage.

Diagnostic criteria for Avoidant Personality Disorder:

A. A pervasive pattern of social discomfort, fear of negative evaluation, and timidness, beginning by early adulthood and present in a variety of contexts, as indicated by at least *four* of the following:

1. is easily hurt by criticism or disapproval
2. has no more than one close friend or confidant, other than first-degree relatives
3. is unwilling to get involved with people unless certain of being liked
4. avoids social or occupational activities that involve significant interpersonal contact
5. is reticent in social situations because of the fear of saying something inappropriate or foolish, or being unable to answer a question
6. fears being embarrassed by blushing, crying, or showing signs of anxiety in front of other people
7. exaggerates the potential difficulties, physical dangers, or risks involved in doing something outside his or her usual routine (but otherwise ordinary)

Dependent Personality Disorder (301.60)

Essential feature. A pervasive pattern of dependence and submissive behavior.

Associated features. Symptoms of other Personality Disorders are common, as are anxiety and depression. Self-deprecation is common in these individuals and is generally aimed at getting others to care for them or take over their lives.

Predisposing factors. Chronic physical illness and Separation Anxiety Disorder may be predisposing factors.

Differential diagnosis. Although dependent behavior is common in Agoraphobia, there is little other similarity.

Diagnostic criteria for Dependent Personality Disorder:

A. A pervasive pattern of dependent and submissive behavior, beginning by early adulthood and present in a variety of contexts, as indicated by at least *five* of the following:

1. is unable to make everyday decisions without an excessive amount of advice or reassurance from others
2. allows others to make most of his or her important decisions (e.g., about living arrangements or work)
3. agrees with people even when he or she believes they are wrong, because of a fear of being rejected or abandoned
4. has difficulty initiating projects or doing things on his or her own
5. volunteers to do things that are unpleasant or demeaning, in order to get others to like him or her
6. feels uncomfortable or helpless when alone and goes to great lengths to avoid being alone
7. feels helpless, or even devastated, when close relationships are terminated
8. is frequently preoccupied with fears of being abandoned
9. is easily hurt by criticism or disapproval

Obsessive Compulsive Personality Disorder (301.40)

Essential features. Pervasive perfectionism and inflexibility. The patient's overly strict, often unattainable standards frequently interfere with completion of tasks or projects, although he or she strives for perfection.

Preoccupation with rules, efficiency, or trivia interferes with the ability to take a broad view of situations. There is often a preoccupation with work, to the exclusion of pleasure and interpersonal relationships. Logic and intellect are frequently substituted for affective behavior (for which there may be little tolerance, particularly to affect in others). One may fantasize about relaxation, pleasure, or finishing a task; however, such goals and rewards are often postponed in favor of focus on the form or process of the work. Decision making is difficult and fraught with ambivalence and avoidance. Harsh judgments of oneself and others are common.

Associated features. Associated features include complaints of difficulty expressing tender feelings (often expressed in distress or complaints about being "unable to love"). Depression is fairly common, as is frustration when the patient's strong need to be in control of both self and environment is thwarted.

Complications. In addition to psychiatric complications, such as Obsessive Compulsive Disorder, Mood Disorder, or Hypochondriasis, the "Type A" personality traits sometimes associated with increased incidence of myocardial infarction are frequently found in individuals with Obsessive Compulsive Personality Disorder.

Differential diagnosis. Obsessive Compulsive Disorder, by definition, includes true obsessions and compulsions, which are *not present* in this Personality Disorder. Some patients fill criteria for both diagnoses, in which case both should be coded. **134**

Diagnostic criteria for Obsessive Compulsive Personality Disorder:

A. A pervasive pattern of perfectionism and inflexibility, beginning by early adulthood and present in a variety of contexts, as indicated by at least *five* of the following:
   1. perfectionism that interferes with task completion
   2. preoccupation with details, rules, lists, order, organization, or schedules to the extent that the major point of the activity is lost
   3. unreasonable insistence that others submit to exactly his or her way of doing things, *or* unreasonable reluctance to allow others to do things because of a conviction that they will not do them correctly

4. excessive devotion to work and productivity, to the exclusion of leisure activities and friendships (but not related to obvious economic necessity)

5. indecisiveness, in which decision making is either avoided, postponed, or protracted. This does not include indecisiveness related to excessive need for advice or reassurance from others

6. overconscientiousness, excessive scrupulousness, and inflexibility about matters of morality, ethics, or values (not accounted for by accepted cultural or religious identification)

7. restricted expression of affection

8. lack of generosity in giving time, money, or gifts, when no personal gain is likely to result

9. inability to discard worn-out or worthless objects, even when they have no sentimental value

Passive Aggressive Personality Disorder (301.84)

Essential feature. A pervasive pattern of passive resistance to demands for adequate social and occupational performance. The resistance is expressed indirectly rather than directly and leads to social and occupational ineffectiveness, even when more assertive and effective behavior is clearly possible. It is assumed that these individuals are passively expressing covert or unconscious aggression or can only carry out normal aggressive impulses in a passive way. They obstruct others' efforts and are often seen as resistive, procrastinating, stubborn, or forgetful. Other people often infer that they are behaving in this way on purpose (particularly since the behavior is chronic), or at least feel frustrated by them.

Associated features. Expressions of pessimism, without realizing that their own behavior has created their difficulties, are typical, as are dependency and lowered self-confidence.

Predisposing factors. There is some evidence that Oppositional Defiant Disorder in childhood or adolescence predisposes one to Passive Aggressive Personality Disorder.

Differential diagnosis. The symptoms may be similar to those of Oppositional Defiant Disorder, which preempts the diagnosis for patients under 18. As in the case of other Personality Disorders, some of the symptoms (in this case passive aggressive maneuvers) are seen in normal people from time to time.

Diagnostic criteria for Passive Aggressive Personality Disorder:

A. A pervasive pattern of passive resistance to demands for adequate social and occupational performance, beginning by early adulthood and present in a variety of contexts, as indicated by at least *five* of the following:
   1. procrastinates
   2. becomes sulky, irritable, or argumentative when asked to do something he or she does not want to do
   3. seems to work deliberately slowly or to do a bad job on tasks that he or she does not want to do
   4. protests, without justification, that others make unreasonable demands on him or her
   5. frequently avoids obligations by claiming to have "forgotten"
   6. believes (or at least states) that he or she is doing a much better job than others think
   7. resents useful suggestions from others concerning how he or she could be more productive
   8. obstructs the efforts of others by failing to do his or her share of the work
   9. unreasonably criticizes or scorns people who are in positions of authority

Personality Disorder Not Otherwise Specified (301.90)
This is a residual category for patients not classifiable as having any of the specific Personality Disorders above, yet who have pervasive, persistent personality traits, beginning by early adulthood and present in a variety of contexts, which cause significant social, academic, or occupational impairment or subjective distress. Such disorders may contain features of several Personality Disorders but not be sufficient for any specific one.

When requirements of pervasiveness, breadth of presentation, chronicity, and impairment or distress are met, this NOS category may be used to describe other personality syndromes not listed as Personality Disorders in DSM-III-R (e.g., impulsive, immature, self-defeating, or sadistic personality disorder), based on the clinician's judgment. In such instances, the clinician should note the specific disorder in parentheses, in a form such as "Personality Disorder NOS (Self-defeating Personality Disorder) (301.90)."

DIFFERENCES BETWEEN DSM-III AND DSM-III-R PERSONALITY DISORDERS

- The DSM-III-R Diagnostic Criteria format is more consistent from disorder to disorder, and current and long-term functioning are more specifically defined.
- "Restricted affectivity" is no longer a requirement for *Paranoid Personality Disorder* and has been added to *Schizoid Personality Disorder*.
- *Schizoid Personality Disorder* may now be considered in childhood and concomitantly with *Schizotypal Personality Disorder*.
- Odd, eccentric, or peculiar behavior or appearance has been added to the list of possible criteria for *Schizotypal Personality Disorder*.
- References to suicidal behavior have been removed from possible criteria for *Histrionic Personality Disorder*, further differentiating it from *Borderline Personality Disorder*, and a reference to characteristic style of speech has been added.
- Preoccupation with envy has been included in the possible criteria for *Narcissistic Personality Disorder*.
- For *Antisocial Personality Disorder*, an item has been added to describe absence of guilt or remorse.
- *Avoidant Personality Disorder* has been significantly redefined to highlight its phobic characteristics (cf., "phobic character") rather than response to rejection. It may now be diagnosed concomitantly with *Schizoid Personality Disorder*.
- Lack of self-confidence was felt to be insufficiently specific as an item defining *Dependent Personality Disorder* and was deleted.
- DSM-III's "Compulsive Personality Disorder" has been renamed *Obsessive Compulsive Personality Disorder*, as this better describes the clinical entity.
- *Passive Aggressive Personality Disorder* may now be diagnosed in the presence of other Personality Disorders.
- Atypical, Mixed, or Other Personality Disorder is now *Personality Disorder NOS*.

CASE VIGNETTES

Case Example 1

A 41-year-old office clerk complains that she has unfairly been passed over for promotion by a boss and a civil service system that are, in her words, "incredibly stupid." She has sought information from others about why she hasn't gotten bonuses or promotions, even though her department is quite productive. She resents and belittles their observations that she is always late with her work and slows down office projects by always being the last person finished. She feel she is last because she is always given the hardest, most odious tasks; her co-workers disagree.

She is intelligent and truly feels she is doing a very good job, but she has received mediocre performance ratings from every department in which she has worked. The managers of the government agency for which she works would prefer to fire her, but are reluctant to do so since she has worked in the same, obstructive, way for longer than any of them has been with the agency.

Discussion

There is no indication of inability to do her work or of more significant paranoia. No mention was made of transient (e.g., V code) occupational problems or Axis I symptoms; rather, the problem is chronic and pervasive and fits the relevant Axis II criteria. Deferred Axis I diagnosis (799.90) would be correct as well.

Diagnosis

> Axis I   V71.09   No diagnosis or condition
> Axis II   301.84   Passive Aggressive Personality Disorder

Case Example 2

For as long as the local residents can remember, this 56-year-old, single high-school graduate has lived alone a couple of miles outside of town. Although often seen along the road, and occasionally in town, he doesn't frequent the local bars or cafés and has never been known to socialize. He makes his living fixing things, at which he is quite adept, but chooses not to open a shop in town. He seems indifferent to praise, advice, or complaints from his customers, generally answering with a nondescript shrug and continuing his work. He has never been married and did not attend either his sister's wedding or his parents' funerals, all of which occurred within the county. When passersby offer greetings or friendly conversation, he remains aloof, barely acknowledging their comments. He has no complaints or psychiatric symptoms which trouble him. He has never been in trouble with the law and has had no known hallucinations, delusions, or psychiatric treatment.

Discussion
The chronic, pervasive personality disorder has some paranoid and avoidant characteristics, but the diagnosis is quite clear. There is no indication of an accompanying Axis I disorder.

Diagnosis

Axis I V71.09 No diagnosis or condition
Axis II 301.20 Schizoid Personality Disorder

Chapter 27

V Codes for Conditions Not Attributable to a Mental Disorder That Are a Focus of Attention or Treatment

These categories, which should not be listed as "diagnoses" or as evidence of mental illness, fill a need for description of conditions which reasonably are of clinical interest, or which require attention or treatment. The V-code listings correspond to the ICD-9-CM "Supplementary Classification," as relevant for psychiatrists. They are briefly addressed in DSM-III-R.   **136**

Other V codes, as well as "E codes," are listed in ICD-9-CM. Some of those which are useful in clinical practice, but are not in DSM-III-R, are listed in the next chapter.

Academic Problem (V62.30)
This category is appropriate when the focus of attention or treatment is an academic problem not apparently due to a mental disorder (e.g., underachievement in the absence of a Specific Developmental Disorder or other clinical explanation for the problem).

Adult Antisocial Behavior (V71.01)
This code implies antisocial—e.g., criminal—behavior not due to a mental disorder.   **137**

Borderline Intellectual Functioning (V40.00)
Note: Coded on Axis II.

This category is appropriate for individuals whose intellectual functioning appears to be between that of normal and mentally retarded individuals. The generally accepted "borderline" range is a measured IQ of 71 to 84. Differential diagnosis with mental retardation may be difficult, particularly when there are social or clinical factors that make meaningful measurement of intelligence difficult (e.g., presence of mental illness, language difficulties, or cultural differences between the individual and the evaluator).

Childhood or Adolescent Antisocial Behavior (V71.02)
This category is appropriate when antisocial behavior, including criminal behavior, in a child or adolescent is apparently not due to mental disorder and does not fit criteria for any DSM-III-R diagnosis.

Malingering (V65.20)
138 Malingering implies intentional faking or gross exaggeration of physical and/or psychological symptoms, which is motivated by a clear expectation of personal gain (e.g., money, avoiding work, evading criminal prosecution, obtaining drugs). It should be differentiated from Factitious Disorder by the presence of external incentives (rather than the intrapsychic ones of Factitious Disorder). It should also be differentiated from the several Dissociative and Somatoform Disorders (q.v.).

DSM-III-R lists four items that should lead the clinician to suspect malingering. This Training Guide urges caution when actually coding Malingering. The four items are:

1. Medicolegal context of presentation (e.g., referral by an attorney).
2. Marked discrepancy between the person's claimed stress or disability and the objective findings.
3. Lack of cooperation during the diagnostic evaluation and in complying with the prescribed treatment regimen.
4. Presence of Antisocial Personality Disorder.

Marital Problem (V61.10)
This category should be used when the focus of attention or treatment is a marital problem that is apparently not due to a mental disorder. Marital conflict in itself should not be considered mental illness.

Noncompliance with Medical Treatment (V15.81)
This category may be used when the focus of attention or treatment is refusal of medical treatment, perhaps related to religious beliefs, personal value judgments about the risks and benefits of treatment, or simply

disagreement with medical recommendations. This category should not be used if the noncompliance appears to be due to a mental disorder.

Occupational Problem (V62.20)
This category is used when the focus of attention or treatment is occupational, such as dissatisfaction with one's job, and apparently not due to a mental disorder.

Parent-Child Problem (V61.20)
This category may be used, for example, for conflict between a healthy child or adolescent and his or her parents which falls within the normal range of developmental experiences.

Other Interpersonal Problem (V62.81)
This category may be used, for example, for counseling concerning difficulties with co-workers or "romantic partners."

Other Specified Family Circumstances (V61.80)
This category may be used when the focus of attention or treatment is a family circumstance not apparently due to a mental disorder, but not a parent-child or a marital problem. Interpersonal difficulties with other relatives are examples.

Phase of Life Problem or Other Life Circumstance Problem (V62.89)
Examples of some problems that might be listed here include those associated with going to a new school, leaving home, beginning a new career, or adapting to retirement.

Uncomplicated Bereavement (V62.82)
This category should be used to describe normal reactions to significant loss, particularly the death of a loved one. Depressive syndromes may be normal in such situations, but appropriate handling of feelings and situations by the individual, over time, with normal resolution of the symptoms, should preclude diagnosis of a mental disorder and suggest a V code. It should be noted that "normal" feelings, behaviors, and durations of grief vary considerably in different cultural groups.

DIFFERENCES BETWEEN DSM-III AND DSM-III-R V CODES

- *Borderline Intellectual Functioning* is now coded on Axis II.

CASE VIGNETTE

A 40-year-old man has been arrested for the fifteenth time since he finished high school, this time for armed robbery. He was on parole when he committed the alleged offense. He has never held a job, other than criminal behavior, for more than six months. He has been married and divorced twice and has often been cited for failure to pay child support. He gets into fights often, both when intoxicated and when sober. He is impulsive and irresponsible, and at one time he traveled with a partner from town to town robbing filling stations and convenience stores. Although a frequent drinker and known to be a former user of marijuana and amphetamines, he denies alcohol or drug problems at present. Further information about substance abuse is being sought.

As a child and adolescent, he was considered intelligent and prone to manipulate others to get his way. He graduated from high school with good marks and attendance, was arrested once (for possession of alcohol) at age 16, and was not known to be particularly dishonest, cruel, or aggressive.

Discussion

The lack of antisocial behavior or clear-cut conduct disorder before age 15 eliminates Antisocial Personality. Although no other specified DSM-III-R Personality Disorder appears likely, the pervasive, maladaptive quality of this person's behavior and lifestyle, and his marked social impairment, make an "NOS" Axis II diagnosis tempting. One should be cautious about equating a Personality Disorder diagnosis with "mental illness" in chronically antisocial people, especially when it may be used to excuse them from responsibility for their behavior. A "deferred" (799.90) or "no diagnosis" (V71.09) Axis II code could also be defended.

There is insufficient information for an Axis I diagnosis of Psychoactive Substance Use Disorder, but it is probable, and further information is being sought.

V Code Condition

      Axis I V71.01 Adult Antisocial Behavior
               799.90 Diagnosis or condition deferred
      Axis II 301.90 Personality Disorder Not Otherwise Specified

Chapter 28

Additional DSM-III-R Codes

The clinician should not hesitate to use the following codes when clinical information is insufficient to make an accurate diagnostic judgment, or when no diagnostic criteria are met. **139**

Unspecified Mental Disorder (Nonpsychotic) (300.90)
This category should be used when the clinician feels that a mental disorder is present, and when enough information is available to rule out a psychotic disorder but further specification is not possible. It is a residual category. The diagnosis may later be changed to a specific disorder. This category may also be used for specific mental disorders not included in DSM-III-R, provided the clinician exercises careful diagnostic judgment.

No Diagnosis or Condition on Axis I (V71.09)
This category should be used when no Axis I diagnosis is felt to be present, and there is sufficient clinical information to make this judgment. There may or may not be an Axis II diagnosis or condition.

Diagnosis or Condition Deferred on Axis I (799.90)
This category should be used when there is insufficient information to make any diagnostic judgment concerning an Axis I diagnosis or condition.

No Diagnosis on Axis II (V71.09)
This category should be used when no Axis II diagnosis is felt to be present, and there is sufficient clinical information to make this judgment. There may or may not be an Axis I diagnosis or condition.

Diagnosis Deferred on Axis II (799.90)
This category is used when there is insufficient information to make a diagnostic judgment about an Axis II diagnosis.

CHANGES BETWEEN DSM-III AND DSM-III-R ADDITIONAL CODES

- DSM-III-R has included an appendix with three "Proposed Diagnostic Categories": *"Late Luteal Phase Dysphoric Disorder," "Self-defeating Personality Disorder,"* and *"Sadistic Personality Disorder."*

Appendix I:
Additional Case Vignettes

The following case vignettes illustrate the use of all five DSM-III-R axes in clinical situations. The examples are written to illustrate clearly one to three disorders, on Axes I and/or II, with little ambiguity so long as one carefully uses the DSM-III-R concepts and criteria.

CASE VIGNETTE 1

On a routine visit to the apartment of Mr. R., a 29-year-old man, a welfare worker notes that his daily living skills are impaired and he struggles to maintain personal independence and self-sufficiency. The welfare worker's notes indicate that Mr. R.'s household functioning has always been at about this level.

Mr. R. had generalized delays in intellectual and social development, but grossly normal developmental stages once they were reached. His full-scale "IQ" was measured as 56 at age seven and 64 at age 13. He is otherwise physically healthy, and has not required medical care for years.

He was told a few weeks ago that the sheltered workshop where he is employed will soon be closing. He will be transferred to a workshop further from home, in an unfamiliar part of town. The welfare worker notes that he is quite worried and nervous about his change, feels hopeless about his ability to adapt to it, cries while the welfare worker is there, and has often skipped work since hearing the news. His work record had been almost spotless since starting his job three years ago.

Discussion

There is a recent identifiable psychosocial stressor, with an excessive, maladaptive reaction. Although Mr. R. apparently has not really lost his job, he fears the consequences of the job change.

The symptoms includes anxiety, depression, and conduct disturbance (e.g., avoiding work). There is no mention of chronic or more pervasive symptoms which might indicate other mood or behavior disorders. The symptoms of social and intellectual deficit began before age 18 and involve general (not specific, as in the Specific Developmental Disorders) delays in normal development. Development proceeded in a routine fashion except for those delays, differentiating this disorder from the Pervasive Developmental Disorders.

Mr. R.'s global functioning was stable, although not optimal, until he recently became more upset and his job attendance and behavior began to deteriorate.

Diagnosis

Axis I	309.40	Adjustment Disorder with Mixed Disturbance of Emotions and Conduct
Axis II	317.00	Mental Retardation, Mild
Axis III		No known diagnosis
Axis IV		Psychosocial stressor: job change
		Severity: 3—moderate (acute event)
Axis V		Current GAF: 45; highest GAF in past year: 60

CASE VIGNETTE 2

A 24-year-old man, Mr. S., is referred by a urologist after requesting sex reassignment surgery. He describes being very uncomfortable with his male sexuality, at least since adolescence. He regularly dresses in female attire and recalls his mother dressing him as a girl when he was very young. She thought he looked "cute" and once showed him off to her friends. Mr. S. has used hormones for several years, both prescribed and illicit, to feminize his physical features. He blames his lack of success at becoming "the woman of my dreams" for the almost continuous depression he has felt since adolescence, with insomnia, lack of energy, and pessimism regarding hopes for a rewarding life.

The patient has a number of effeminate and histrionic characteristics, but does not appear to meet criteria for any DSM-III-R Personality Disorder.

Mr. S. is employed as a waiter in an expensive restaurant. He engages in social activities with both heterosexuals and overt homosexuals and occasionally has homosexual liaisons. He is most comfortable when "in drag" and has picked up men who did not know his true sex. This behavior is somewhat dangerous; he has been beaten up twice this year.

He lost a very close friend to AIDS a few months ago, and his father died during the past year. Although no longer grieving, he feels quite alone much of the time. He worries a lot about AIDS.

The urologist reports that Mr. S. was found to have nonspecific urethritis and prostatitis. He takes anticonvulsant medication to control seizures which began after he was beaten two years ago.

Discussion

The cross-dressing is associated with a chronic wish to change sex, differentiating it from Gender Identity Disorder of Adolescence or Adulthood and from Transvestic Fetishism. There is no mention of psychosis or delusions to indicate Schizophrenia or a similar disorder. The chronic depression meets criteria for Dysthymia, appears to be secondary to the Transsexualism, and apparently started before age 21.

The "severe" level of psychosocial stressors is the result of the combination of losses and assaults the patient has sustained; some clinicians might consider the combination to reach "extreme" proportions. His Global Assessment of Functioning reflects the dangers to which he exposes himself, in spite of his socializing, lack of reported suicidal ideation, and ability to keep a good job. The "highest level in past year" figure is somewhat arbitrary in this case; he has apparently not been much better than he is at present.

Diagnosis

Axis I   302.50   Transsexualism, "Unspecified"
           300.40   Dysthymia, Secondary Type, Early Onset
Axis II   V71.09   No diagnosis on Axis II, but histrionic traits
Axis III   Epilepsy, probably traumatic, by history
                  Prostatitis and urethritis, nonspecific
Axis IV   Psychosocial stressors: Deaths of father and close friend, assaults, epilepsy
                  Severity: 4 — severe (predominantly acute)
Axis V   Current GAF: 55; highest level in past year: 65

CASE VIGNETTE 3

Ms. T. is a fairly attractive, 34-year-old woman who presents to a community mental health center for evaluation. She recently saw a television program about biological treatments for depression and feels she has many of the symptoms mentioned. During an interview she reports frequent dysphoria, with chronic feelings that reflect more emptiness and boredom than depression. She has no trouble sleeping, has a good appetite, and rarely cries, "except when I get mad." She has had no manic or hypomanic episodes.

A friend, supplying corroborating history, reports that Ms. T. often gets angry. During these times, she is childishly demanding, drives recklessly, and has taken or threatened overdoses a number of times. She has also cut her wrists, superficially, "just to *feel* something." She has children aged 11 and 14, who often seem to take care of her more than she takes care of them. She has "been like this all her life."

She feels depressed at times, but says her moods shift frequently (sometimes every few hours or so) from depression to anxiety to being so irritable that "three husbands couldn't take it and left." At other times, she says that *she* was the person who left the marriages, because of chronic uncertainty about her goals, values, and marital needs. She says she has met a lot of men she thought would make princelike husbands, but "they turned out to be frogs."

Ms. T. has seen many general and psychiatric physicians over the years, who have prescribed various psychotropic medications. She was in a mental hospital for six days a few years ago because "I just went crazy. I needed some time to think." She has gotten large prescriptions for benzodiazepine anxiolytics "and a lot of stuff like Valium," which she has taken for "nerves." She admits that she often takes more than she should, "to block everything out," in spite of several warnings from her employers and friends about overuse.

Ms. T. lost her last job — she is a licensed vocational nurse — after six months of employment, because she "couldn't take the B.S." She has been looking for another job for several months. She has many financial problems: her ex-husband refuses to pay her alimony and child support, and she had to move into a rented mobile home about six months ago.

Discussion

Ms. T. has a lifelong, pervasive, maladaptive personality pattern best described as "Borderline." Although she is uncomfortable much of the time, her dysphoria seems related to her personality disorder. She does not fit criteria for any specific mood disorder, nor is there any stressor specifically associated with onset of her symptoms which would make Adjustment Disorder an appropriate diagnosis. She has a number of "enduring" psychosocial stressors.

Diagnosis

Axis I	305.40	Benzodiazepine Abuse
Axis II	301.83	Borderline Personality Disorder
Axis III		No diagnosis apparent
Axis IV		Psychosocial stressors: unemployment, financial problems, change of residence
		Severity: 4 — severe (predominantly enduring)
Axis V		Current GAF: 55; highest level in past year: 60

CASE VIGNETTE 4

Ms. U., a 33-year-old lawyer, has had recurrent bouts of depression every two or three years, during which she has several months of anhedonia, terminal insomnia, difficulty concentrating, strong feelings that she is a terrible attorney, and thoughts of suicide. Between depressive episodes, she has few affective symptoms, is very successful in her practice, and enjoys a good marriage and family life.

Ms. U. began to get depressed again a month ago. Her psychiatrist prescribed an antidepressant, imipramine. Instead of improving over several weeks as in the past, she rapidly became psychotic, with initially euphoric mood, followed by unreasonable anger and irritability. Her need for sleep decreased to only two or three hours a night, with no indication of fatigue. She began to go to her office very late at night and to call clients at odd hours, telling them that she had "wonderful" ideas for solving the state's economic problems through "megamergers." This behavior quickly threatened her practice and strained her home life, and she was hospitalized.

Physical examination was negative except for essential hypertension, which has been controlled with a mild diuretic. There is no indication that her symptoms are caused or affected by the diuretic, environmental exposures, or intercurrent physical illness (such as viral infection). Careful thyroid evaluation reveals normal functioning. There is no history of substance abuse.

Ms. U. has had no major losses or life changes during the past year. Her recent depressive episode does not seem to be related to external stress or to season of the year. Her father had "mood swings," drank a lot, and died several years ago in an auto accident.

Discussion
Ms. U. initially met criteria only for Major Depression, Recurrent, but an underlying predisposition to Bipolar Disorder has apparently manifested itself in a manic episode. The fact that it was precipitated by antidepressant treatment does not indicate an Organic Mental Disorder. Careful efforts to find physical illness or psychosocial stressors related to the acute manic psychosis were unsuccessful. Although currently functioning poorly, she has been free of symptoms within the past year.

Diagnosis

Axis I	296.42	Bipolar Disorder, Manic, moderate (current exacerbation precipitated by antidepressant medication)
Axis II	V71.09	No diagnosis
Axis III		Essential hypertension, mild, in remission
Axis IV		Psychosocial stressors: none apparent relevant to this disorder
		Severity—1
Axis V		Current GAF: 31; highest in past year: 90

CASE VIGNETTE 5
Ms. V. is a 56-year-old woman with a long history of alcohol abuse in which she drinks heavily and continuously, is intoxicated most of the time, has a high tolerance for alcohol, and has been unable to work (and would rather drink than work) for several years. She presented to the county "detox" facility four weeks ago. Her withdrawal from alcohol was stormy, in spite of clinical monitoring, although seizures and "DTs" were prevented. She has received large doses of thiamine and nutritional supplements since admission, and she is soon to be discharged from a four-week rehabilitation program.

Her physical evaluation reveals significant elevations in hepatic function tests, mild scleral jaundice, an enlarged liver, mild ataxia, positive Romberg test, and multiple healing scrapes and excoriations. A heavy smoker, she has trouble catching her breath and has a decreased timed, forced expiratory volume. There are no signs of significant heart disease.

The program staff notice continuing confusion and social impairment, manifested by short- and long-term memory deficits, inability to plan reasonably for her discharge, poor judgment in day-to-day matters, and significant disturbances in her ability to name common items and "find the right word" in conversation. The staff is pessimistic about her ability to live independently, although she does not require constant supervision.

During the past year, Ms. V. has lived in rooming houses and, for a while when her welfare check was delayed, on the street. She does not recall any significant acute psychosocial stressors. Her memory deficit and the complex relationship of her chronic drinking pattern to possible signs of other disorders make further diagnosis difficult at this time. She denies abusing other substances, severe depression or anxiety, and mental hospitalization other than for alcohol-related care. There are no family or friends to help in gathering further history.

Discussion

Ms. V. has continuing organic sequelae of chronic alcohol use and dependence. Her dementia persists after four weeks without alcohol and is not limited to memory impairment. If the dementia eventually remits and she is left with memory problems, she may meet criteria for Alcohol Amnestic Disorder. She does not currently show signs of delirium or hallucinosis.

The lack of clear past history regarding anything except drinking makes Axis II diagnosis impossible at this time. It cannot be said that she does not have a personality disorder, but only that the diagnosis must be deferred. Her poor, sometimes chaotic living conditions constitute severe, enduring psychosocial stressors which are pressed to "extreme" by the physical and emotional results of her alcoholism. Even after alcohol withdrawal and a rehabilitative program, her general functioning is seriously impaired by her dementia.

Diagnosis

Axis I	291.20	Dementia Associated with Alcoholism, moderate
	303.90	Alcohol Dependence, severe
Axis II	799.90	Diagnosis deferred
Axis III		Probable hepatic disease, alcohol-related
		Probable chronic obstructive pulmonary disease
Axis IV		Psychosocial stressors: poverty, dangerous living situation, ongoing serious illness
		Severity: 5 — extreme (predominantly enduring)
Axis V		Current GAF: 32; highest in past year: 32

CASE VIGNETTE 6

Jim, a 13-year-old boy, has been brought to a child guidance counselor. His mother, a recently divorced single parent, is concerned about a drop in average grades from "A" to "B" and wants to "stop trouble before it starts."

Jim is a likable boy, who blames the drop in grades on his transfer to a new school. He doesn't see many problems in his life, although he wishes to live with his father. He sleeps well, has many friends, and there have been no apparent changes in his interests, energy level, or the like. There have been no complaints from teachers or others about his behavior.

His mother perceives a few more problems, however. She disagrees with him about his choice of clothes and haircut (or lack thereof), although she admits their arguments rarely reach major proportions. She fears she will not be able to be "both mother and father" for him, particularly during his current puberty. She wants to be sure she isn't making Jim the recipient of her anger toward his father. She is an insightful woman, with no personal or family history of psychiatric problems.

Discussion

There is no indication of serious psychopathology in this young man, but his mother feels that his behavior—and particularly their parent-child relationship—deserves attention. It is important to avoid a false "diagnostic" label.

Diagnosis

Axis I	V61.20	Parent-Child Problem
Axis II	V71.09	No diagnosis on Axis II
Axis III		No diagnosis apparent
Axis IV		Psychosocial stressors: parental divorce
		Severity: 4—severe (acute)
Axis V		Current GAF: 80; highest in past year: 90

Appendix II: ICD-9-CM V Codes and E Codes Not Listed in DSM-III-R

These codes may be useful in certain administrative or research settings. Many others are listed in ICD-9-CM. **140**

ADDITIONAL V CODES

V11.x Personal history of mental disorder (not mood disorder or schizophrenia "in remission").   .0 = Schizophrenia; .1 = Affective Disorder;   .2 = Neurosis;   .3 = Alcoholism; .8 = Other mental disorder;   .9 = Unspecified mental disorder

V60.x Housing, household, or economic circumstances.   .x codes type of housing problem.

V62.0 Unemployment.

V62.1 Adverse effects of work environment.

V62.4 Social maladjustment, including deprivation, discrimination, isolation, or persecution.

V62.5 Legal circumstances, including imprisonment, investigation, litigation, or prosecution.

V62.9 Unspecified psychosocial circumstance.

V63.x Unavailability of other medical facilities for care.

V63.0 Residence remote from health care facility.

V63.2 Person awaiting admission to adequate health care facility elsewhere.

V65.x   Other persons seeking consultation without complaint or sickness.

V65.1   Person consulting on behalf of another person, e.g., for advice about an absent third party.

V65.4   Counseling not elsewhere specified, including explanation of findings, treatment plan, or medication; health education or advice.

V65.5   Person with feared complaint for whom no diagnosis was made.

V67.3   Follow-up examination following psychotherapy or other treatment for a mental disorder.

V68.0   Encounter for issuance of medical certificates, including fitness or incapacity (e.g., for work, school, or duty).

V68.2   Request for expert evidence.

V68.81 Encounter for referral without examination or treatment.

V68.9   Encounter for unspecified administrative purpose.

V70.1   General psychiatric examination, requested by authority.

V70.3   Other medical examination for administrative purpose, including immigration, licenses, adoption, marriage, insurance, school, sports.

V70.5   Health examination of defined subpopulation, including military persons, institution inhabitants, employees or job applicants, students.

V70.7   Examination for normal comparison or control in clinical research.

V79.x   Special screening for mental disorders and physical handicaps. .0 = Depression; .1 = Alcoholism; .2 = Mental Retardation; .3 = Early childhood developmental handicaps; .8 = Other, specified; .9 = Unspecified.

E CODES LISTED IN ICD-9-CM (DSM-III-R DOES NOT LIST E CODES)

E85x.x through E86x.x cover accidental poisoning (not suicide attempt), including poisoning by *accidental* taking or overdose of medications.

E850.x Analgesics, and so forth, including heroin, methadone.

E851   Barbiturates.

E852.x Sedatives, hypnotics.

E853.x Tranquilizers, including neuroleptics.

E854.x Other psychotropic agents, including antidepressants, stimulants, hallucinogens.

E855.x Other CNS-active drugs, including antiparkinsonian drugs.

E860.x Alcoholism not elsewhere specified.

E950 through E959 cover suicide, attempted suicide, and other intentionally self-inflicted injuries.

E950,1,2 Self-inflicted poisoning.

E953.x Hanging, other suffocation.

E954 Drowning.

E955.x Firearms and explosives.

E956 Cutting and piercing instrument.

E957.x Jumping from a high place.

E958.x Other or unspecified means.

E959 Late effects (one year or more after attempted injury).

E96x.x Injury caused by assault or otherwise purposely inflicted by another person (the patient is the victim).

E960.0 Unarmed fight, brawl.

E960.1 Rape.

E961–E969 Assault with weapon.

E965.x Firearm.

Glossary of Terms Used in DSM-III-R and in This Guide

Note: The names of specific mental disorders are defined in the text and are not listed in this glossary.

Abstracting, Abstracting Ability—Referring to one's ability to use abstract, symbolic thought, as differentiated from concrete or literal thought.

Acute—Current; currently visible; related to the present or recent past; not *chronic* (q.v.).

Affect—The outward, often facial, manifestation of subjective feelings or emotions.

Agnosia—An inability to recognize and name objects.

Agoraphobia—A morbid fear of, and intolerance for, unfamiliar surroundings or open spaces.

Akinesia—Lack of movement.

Alcoholism—Any of several syndromes (e.g., "gamma alcoholism"), sometimes culturally determined and often associated with alcohol dependence or alcohol abuse.

Ambivalence—Vacillation between/among two or more thoughts or feelings; indecision, perhaps to a pathological extent; also, coexistence of contradictory feelings or impulses toward something.

Amenorrhea—Absence of menses.

Anergia—Loss of strength or energy; feeling of loss of strength.

Anhedonia—An inability to experience pleasure.

Anorexia—Absence of appetite or eating; refusal to eat.

Anxiety—A feeling of apprehension or uneasiness, similar to fear, from the anticipation of internal or external danger. The source of the danger, in some definitions, is unknown. In psychoanalytic theory, the danger stems from threats (usually unconscious) to the ego.

Anxiolytic—Referring to the amelioration of anxiety; as a noun, a class of medications that alleviate anxiety.

Apathy—Marked lack of interest or motivation.

Aphasia—Inability to understand or produce language, not related to sensory (e.g., deafness) or motor (e.g., dysarthria) deficit.

Aphonia—Inability to speak or produce normal speech sounds.

Apraxia—Absence of a motor skill not explained by simple weakness or previously existing incoordination.

Arylcyclohexylamine—Any of a class of psychoactive substances which includes phencyclidine (PCP).

Associations—With respect to thought process, the relationship (normal or abnormal) between one idea or thought and the next (see "Tangential," "Loose," "Circumstantial," "Clang").

Asterixis—A neurological sign characterized by flapping of the hands, associated with toxic or metabolic encephalopathy.

Ataxia—Muscle incoordination, especially of gait.

Athetoid—Refers to slow, regular, twisting motion of limbs.

Autistic—Refers to autism (q.v., in text); referring to marked disturbances in relating to, and apparent unawareness of, others and one's environment.

Autonomic—Refers to normally involuntary innervation of cardiac and smooth muscle tissue (e.g., internal organs).

Belle Indifférence—An apparent indifference to symptoms that are expected to elicit worry or distress (also *"la belle indifférence"*).

Benzodiazepine—A class of antianxiety and hypnotic medication.

Bereavement—Grief over a loss.

Bestiality—See "Zoophilia"; also, the practice of sexual activity with nonhuman animals.

Biopsychosocial—Refers to the multideterminate nature of psychiatric syndromes and disorders and multideterminate approaches to their understanding and treatment.

Blocking—An interruption, caused by psychological factors unconscious or unknown to the individual, of one's communication before a thought or idea has been completed and preventing its completion.

Blunted—With respect to affect, marked reduction in normal intensity.

Bulimia—Episodic, usually uncontrollable, eating binges, sometimes accompanied by ingestion of large amounts of food. Self-induced vomiting or diarrhea is characteristic.

Butyrophenone—In psychopharmacology, a class of antipsychotic medications.

Caffeinism—An organic syndrome caused by (usually chronic) caffeine intoxication.

Cannabis—Marijuana.

Cardiac Neurosis—The fear or erroneous belief that one has heart disease; also, a feeling of physical incapacity related to past heart disease, out of proportion to one's actual disability, related to fear of having a heart attack.

Catalepsy—Diminished responsiveness, often trancelike; may be related to organic or functional disorders or hypnosis.

Cataplexy—Episodic loss of muscle tone, often to the extent of falling, triggered by strong emotions.

Catatonic—Refers to any of several marked motor anomalies, generally described as related to a psychosis, including excitement, stupor, rigidity, and waxy flexibility.

Cerea Flexibilitas—Waxy flexibility (q.v.).

Choreiform—Writhing.

Chronic—Long-lasting; not acute or limited to the present.

Circadian—Referring to one day (24 hours), especially 24-hour biological rhythms.

Circumstantial—When referring to thought process, describes conversation or a train of thought that wanders from the point, but eventually returns to it.

Clairvoyance—The experience or feeling of being able to sense others' thoughts (not usually considered psychotic).

Clang—With respect to associations or thought process, speech or train of thought largely governed by sound or rhyme, rather than by logic (e.g., "Turn on the light, bright; bright enough to bite. Watch out for biting dogs.").

Complex Tics—Tics that involve more extensive behaviors than simple motor tics (e.g., grooming behaviors, coprolalia).

Complication—A feature or characteristic, often separate from the natural course of the disorder or illness, which worsens it or otherwise interferes with treatment.

Compulsion—A repetitive, purposeful behavior performed in response to an obsession, with certain rules, or stereotypically, even against the performer's wishes.

Concordant—In genetics, refers to two genetically related (especially twin) animals or people with the same characteristic or trait.

Concrete—Referring to literal thought, as differentiated from abstract, symbolic thought.

Confabulation—Creation of inaccurate memories or fabrications, unconsciously, to substitute for unrecalled events.

Congenital—Present at birth (but not implying genetic or familial transmission).

Conjugal—Refers to marital, especially sexual, relationships.

Constricted—With respect to affect, a reduction or circumscribing of range and/or intensity.

Constructional Apraxia—Loss of the ability to produce or copy drawings, shapes, or designs.

Continence—The ability to control voluntarily one's urination or defecation.

Conversion—Refers to a physical symptom or dysfunction that unconsciously expresses an emotional conflict or need.

Coprolalia—Pathological use of obscene or unacceptable words.

Coprophilia—Reliance on feces as a primary source of sexual gratification.

Covert—Hidden.

"Crack"—Purified cocaine alkaloid (also called "freebase").

Custodial—Refers to clinical care that supplies needs but does not engage in active treatment.

Defense Mechanism—See "Neurotic Defense Mechanism."

Delirium—An acute, organically caused brain disorder characterized by confusion and altered consciousness.

Delirium Tremens—A severe, life-threatening delirium caused by withdrawal from excessive alcohol intake.

Delusion—A fixed, false belief not ordinarily accepted by other members of an individual's culture.

Dementia—An organically caused mental disorder characterized by loss of previously held mental abilities, including intellect, memory, and judgment.

Depersonalization—A feeling of not being oneself or of being detached from oneself or the environment.

Depressant—In pharmacology, refers generally to central nervous system sedation (but not usually to depressed mood).

Depression—A sad, despairing, or discouraged mood; such a mood or feeling sufficient to be a symptom of a mental disorder; a syndrome (e.g., "Major Depression") characterized by depressed mood.

Derailment—A disorder of thought process in which one's thoughts unexpectedly and inappropriately leave the topic.

Derealization—A feeling of detachment from the environment or from reality.

Dereistic—Refers to feelings or thoughts that are grossly illogical, not in accordance with reality.

Differential Diagnosis—Those diagnoses or disorders which fit, or nearly fit, a patient's symptoms, and which must be ruled in or out in order to arrive at a provisional, tentative, or final diagnosis.

Diplopia—Double vision.

Diurnal—Daily.

Dizygotic—Refers to multiple fetuses (e.g., fraternal twins) developed from more than one zygote.

Dysarthria—Difficulty in speech production related to anatomical or coordination deficit.

Dysfluency—A disturbance of language fluency.

Dyskinesia—Movement disorder involving involuntary muscle contractions. It may be mild (e.g., benign orofacial dyskinesia) or severe (e.g., hemiballismus).

Dyslexia—A difficulty, not related to ordinary schooling, in understanding or manipulating words (e.g., in reading).

Dysmenorrhea—Irregularity, pain, or other abnormality of menses.

Dysmorphophobia—Preoccupation with an imagined defect in appearance; Body Dysmorphic Disorder.

Dysphonia—A disturbed ability to create or understand sounds.

Dysphoric—Uncomfortable, painful.

Dyssomnia—A disorder of sleep, whether organic or functional.

Dystonic—With respect to movement, refers to involuntary, often painful or disfiguring muscle contractions; also, not in agreement with (see "Ego-dystonic").

Echokinesis—Pathological imitation of another's movements.

Echolalia—Pathological imitation of a just-heard word or sound.

Ego—Literally, the self, referring to one's inner self or personality; in psychoanalytic theory, a major part of the (largely unconscious) psychic apparatus, which is primarily responsible for defense mechanisms and mediates between the primitive (id) and consciencelike (superego) parts.

Ego Boundary—The conceptual delineation between oneself (especially the perception of oneself) and the external world.

Ego-alien—Foreign to one's view of oneself.

Ego-dystonic—Inconsistent with an acceptable view of oneself.

Ego-syntonic—Consistent with an acceptable view of oneself.

Empathy—Being aware of another's feelings as if through his eyes, e.g., "putting oneself in another's shoes."

Encapsulated—Circumscribed, well delineated (e.g., referring to delusions—see "Fragmented").

Encephalopathy—Any organic disease of the brain.

Endogenous—Arising from intrapsychic causes (see "Reactive").

Epileptic Equivalent—Motor, sensory, autonomic, or emotional feelings or behavior that is ictal in nature. Also called "seizure equivalent."

Erotomania—A delusion of idealized, secret romantic love, usually involving a famous or highly visible person.

Essential Features—Characteristics required in order for a diagnosis to be made.

Etiology—Cause.

Euphoria—An extraordinary feeling of happiness or well-being.

Exacerbate—Make worse.

Expressive—In language, refers to the construction, production, and expressing of communication, largely words.

Factitious—Refers to symptoms or disorders voluntarily produced by the patient for unconscious reasons (separate from "malingering") (see also "Munchausen's Syndrome").

Familial—Transmitted within families, not necessarily genetically (see "Hereditary," "Congenital").

Fetish—A body part or nonliving object, not usually associated with sexual excitement, which causes inordinate sexual arousal in an individual; the condition of being attracted to such an object.

First-Degree Relative—In genetics, a parent, full sibling, daughter, or son.

Flagellation—Beating, usually whipping, with a sexual, religious (e.g., absolving), or self-punitive context; slang for masturbation.

Flashback—An intense, dissociative experiencing of a past event (reality-based or substance-induced) or feeling.

Flight of Ideas—Rapid movement from topic to topic, out of proportion for ordinary conversation, usually verbal.

Florid—Highly visible, unmistakable; "in full bloom."

Folie à Deux—A condition in which two people, usually living together, affect each other's psychotic syndromes in such a way that when one is symptomatic, the other improves.

Formication—A tactile hallucination of insects crawling on or under one's skin.

Fragmented—Not whole; poorly circumscribed (e.g., referring to delusions—see "Encapsulated").

"Freebase"—Purified cocaine alkaloid (also, "crack").

Functional—Usable; able to function; with respect to psychiatric disorders, those not associated with known or presumed anatomical, physiological, or other "organic" causes.

Gamma Alcoholism—An alcohol abuse syndrome characterized by the inability to stop drinking once one begins.

Ganser Syndrome—A dissociative syndrome occasionally seen under conditions of isolation or incarceration.

Globus Hystericus—Emotional feeling of "lump in the throat."

Gran Mal—A form of seizure including both loss of consciousness and generalized movements (also "Grand Mal").

Grandiose—Referring to size or importance greatly out of proportion with reality.

Hallucination—A sensory experience in the absence of external stimulation of the relevant sensory organ. Hallucinations are separate from thoughts, feelings, obsessions, and illusions (q.v.) and are experienced as if they were real.

Hallucinogen—A substance that induces hallucinations.

Hallucinosis—Hallucinations during clear consciousness, usually organically caused (e.g., "alcoholic hallucinosis").

Hebephrenic Schizophrenia—A non-DSM-III-R term for Schizophrenia, Disorganized Type; "Hebephrenia" connotes inappropriate, shallow, silly affect and behavior.

Hemiballismic—Refers to gross, irregular movements of large parts of the body.

Hereditary—Having to do with genes and/or chromosomes; genetically transmitted (see "Familial," "Congenital").

Hostile-Dependent—Refers to a situation in which one's dependence on someone or something engenders guilt, irritation, or inconvenience in the dependent individual, leading to anger against the object being depended upon. As a personality trait, refers to a person who is routinely dependent on others but hostile toward them because of the feelings and conflicts associated with that dependency.

Hyperacusis—Overarousal; hypersensitivity to sensory stimulation.

Hypervigilance—A condition of emotional and physiological preparedness, to an unnecessary extent, in anticipation of an anxiety-producing stimulus.

Hypnagogic—Refers to the semiconscious state just before sleep.

Hypnopompic—Refers to the state just before, or during, awakening from sleep.

Hypnotic—In pharmacology, a medication to induce sleep.

Hypomania—An elevated, expansive, or irritable mood, perhaps euphoric, associated with increased physical activity, but not to the point of mania (q.v.).

Hypoxyphilia—The practice of strangling or suffocating oneself almost to the point of unconsciousness for sexual stimulation.

Hysterical—Histrionic; referring to a Conversion Disorder; having flamboyant, superficially stereotypic gender characteristics; frightened or panicked to the point of being out of control. (Note: The many meanings of this disorder in clinical and lay settings often make its understanding in any one context difficult.)

Idea of Reference—An idea, short of a delusion, that occurrences or objects in the environment have particular, special meaning for oneself.

Identity—The sense of self, providing a unity of personality over time.

Idiosyncratic—Characteristic of one individual; limited to one person.

Illusion—The misperception or misinterpretation of an external stimulus, differentiated from hallucinations by the presence of some form of sensory stimulation.

Immediate Memory—The ability to recall items immediately after hearing or seeing them (also, "reflex memory").

Incidence—In epidemiology, the number of new cases that occur over a given period of time (see "Prevalence").

Incontinence—Inability to control urination or defecation.

Infibulation—Piercing the skin, especially for sexual reasons.

Insufflation—"Snorting" or sniffing, as with powdered cocaine.

Intoxication—An acute, organic mental disturbance caused by a chemical agent. The agent may be prescribed or not and may be internally produced (e.g., from infection).

Involuntary—Not under conscious control.

Involutional—Refers to the menopausal or postmenopausal period of life, and especially depressive disorders arising at that time.

Jacksonian—In epilepsy, seizures with localized convulsive movements without loss of consciousness.

Kleine-Levin Syndrome—Episodic hypersomnia, beginning in adolescence and associated with bulimia.

Klismaphilia—Reliance on enemas as a primary source of sexual gratification.

Klüver-Bucy Syndrome—Primitive impulse-control symptoms associated with memory defect and other changes, caused by loss of both temporal lobes.

Korsakoff's Psychosis—A psychosis characterized by confabulation, often related to chronic alcoholism (see "Wernicke's Encephalopathy").

La Belle Indifférence—see *"Belle Indifférence."*

Labile—Rapidly shifting; unstable.

Lacrimation—Tearing.

Lanugo—A type of hair found on fetuses and newborn babies.

Lesch-Nyhan Syndrome—A metabolic defect associated with mental retardation.

Limited Symptom Attack—In Anxiety Disorders, a single or small number of symptoms of anxiety that do not meet DSM-III-R criteria for panic attacks.

Loose—With respect to associations or thought process, lack of logical connection between one's thoughts, usually expressed in conversation.

Loosening of Associations—An unconscious shifting of thoughts or ideas among unrelated (or obliquely related) topics, generally manifested in one's speech.

Macropsia—The illusion that objects appear larger than they actually are.

Magical Thinking—The belief that one's thoughts, ideas, or actions will affect the environment, counter to cause-and-effect rules.

Malingering—Voluntary producing of symptoms or disorders for conscious reasons of personal gain (separate from "factitious").

Mania—Extremely elevated, expansive, or irritable mood associated with marked physical activity, sometimes to the point of physical danger (see "Hypomania").

Melancholia—Severe, anhedonic depression (implies an endogenous source).

Metaphorical Language—Idiosyncratic communication meaningful only to those familiar with the speaker's (a child's) past experience.

Micropsia—The illusion that objects appear smaller than they actually are.

Milestones—The significant accomplishments of human growth and development (e.g., walking unassisted, speaking in sentences), especially the ages at which they occur.

Monoamine Oxidase Inhibitor (MAOI)—In psychopharmacology, a class of antidepressant medication.

Monozygotic—Refers to multiple fetuses (e.g., identical twins) developed from a single zygote.

Mood—Breadth of sustained emotion (e.g., sadness, euphoria); a pervasive and sustained emotion.

Mood-congruent—Apparently consistent with the mood being exhibited (e.g., mood-congruent behavior).

Mood-incongruent—Not consistent with the mood being exhibited.

Morbid—Occurring during or after an exacerbation of a disease; severe, predisposing to serious illness or other problems (e.g., morbid obesity).

Multiaxial—Refers to several classes of information used in psychiatric evaluation. DSM-III-R uses five axes, the first three of which constitute the official diagnostic assessment.

Munchausen's Syndrome—A factitious (i.e., voluntary but unconsciously motivated) disorder or set of symptoms.

Myoclonic—Refers to irregular, brief, usually generalized muscle contractions.

Narcissism—focus on and regard for oneself, to either a healthy or abnormal extent.

Narcolepsy—A hypersomnia-related disorder characterized by involuntary, episodic falling asleep, usually for only a few seconds or minutes.

Narcotic Antagonist—A drug that counteracts the physiological effect of a narcotic.

Necrophilia—Reliance on dead sexual objects (in reality or fantasy) as a primary source of sexual stimulation.

Negative Symptoms—With respect to schizophrenia, often subtle but pervasive absence of normal thought or behavior, as differentiated from presence of abnormal symptoms. Negative symptoms include absence of normal affect or social interaction.

Negativism—Active or passive resistance, e.g., to movement (as in catatonia) or to verbal responsiveness (as in autism).

Neologism—A "word" invented by an individual, usually having an idiosyncratic meaning.

Neuroleptic—In common usage, referring to antipsychotic medication; also, a neuroleptic medication.

Neurotic—Referring to internal, unconscious conflict; referring to a neurosis (e.g., a neurotic disorder or conflict characterized by unconscious defense mechanisms).

Neurotic Defense Mechanism—An unconscious pattern of feelings, thoughts, or behaviors designed to prevent or alleviate anxiety that stems from internal conflict. Their presence, in combinations called defensive systems, is generally normal and adaptive, but in many people reaches maladaptive proportions. Some examples include denial, displacement, intellectualization, projection, rationalization, reaction formation, and undoing. All defense mechanisms involve repression, which is the mechanism by which the person prevents unconscious material from reaching awareness. Some writers describe some "defense mechanisms" as voluntary.

Nihilistic—Referring to nonexistence or lack of existence, e.g., of oneself.

Nonrestorative Sleep—Sleep that does not satisfy one's need for sleep.

"Normative"—In DSM-III-R, usually synonymous with "normal."

Nystagmus—A rhythmic motion of the eyeballs, sometimes in response to certain neurological tests.

Obsession—A persistent, intrusive thought or impulse.

Opioid—In pharmacology, any of a class of drugs or other substances with actions similar to opium.

Organic—Referring to the physiological functioning of living tissue, e.g., brain tissue, at any level (anatomical, chemical, electrical, other).

Overt—Open, easily seen.

Palilalia—Pathological repeating of one's own sounds or words.

Palpitations—Bursts of rapid or irregular heartbeats (sometimes "flutter"), usually real, but may be imagined.

Panic Attack—A discrete period of intense fear or anxiety, usually associated with unconscious, internal conflict rather than external objects or events.

Parallel Play—In young children, play with another child, but not involving interpersonal interaction.

Paranoia—A condition of oversuspiciousness, sometimes to a grossly unrealistic, even psychotic extent; old term (usually *"paranoia vera"*) for Delusional Disorder.

Paraphilia—Any of a class of recurrent, intense, pervasive sexual urges or fantasies which are associated with psychosocial dysfunction and/or are not socially acceptable; commonly synonymous with "sexual deviation."

Parasomnia—Any of several disorders characterized by symptoms that occur just before, during, or just after sleep (differentiated from the disordered sleep of "dyssomnia").

Paresthesia—Numbness or tingling, usually of the extremities.

Partialism—In paraphilias, focus on particular, nonsexual parts of the body as a primary source of sexual stimulation.

Passive Aggressive—Refers to aggressive behavior manifested in passive ways (e.g., by obstructionism or purposeful inefficiency).

Pathognomonic—Referring to a symptom or sign that is found in only one disease or disorder, and in no other.

Pathological Intoxication—Intoxication, generally from alcohol, in response to only a small amount of intoxicant, and out of proportion to that amount.

Pathophysiology—Organic abnormality related to disease.

Pavor Nocturnus—Sleep terror disorder (q.v. in text).

Perseveration—Persistent, often rhythmic repetition of words or ideas, not generally controllable by the individual.

Personality Trait—An enduring pattern of perceiving, relating to, and thinking about the environment and oneself, exhibited in a wide range of social and personal contexts.

Pervasive—Broadly and comprehensively found; involving all or almost all things.

Petit Mal—A form of seizure that involves loss of consciousness without convulsive movements (also *"Petite Mal"*).

Phenomenologic—Referring to descriptions or descriptive characteristics. DSM-III-R descriptions of disorders are generally phenomenologic (i.e., based on observations) rather than etiologic (based on cause of symptoms).

Phenothiazine—In psychopharmacology, a class of antipsychotic medications.

Phobia—A persistent, irrational, morbid fear of an object or an activity, recognized by the individual as unreasonable but nevertheless leading to significant avoidance of the "phobic object."

Piloerection—Stiffening or raising of the hair on one's body.

Postpartum—After delivery of one's child.

Poverty of Speech—Restricted quantity of speech. Differentiated from "poverty of speech content," which implies adequate quantity but little information.

Predisposing Factors—Things or events that increase the likelihood that a particular disorder will develop.

Premorbid—Before the onset of illness, "baseline."

Preoccupation—A repetitive, often continuous thought or focus of one's thoughts (see "Obsession").

Presenium—The period just before old age.

Pressure of Speech/Pressured Speech—Accelerated, often loud and emphatic speech which is difficult to stop and may continue even in the absence of a listener.

Prevalence—In epidemiology, the number of cases present in a population at a particular point in time (see "Incidence").

Primary Gain—The unconscious gratification, from alleviation of neurotic conflict, which motivates neurotic behaviors (e.g., somatoform symptoms) (see "Secondary Gain").

Prodromal—Premonitory; preparatory.

Prognosis—A prediction of the outcome of an illness or disorder, based on clinical experience with similar cases.

Provisional Diagnosis—An uncertain diagnosis, based on incomplete information and subject to change.

Pseudodementia—A dementialike syndrome not actually related to organic illness.

Pseudologia Fantastica—The telling of elaborate lies.

Psychoactive—In pharmacology, having some effect on the psyche, emotions, or psychiatric/psychological symptoms.

Psychogenic—Caused by the emotions or psyche.

Psychomotor—A combination of physical and mental.

Psychomotor Agitation—Continuous activity (often with pacing, wringing of the hands, or inability to sit still) related to emotional distress.

Psychomotor Retardation—General slowing of emotional and physical responses.

Psychosocial—Refers to a combination of psychological and social factors or interventions.

Psychosomatic—Referring to the interaction between the mind and body, especially illnesses in which emotional disorder or conflict gives rise to—or significantly affects—physical signs or symptoms. Closely related, or identical, to "psychophysiological," in which physiological mechanisms are affected by emotional factors.

Psychotic—Refers to serious impairment in reality testing, with inaccurate perceptions and/or thoughts about external reality (implying the creation of a new, internal reality).

Querulous Paranoia—A delusion of injustice that one feels must be remedied by legal action.

Reactive—Referring to symptoms associated with, or exacerbated by, one's external environment (as opposed to the intrapsychic environment); more properly, emotional symptoms that change (e.g., get better or worse) with changes in the external environment (see "Endogenous").

Recent Memory—In the mental status examination, memory for items or names three to five minutes after hearing them.

Receptive—In language, refers to the taking in, processing, and interpretation of sensory input, generally words.

Reciprocal Play—In children, play that involves interacting with another child (see "Parallel Play").

Remission—An abatement of symptoms, commonly to the point at which no indication of disease is present (but not "cure").

Remote Memory—In the mental status examination, memory for items or events that occurred in the distant past.

Rhinorrhea—Nasal discharge.

Ritualistic—Refers to an activity, usually repetitive, employed for a magical or anxiety-relieving, often idiosyncratic purpose.

"Rum Fits"—Seizures precipitated by alcohol withdrawal.

Rumination—Obsessive repeating of a thought or idea; in infants, regurgitation and reswallowing of food.

Scanning—A condition, often associated with hypervigilance, in which one tries intensively to be aware of his environment, in fear or anticipation of an anxiety-producing event.

Scapegoating—In families or groups, the unconscious appointing of one member to represent the pathological characteristics of the group.

Scatologia—Lewd or obscene speech.

Seasonal Depression—Depression whose symptoms are regularly associated with a particular time of year, often winter.

Secondary Gain—Indirect gratification or reward, not consciously sought, from illness or symptoms. Easily confused with "primary gain" (q.v.) and direct rewards for malingered symptoms.

Seizure Equivalent—See "Epileptic Equivalent."

Self-esteem—Regard for oneself.

Self-image—One's mental picture of oneself, particularly with regard to strengths, weaknesses, expectations, and ethics.

Senium—Old age.

Sensory—Related to the senses (e.g., sight, smell, touch); differentiated from "motor."

Sign—A manifestation of a pathological condition observed (directly or indirectly) by an examiner rather than subjectively experienced by the individual.

Simple Schizophrenia—A non-DSM-III-R classification that refers to a form of schizophrenia without florid symptoms.

Simple Tics—Reasonably delimited tics (q.v.), such as eye blinking, grimacing (see "Complex Tics").

Sleep Apnea—Any of several physiologically based conditions in which one stops breathing while asleep.

Sleep Paralysis—Inability to move just before falling asleep, or just after awakening.

Sleep-related Myoclonus—Myoclonus (q.v.) that occurs exclusively during, or is related to, sleep.

Sleeptalking—A non-REM parasomnia similar to, and probably related to, sleepwalking.

Somatic—Referring to the body or human biology.

Somatopsychic—Referring to psychological symptoms caused or exacerbated by somatic illness or injury.

Specific Phobia—A simple phobia (i.e., one with a circumscribed, not vague, stimulus), agoraphobia, or Social Phobia.

Speech melody—The intonation or inflection of one's speech.

"Speedball"—Any of several combinations of abusable drugs, especially cocaine and heroin mixed in a syringe.

Stammering—An impairment in speech fluency similar to stuttering.

Startle Response—A condition, often related to hypervigilance (q.v.), in which an individual reacts abruptly, and out of proportion, to a minor physical stimulus.

Stereotyped/Stereotypic—Refers to movements or verbalizations repeated mechanically, without apparent purpose (see "ritualistic").

Stressor—An object or situation, real or symbolic, that gives rise to stress.

Subacute—Having the potential to become acute; likely to become acute.

Superego—In common usage, the "conscience"; in psychoanalytic theory, that portion of the psyche formed by identification with and introjection of parental characteristics that foster ethics, empathy, and self-criticism.

Surrogate—Substitute.

Symbolic—Substituting for a real feeling, memory, object, or event. In a psychodynamic context, the thing symbolized is unconscious, and the symbol may bear only an indirect relationship to it.

Sympathomimetic—Referring to a substance whose action mimics that of the sympathetic nervous system.

Symptom—An outward manifestation of a pathological condition, especially a subjective complaint.

Tangential—Refers to thoughts or words that depart from the current train of thought in an oblique or irrelevant way.

Terminal Insomnia—Awakening several hours earlier than planned, with an inability to return to sleep.

Thought Broadcasting—The delusion that one's thoughts can be heard by others.

Thought Insertion—The delusion that others have placed thoughts in one's mind.

Thought Withdrawal—The delusion that thoughts have been removed from one's mind.

Tic—An involuntary, rapid, recurrent, nonrhythmic, stereotyped motor movement or vocalization.

Tolerance—In pharmacology, physical habituation to a drug (prescribed or not) leading to loss of its effect unless the dose is increased (not synonomous with "addiction"); generally, loss of effectiveness of a particular treatment or stimulus at its current level.

Toucherism—Frotteurism, but sometimes distinguished from Frotteurism by its fondling characteristics.

"Trailing"—The auditory illusion that sounds echo or persist.

Trance—A nonorganic alteration of consciousness, voluntarily (e.g., during hypnosis) or involuntarily (e.g., during a dissociative disorder) produced.

Trichophagy—The mouthing or eating of one's hair.

Tricyclic—In psychopharmacology, a class of antidepressant medication.

Unconscious—Out of awareness; not under voluntary control; that part of the psyche not available to voluntary awareness or control.

Urophilia—Reliance on urine as a primary source of sexual gratification.

Vertigo—A feeling of dizziness, usually including the sensation that one's environment or oneself is moving.

Visual Tracking—Following objects with one's eyes.

Voluntary—Under conscious control.

Vorbeireden—A psychological symptom involving giving "near-miss" answers or talking past the point, done consciously in Factitious Disorder and unconsciously in Ganser Syndrome.

Waxy Flexibility—A symptom of catatonia characterized by the ability of an examiner to move the patient's body or limbs into different positions, which are then held indefinitely by the patient (also *"Cerea Flexibilitas"*).

Wernicke's Encephalopathy—Central nervous system dysfunction due to thiamine deficiency, as in chronic alcoholism (part of Wernicke-Korsakoff syndrome).

Zoophilia—Reliance on sexual activity with nonhuman animals (in reality or fantasy) as one's primary source of sexual stimulation.

Index

263